Loyal to the Sky

Loyal to the Sky

Notes from an Activist

MARISA HANDLER

BERRETT-KOEHLER PUBLISHERS, INC.
San Francisco
a BK Currents book

Berrett-Koehler Publishers, Inc.
235 Montgomery Street, Suite 650, San Francisco, CA 94104-2916
Tel: (415) 288-0260   Fax: (415) 362-2512   www.bkconnection.com

ORDERING INFORMATION

QUANTITY SALES. Special discounts are available on quantity purchases by corporations, associations, and others. For details, contact the "Special Sales Department" at the Berrett-Koehler address above.

INDIVIDUAL SALES. Berrett-Koehler publications are available through most bookstores. They can also be ordered directly from Berrett-Koehler: Tel: (800) 929-2929; Fax: (802) 864-7626; www.bkconnection.com

ORDERS FOR COLLEGE TEXTBOOK/COURSE ADOPTION USE. Please contact Berrett-Koehler: Tel: (800) 929-2929; Fax: (802) 864-7626.

ORDERS BY U.S. TRADE BOOKSTORES AND WHOLESALERS. Please contact Publishers Group West, 1700 Fourth Street, Berkeley, CA 94710. Tel: (510) 528-1444; Fax (510) 528-3444.

Berrett-Koehler and the BK logo are registered trademarks of Berrett-Koehler Publishers, Inc.

Printed in the United States of America

Berrett-Koehler books are printed on long-lasting acid-free paper. When it is available, we choose paper that has been manufactured by environmentally responsible processes. These may include using trees grown in sustainable forests, incorporating recycled paper, minimizing chlorine in bleaching, or recycling the energy produced at the paper mill.

LIBRARY OF CONGRESS CATALOGING-IN-PUBLICATION DATA

Handler, Marisa, 1976–
Loyal to the sky: notes from an activist / by Marisa Handler.
    p. cm.
ISBN-13: 978-1-57675-392-7 (hardcover)
ISBN-10: 1-57675-392-1 (hardcover)
    1. Handler, Marisa, 1976– 2. Journalists — United States — Biography. 3. Political activists — United States — Biography. I. Title.
PN4874.H226A3 2007
070.92 — dc22
[B]
                                                                    2006025734

First Edition
12 11 10 09 08 07   10 9 8 7 6 5 4 3 2 1

Copyediting: Amy Einsohn. Interior design and production: Valerie Brewster, Scribe Typography. Proofreading: Todd Manza, Manza Editorial; Don Roberts. Indexing: Rachel Rice, Directions Unlimited.

for my parents,
Rosemund and Frank Handler,
who taught me, by example, to open my mind
and then speak it

AUTHOR'S NOTE

The accounts in this book are all based on real people and events, but some have been condensed or conflated. Names have been changed in some places, and a few of the characters are composites. I have on occasion altered the setting or timing of a revelation or personal experience. But throughout the book I have searched for and striven to relate the heart of the story—my own, as well as those of the individuals and communities I have been blessed to encounter along the way.

Page vii used by permission of Joanna Macy

The illustration for the poster on page 125 appears by permission of the artist, Mona Caron. © 2003 by Mona Caron. The text for the poster was written by Chris Carlsson and is used with his permission. © 2003 by Chris Carlsson.

Full texts of the article by Patrick Reinsborough mentioned in chapter 7 and the article by Ilyse Hogue and Patrick Reinsborough mentioned in chapter 8 are posted at www.smartmeme.com.

You come and go. The doors swing closed
ever more gently, almost without a shudder.
Of all who move through the quiet houses,
you are the quietest.

We become so accustomed to you,
we no longer look up
when your shadow falls over the book we are reading
and makes it glow. For all things
sing you: at times
we just hear them more clearly.

Often when I imagine you
your wholeness cascades into many shapes.
You run like a herd of luminous deer
and I am dark, I am forest.

You are a wheel at which I stand,
whose dark spokes sometimes catch me up,
revolve me nearer to the center.
Then all the work I put my hand to
widens from turn to turn.

I, 45 from *Rilke's Book of Hours: Love Poems to God;*
translation by Joanna Macy and Anita Barrows

Contents

Foreword

by Rebecca Solnit

Marisa Handler's luminous tale of coming to activism issues an invitation to read your own life as an awakening. You can either examine your own past to realize that you have been educated and molded, or you can decide to live your life as an adventure and a pilgrimage toward a better world, moving rather than standing still, changing rather than settling. For the point of her book is not that she is extraordinary, but that ordinary life throws all of us fodder and curveballs that invite us to learn, to commit, to keep traveling, to keep discovering. She *is* exceptional in that she sought as much as she stumbled across the situations and conversations that shaped her journey and her coming of age, and that her pilgrimage traverses four continents, and that she made so much of what she found. Still, the same developments could have taken place in the life of someone who stayed home in Oklahoma or Manitoba and paid attention there to the politics of race, money, foreign policy, war and peace, the troubles and demands that are everywhere. But those continents do make the story more exciting; she is fortunate to have had a global cast of characters play a part in her awakening to problems that are themselves often global, though she made her own fortune in choosing to accept the challenges posed along each step of the way.

For these are the essential steps toward being an activist: to see injustice, to do something about it, to be willing to risk, to be unpopular or out of step, to change your life. It's a challenge that she accepts almost as an inevitability on the playground in the first pages of *Loyal to the Sky* and that only later brings her joy and allies. So many, too many, of us either shrug off these pangs of conscience or wring our hands, believing that we can do nothing about them. Marisa Handler shows hope is both possible and justified. Perhaps the one thing I missed in this book is the (wildly encouraging) background that many of the political actions she describes from within, as a participant, have changed the world. The Free Trade Area of the Americas began to crumble that week in Florida and is now in shambles. Nepal's popular uprising in the spring of 2006 brought democracy back to the country. Legislation on closing the School of the Americas in Fort Benning, Georgia, continues to gain support, and Latin American countries are withdrawing from its sinister training programs. You *can* change the world; you can accept the challenge injustice issues. It won't make your life easier, but it might make it worth living or let you live with yourself. And it might save someone's else life or help defend something larger than any single one of us—a culture, an ecosystem, a principle.

The book describes a series of conundrums and paradoxes—racism in the United States, the country that Handler's parents chose as the antithesis of apartheid-era South Africa; the mixed wonders and limits of the very different traditional cultures she encounters; the Gordian knot that is Israel and her own status as a Jew; the grassroots activists' achievement of necessary intervention, despite their aggravating pursuit of perfection. Maybe what I love most about the book is the grace with which she accepts these challenges—the challenge not just of being engaged but also of understanding and accepting the contradictions, impurities, and complications of each side, each possible position, and of not surrendering to indifference, ambivalence, or a quest for personal purity that makes alliance or action impossible. There's a wonderful passage in which she describes a struggle, this time inside herself, in Nepal: "I have my ideas. I love my ideas. I bask in them, cling to them, noisily impose them. And then I move beyond my bubble and they get wrecked. I grieve them. They really were beautiful, in their oblivious idealism, in their purity. Later I am grateful.... Life, it seems, pushes me ever wider, deeper, in an ongoing struggle to accommodate things I never imagined existed."

The most high-minded excuse for doing nothing is that the means with which to do it or the company you'd keep are flawed, the justification that you're keeping your hands clean (which is another way to say that you'll save only yourself). There are unambiguous realities in this book—the reality of poverty and of exploitation—but every situation still requires a tightrope-walker's balancing act: of pragmatism and idealism, of solidarity and independent-mindedness, of purposefulness and flexibility. And this is where the book becomes more than a conventional tale of an activist's evolution: spirituality, eventually in the clear form of Buddhism, enters in, and Buddhism itself offers the nonattachment, the recognition of ephemerality and the need to let go, the sense of life as an ever-moving river, that helps Marisa make sense out of all that she witnesses and does. At a very young age, she has gone very far. This book is an invitation to the rest of us to keep going.

Acknowledgments

Indeed it takes a village, and in this case, a global one.

First and foremost, thank you to the millions of people across the planet working to make their communities and this earth a better place. Your dedication and love are changing the world in ways visible and yet to unfold. You are the inspiration for this book and our hope for the future.

It has been a great honor to have as my editor Johanna Vondeling, without whom this book wouldn't exist and would most certainly not be what it is today. Her insights and vision were transformative. Her dedication and patience were awe-inspiring. Also great gratitude to all the incredible staff at Berrett-Koehler for their enthusiasm, expertise, and commitment to a better world. My thanks as well to Amy Einsohn, my copyeditor, for polishing this book with such a keen eye.

I am particularly grateful to my sister Gabrielle Handler Marks and my brother-in-law Donald Marks, who have been a constant source of support and generosity.

Thank you to my own community, the San Francisco Buddhist Alliance for Social Engagement household, which has stood by me with support and encouragement throughout the creation of this book. Scott Boultinghouse, Diane Gregorio, and Hugo Medina: each of you has reminded me on a daily basis what it means to live with wisdom and compassion.

I am deeply indebted to Michael Lerner, Michael Nagler, and Sharif Abdullah, each of whom has mentored me at a crucial phase in my own development, and whose lives stand as towering examples of courage and vision.

My huge gratitude to my parents for their love and support, and to my brother Marc Handler for his humor and faith in me.

Much appreciation to my friends from Code Orange, who have been inimitable *compañeros* and judicious teachers along this path.

My thanks to Nina and Trevor Blanc and to Noa Marks, who masterfully fulfilled the often-demanding task of keeping me silly.

Thank you to Peter Barnes and the Mesa Refuge, for the gift of time and space to simply write.

For numerous forms of support, I am indebted to Nancy Shaw, Elizabeth Zarek, Rebecca Solnit, David Solnit, Rachael Cunningham, Eddie Foronda, and Jonathan Raymond.

For advice and encouragement, I am very grateful to Christopher Cook, Nicole Monastersky Maderas, Caryn Mandelbaum, Hannah Acevedo-Schiesel, Danielle Monastersky, Remi Cohen, Darren Noy, Jo Ellen Green Kaiser, Michael Chorost, and Mark Abel.

Loyal to the Sky

One:

Cape Town

Lunchtime at Camps Bay Primary School is when things tend to go severely wrong. Outside the structure of a syllabus, beyond the rigorous scrutiny of our teachers, I reliably blunder. These forty-minute daily ordeals typically consist in no small portion of us prattling about what our parents prattled about over the last night's supper table. Election time is no different.

"Who are your parents voting for?" Joan turns to Catherine first. Joan is my best friend, and the only girl who can legitimately kick my ass at the hundred-meter sprint. Of course, going to an all-white public school does cut out a good chunk of the competition.

"The Nats, obviously." Catherine nibbles delicately on the edge of her sandwich. Blond, green-eyed, and irritatingly demure, Catherine is the resident beauty in Standard 4P, Camps Bay Primary. At least half of the boys sitting on the other end of the playground spend lunchtime gazing at her with unadulterated longing. I, on the other hand, wend my way from one humiliating, clumsy crush to the next. Any attention I do get from boys is strictly limited to my skinny legs or massive, unwieldy glasses. Following the purchase of our house in Camps Bay, a sleepy beach suburb of Cape Town, my parents had been feeling a tad pinched when it came to finances. My mother succeeded in convincing my sister and me that her old frames were just perfect for us. Given that my vision verges on legally blind, the abnormally thick, oversized lenses make for a fearsome sight.

"How about you?" Joan turns to Meredith. At nine, Meredith's body had blossomed into untimely womanhood. At eleven, she remains the only one among us who can fill a bra without the assistance of socks.

"Mer's tits," says Jonathan West, who sits behind me in class and torments me mercilessly with sharpened pencil points, "could feed all of Africa. Even Ethiopia."

"The Nats," says Meredith, barely glancing up from her chips. I am growing anxious. Joan is working her way methodically through the ranks. Any moment now, she's going to turn to me.

"Deb?"

"Nats."

"Melanie?"

"*Agh* man, the Nats, what do you think? You think they're *dom*? My mom says the PFP would hand this country over to the blacks."

"My dad says the blacks would get rid of us in a minute if they were clever enough," says Catherine.

"My dad says they would kill us and take our homes," says Joan. "But I mean, the blacks are too stupid to even get the washing done properly, so how would they be able to run a country?"

"*Agh* please, that's ridiculous," offers Meredith, coming to life, breasts a-jiggle as she shakes her head in vigorous derision. "There's no way a black could be president. They don't have brains, man, they can only be gardeners and maids. Can you imagine? Hello, Mr. Black President," she pantomimes speaking into a telephone, "can you please bleach Donald's nappies before you meet with all those politicians?" "Yes, madam, of course madam, the nappies are in the outside sink already." Meredith says this with a thick Xhosa accent, and we all screech with laughter. I know it's wrong, though. I know it, but I'm terrified of what's about to come.

Joan resumes the reins. "Lauren?"

"Nats."

"Marisa?" Her cool blue gaze meets mine. I look at the ground.

These days, the casual observer might wonder: how did apartheid ever happen? When you speak to white South Africans today, no one ever voted for the National Party. The National Party was the bastion of politically sanctioned racism for decades; it spawned bigoted leaders like rounded white peas out of some eugenics-concocted pod. Mysteriously, despite this purported dearth of support among the only population eligible to vote, the National Party won election after election. This collective rewriting of individual political history is a rosy indicator of just how rapidly change can happen: a mere handful of years after apartheid officially ended, white South Africans acquired a conscience. Even, I would venture to say, a sense of shame.

Of course, there were many white South Africans who objected to apartheid for decades, and who played more or less visible roles in the anti-apartheid struggle. My mother, marching against apartheid in the sixties at Johannesburg's University of the Witwatersrand, got beaten over the head with a baton and unceremoniously carted off to jail thanks to her wayward conscience. I was lucky. My parents raised us to question the status quo. "It's not right that the blacks only live in townships outside the city instead of in places like Camps Bay and Clifton," my mother would say, her eyes wide, frightening. "It's not normal to only go to school with white children. This is a very sick country. Do you understand?" I'd nod, attempting to square this insight with the glaring contradiction that was daily life. My mother pointed out time and again that the society in which we lived was unnatural. That, and my parents voted for the Progressive Federal Party —the only party with any constituency that both preached a mild form of equality and, being white, retained legal status. Conservatives alleged the PFP stood for "Packing for Perth," mocking the white liberals emigrating to Australia in subdued droves. The African National Congress—the leading anti-apartheid movement turned governing political party with the establishment of majority rule in 1994—was long underground by the time I hit puberty.

"Marisa?" Joan is waiting expectantly. I say nothing. Slowly the other girls turn toward me, wondering at the silence.

"Marisa?" Now she is impatient, wanting to get on with her show. I keep my eyes on the ground. Twelve identical pairs of brown mary-janes. Twelve pairs of gray kneesocks with our school colors on the top: green, red, yellow. Maybe if I close my eyes and then open them again I'll wake up. I try it. Joan is directly in front of me, feet planted apart, arms crossed, scenting blood.

"Come on man, go already!"

Isn't it enough that my mother never participates in the carpool, steers miles clear of PTA meetings, and refuses to socialize with the other mothers? Must I be put through this, too?

"The PFP," I whisper.

There is a moment of stunned silence, then a babble of shrieked responses. I sit glumly through the hailstorm, eyes on the ground. Finally it eases off into shocked half-phrases. I am shrinking into myself, praying to disappear, to evaporate with a soft pop into thin air, or melt down to an innocuous puddle of green uniform and gray socks. Joan remains positioned in front of me, rigid, furious at how I have failed her. The other girls quiet down, appetites whetted, settling in for the show.

"Do you want to hand South Africa over to the blacks?"

"No. I mean, they do live here also. Actually there's a lot more blacks than whites in South Africa. Did you know that eighty percent—"

"Do you want to hand South Africa over to the blacks?" Joan is very serious now, face still, her stare hard. All of them are watching me in an unearthly silence. I feel waves of panic washing through me. This is my best-friendship on the line. No, this is my entire, precariously balanced, laboriously constructed social status. This is, perhaps, my life.

"I don't think blacks are stupid." I think of the few black people I know, all domestic workers in white homes. I think of the black man I passed in the street with my brother yesterday, of his courteous "Good morning, madam, good morning, little master." I think of Maureen with her plump, open arms, of July with his gentle instructions. "I think they're as clever as us." A hushed uproar rises from the peanut gallery. Joan steps in menacingly.

"Do you want to hand South Africa over to the blacks?"

I've taken risks before. While I want nothing more than to be popular, at times an irksome tendency to do what I feel I should do—without calculating the consequences to my social status—pops up. I'm pretty low on the totem pole as it is, but I've earned myself an unwanted reputation standing up for "fatty" Felicia Sperling, who's at the very bottom. Recently I lectured Felicia at length, telling her it was time for her to speak up for herself, that I just didn't have it in me to keep defending her. Now I meet her eyes. She is sitting somewhat apart from the rest of us, mouth open midchew at the drama. Do I detect a glimmer of sympathy? The rest of the girls follow my gaze like spectators at a tennis match. I look back at Joan.

"I think a black person could be president."

There it is. Frail but clear. My voice.

The tension bursts like a punctured balloon as everyone starts speaking at once. Joan glares at me, jaw clenched. She shakes her head slowly and turns away. That's it. I'm ruined.

I guess that's where it begins. Saying no is hardest the first time. When you are sufficiently privileged that *yes* is handed to you on a platter, when virtually everything around you whispers, hollers, cajoles, winks *yes, yes please, yes now, just say yes*—well, that's when saying no feels impossible. And then out of nowhere you just say it. *No, thank you. Hell no. Not this time.* I don't know what prompts it. Maybe courage. Maybe bravado. Or desperation. But the next time—it may be the next minute, or the next year, or a thousand yeses later—it's a little easier.

People often ask me how it was growing up in apartheid South Africa. It felt normal, I say. It was all I knew. Apartheid only became truly odd, wrong, twisted, once we'd left South Africa. It may be grotesquely warped, but if you are a child born and bred in a segregated society, a rigidly stratified and censored society, it's all you know. I was aware that it was wrong; my mother told me, and when I became very still I felt it. But until I stepped into the multicolored throngs of the San Fernando Valley's Portola Junior High at age eleven in 1988, apartheid South Africa was simply all I knew. I was living the life that had been handed me. Saying no was the exception, not the rule. Yet this timid *no* was where it all began for me. Where I started to trust what ran deeper than the assumptions and conventions of my society. Every society assumes that its way is the norm, the natural way. It takes a flying leap beyond the frame to conceive of other possibilities. To believe in them.

After three generations in South Africa, my parents' decision to emigrate to the United States was simply another stitch in an extended embroidery of migration. We are Jews, and the history of Jews is invariably a meandering, punctuated affair—a series of leaps in the direction of possibilities. At the turn of the twentieth century, my great-grandfather on my father's side, Max Faiman, left his hometown of Gomel, Belarus, on a boat bound for New York. He took a job as an apprentice in a bakery, working such long hours that he never saw daylight. Then someone mentioned South Africa. And again: South Africa. There's gold there, Faiman, diamonds too. Big as your fist, ripe for the picking. South Africa eased its way into Max's bushed brain, hung in the air with the flour, stayed put as palms pressed dough to pastry. Three years after arriving in New York, Max boarded a boat to Cape Town.

I can see my great-grandfather stepping into the harbor, exhausted and stiff-necked, cursing in Yiddish at the goyim pushing and clomping around him. He looks up. There, enshrouded in gauzy wisps of cloud, is Table Mountain: massive, rocky, astonishingly flat. She winks at my great-grandfather, stretches sturdy arms out to him. Below her, the city nestles, a cluster of colonial architecture. And before them all — Max, Table Mountain, the city — before them all: the Atlantic, stretching spread-eagled in sun-drenched abandon, lapping lazily at the quay. Who wouldn't fall in love with Cape Town? What fool would turn his back upon such calculated seduction? My great-grandfather hastily blessed his good fortune, squared his shoulders, and scurried off to build a life. He bought a property on Hanover Street and industriously set about starting his own bakery. For two decades the Faimans lived directly upstairs from the fragrant font of their livelihood: the American Bakery, with the stars and stripes themselves beckoning from the window. The American Bakery, smack in the middle of District Six.

If you go to the District Six museum today, you can find my great-grandfather's bakery on the oversized map of the neighborhood. It was originally an immigrant quarter. As immigrants moved up and out, blacks and coloureds — a culturally distinct population, the product of then-illegal miscegenation — moved in. District Six was one of the only racially integrated urban neighborhoods in the country. Blacks and whites, Jewish immigrants and Muslim descendants of slaves hauled over from Indonesia: you name it, they passed through. Chuckling on their stoops, gossiping over fences, bellowing at each others' kids.

But by the time my parents met and married in 1972, District Six was a wasteland. In 1966, the government had invoked the notorious Group Areas Act, declared Cape Town's center and immediate environs suitable only for white occupation, and proceeded to categorically remove over sixty thousand "unwanted" residents from District

Six to distant townships. The neighborhood was then razed to the ground by bulldozers. Yet all the employment was in the city and its surrounding white suburbs. Most blacks, like our maid Maureen, occupied a tiny room in their employer's household for six days out of the week. On Sundays, they traveled home to the black townships, to their children and families in the squalid, sprawling mazes of Langa, Guguletu, and Khayalitsha.

Between 1950 and 1986, the apartheid government, with its policies of "separate development," forcibly relocated around 1.5 million people of color from cities to rural reservations. The District Six that had been the idyll of my grandmother's childhood had, by the time I was old enough to pay attention, curdled into an ominous place, a name that left only silence or epithets in its wake. When I went back to visit South Africa after graduating from college, I tried to find a trace of District Six. But there was nothing. Undeveloped plots sat eerily in the midst of the city, waist-high grass undulating in the wind.

Max Faiman left his homeland because he believed in possibilities. He marched boldly into paradise, just like my family would nearly a century later. But as we learned in South Africa and then again in the U.S., paradise is problematic. Paradise, as I discovered after significantly more practice saying no, plays favorites. Monogamous to the end, it belongs exclusively to those who own it. As for the rest? Theirs are the lives displaced into ghettos and townships, the dreams deferred. For me, at age eleven, wondering about God and racism and my own place in the scheme of things, caught between a religion that told me I belonged to the chosen people, a society that told me I belonged to a different set of chosen people, and parents who told me everyone was equal, paradise was starting to seem like rather shifty territory.

I walk home slowly, each step miring me further in a sucking swamp of despair. Will anyone in Standard 4P ever speak to me again? Unlikely. I open the gate to our house and walk around to the backyard, across its cement squares, through the back door. Maureen is at the kitchen sink, hands immersed in warm, soapy water. She sees my face.

"What's wrong, baby?"

"Nothing, Mau. I'm hungry."

She pulls her hands out of the water, dries them on a *lappie,* and begins preparing my favorite: toasted cheese and tomato. I drop my backpack on the floor and slump into a chair. Usually this is a happy time: my sister and brother are still at school, so I get an hour alone with Maureen. I watch her broad back as she moves from fridge to counter, counter to toaster, toaster back to fridge. She is wearing the standard uniform: pastel checkered housedress, colorful *doekie* covering her short, wiry hair. I am endlessly fascinated and repelled by her hair, and the various greasy, bitingly sweet products she applies to it. At night, when I visit her in her room, I examine these, stockpiled as they are on a makeshift shelf along with a plastic Jesus, sample bottles of lotion and shampoo, and a dusty assortment of items discarded by my family.

"Mau, do you think a black could be president?"

"What, Mimi?" Maureen turns to me, taken aback.

"Do you think a black could be president?"

She purses her lips over the large gap that was once, who knows how long ago, two front teeth. She lost them during a drunken binge, when she fell into a pole. Although I heard my father speculating, when he thought I was out of range, that it was probably her ex-husband's work.

"No, Mimi. If a black was president this country would be in even worse shape than it already is." Maureen sets my sandwich down in front of me, neatly cut into quarters, and turns back to the sink.

"What, Mau? What are you talking about? Don't you want Nicky and Thobela to be able to live in a house like this?" Nikelwa, Maureen's only daughter, is currently in nursing school, unwed and with a baby on the way. Thobela was recently arrested for dealing *dagga* from our house. I returned home from school one day to find our home teeming with police, Thobela in handcuffs, and Maureen wringing her hands and apologizing tearfully to my parents.

"Blacks too much like to have a good time. Too much alcohol and smoking *dagga.*" Maureen regularly warns me never to drink. Soon after my parents hired her, my mother returned home from work to find the house in disarray. My little brother was screeching from their bedroom, nappy full and stinking, hands and face covered in jam from breakfast. Maureen was passed out on the floor. She had been pilfering from my parents' liquor cabinet, stealthily replacing the booze with water. Instead of firing her, my mother took her to Alcoholics Anonymous. Maureen was the first black member of the Cape Town chapter. She found Jesus. She turned her life around. Today, she speaks on the AA circuit, and is a resolute, fiery coach to others trying to drag themselves back onto the wagon.

"*Agh* man Mau, I don't believe you. This country will never change if everyone thinks like you." I get up, in sudden, ferocious need of her strong arms, wide hips, the pure unalloyed physicality of her. I squeeze her tightly around the waist as she collapses into characteristic giggles.

"No Mimi! Stop! Get off!" She pushes me gently with wet hands. I squeeze tighter and she shrieks with laughter. My love for Maureen is what I will later, when we are long gone, realize is a rare, perhaps once-in-a-lifetime, kind of love. It is naked of fear, resentment, guilt. It is a love in which I have not yet learned to lie. A love wholly uncomplicated in perhaps the only way love can be wholly uncomplicated — when it is far too complicated on the other end. For the love Maureen gives us is love lost to her own three children. Yet any bitterness she feels is kept from us. I sometimes wonder what would happen if my parents stopped paying her. She'd stay, wouldn't she?

I ease up my grip. "Don't you think it's unfair, Mau? Don't you think it's wrong?"

She looks down at me sternly. "God grant me the serenity to accept the things I cannot change, the courage to change the things I can, and the wisdom to know the difference," she pronounces emphatically. She digs in her pocket, and hands me yet another card imprinted in curlicued type with the phrase. I have a veritable collection of them upstairs.

I don't know about God. When Maureen says things like this, I wonder. I used to believe in Him. I would go to the children's services with my grandmother and sister and brother and pray fervently. I prayed so much it stung. Was that God? Those twinges, like a bee pinned to the back of my ribs? Or sometimes, in beautiful places — at the top of Table Mountain, watching the sunset from Camps Bay beach — I would be flooded with something achingly huge, bigger than me or the latest classroom drama, something exquisite and multihued and piercingly clear. Was that God? Or sitting in my classroom, suddenly inundated out of nowhere with a surging love for all the people around me, even Jonathan West, so much love that I had to swallow back tears — perhaps that was God? When I asked the *rebbitzen* at Hebrew school what God was, she said, in her nasal New York accent, avoiding my eyes from beneath her stiff *sheitl:* go ask the rabbi. When I asked the rabbi, he told me he was busy. When I asked my mother, she said God is love. God is good. I like that idea. But what about all the bad? Does God just not care? That seems rather unfair. The *siddur* says that we are God's chosen people. In that case, are all the goyim unchosen? Or are just the blacks unchosen? What about the coloureds? Are they half-chosen? What about my second cousin Lily? Did she get unchosen when she moved in with Nigel? Nigel is coloured, definitely not a Jew. My parents are the only people in the family that still speak to Lily. Lily and Nigel came over for tea, and Lily started crying in the middle of eating her scone. Lily's grandfather refused to speak to her father when he married a goy. Then Lily had children with a coloured, and now her father won't talk to her, even though he's in the hospital with a heart condition.

I used to believe in God, but now He makes less and less sense.

I knew we were leaving South Africa for a good two years before we actually packed up, although my parents swore us to secrecy. It was 1986, directly before my tenth birthday, when the reality of parting from everything I knew first materialized on the horizon. My parents had recently returned from one of their lengthy trips abroad; unknown to me, they had been scouring the U.S. for a possible sponsor, someone to offer to employ one of them and thereby grant us legal status as permanent residents. Blissfully oblivious of their travails — it took four years for our visas to come through — I was immersed in my own universe of thorny dilemmas. I was desperately in love with animals, but my parents refused to get me a pet. I had rescued a baby bird from our pool, inadvertently slaughtered two goldfish through overfeeding, saved innumerable spiders from my sister's merciless heels, and insisted on building a home (with garden) for the peripatetic tortoise in our backyard. But I wanted a real pet.

"Please, Mom," I beg. "Please." It is a warm spring day, early evening, and we are sitting on the tiled patio by our pool. "Just a little doggie."

"No dogs," says my mother firmly. "I've got three kids. That's enough."

"Please please please please please." I adopt what I imagine to be my most ingenuous and winning expression, eyes wide behind my gargantuan frames, eyebrows aloft.

"No Mimi, not a dog."

"You don't know how much I need one."

"No." She is unmoved. I sense I'm getting nowhere on this tack.

"I'll take such good care of him."

"No." Heartless woman! I am despairing, blinking back tears. My mother takes a deep breath, looking before us to the bulky palm tree at the other end of the pool. On summer days we swing from its branches into the water. Every now and then a branch breaks off and we scurry guiltily to cart away the evidence. I look back to my mother. Is it possible she's bending? But she's not looking at the tree. She's looking through it, beyond it, somewhere else altogether.

"Listen Mimi, Daddy and I were talking. If you are willing to be entirely responsible for it, we'll get you a budgie for your birthday."

A budgie! A budgie! Of my own! All right, this isn't a dog, or even a cat, but this is a *real* pet. The possibilities are endless. I'll train the bird to speak. I'll show it off to my friends. It will be mine, all mine, and it will follow me everywhere I go, sitting on my shoulder or perched on my hand—

"Mimi," my mother interrupts my reverie. "We went to America to try to find people to help us move there. We need to leave this country." Her voice is sad in a way that instantly throttles my exuberance. It is sad in a way that is measureless. I have seen my mother cry only once: after her father was killed by a drunk driver. I was five. She stayed in bed for days sobbing. The sadness in her voice reminds me

13

of how she was after she got out of bed. When she wasn't crying anymore, but she should have been.

"South Africa is not going to change," says my mother, looking down at me. She is here again, with me, eyes ruthless. "The whites are not going to give up any power. The blacks won't take it anymore. Daddy and I think there will be a war." Suddenly I am feeling distinctly nauseous. Should she really be talking to me this way? What happened to the budgie?

"We think there is no future in this country," she pummels away. "Most of the other whites are living in denial, diseased with racism, burying their heads in the sand and pretending they can live like this forever." She gestures around us to our house, our pool, the generous expanse of lawn and shrubbery lovingly tended by July. "America is a democracy. Everyone can vote. Black people are equal to white people there. Everyone has the same opportunities no matter what their skin color is. They all have the chance to provide for their families, live anywhere they want, marry whoever they want." I think this over. Sometimes when a black child touches me I feel dirty. Does Lily actually enjoy kissing Nigel? Is it really right for blacks to be able to marry whites? Yesterday at school when I did a handstand Joan yanked me down, scolding me for my carelessness. Two black boys were walking past the fence, and my *broekies* were showing.

"Mimi, are you listening to me?" My mother takes my face in her two hands, tilts it up to meet her eyes. I am overwhelmed with guilt, praying she can't read my thoughts. She's right. And I'm a racist, just like all the white people here who are going to get killed soon. I'm a horrible racist and we're going to America. I push my mother's hands away and look down into the clear depths of the pool, where light dapples the white surface in shimmering waves.

"*Ja*, Mom."

"Do you still want a budgie? Because if you want it, we'll get you one for your birthday. But you must know that one day we're going to leave South Africa, and you can't bring it with us when we do." My mother is normal again, even concerned.

"I still want one."

"Okay, darling. We'll get you a budgie for your birthday then."

I'm getting a budgie even though I don't deserve one because I'm a racist. I should have told Joan that black boys aren't any different from white, but I was too scared, and besides what if she's right? I'm a racist and a coward but I'm getting a budgie. And we're going to America. Where the people on TV live. Where everyone has the funny drawling accent that we in Standard 4P, Camps Bay Primary, imitate with reverence. I guess God forgives me for being racist. We're going to America.

Two:

The Valley

"Hey you! Chica! You!"

He is whistling at me. I keep walking rapidly. Where is homeroom again? Yes, B13, on the other side of the campus. That way, I need to go toward the central lawn and then—

"Hey, you! Girl, I'm talkin' to you!"

Followed by a sodden trill of kisses. People are starting to look. I scurry along, head down. I hate this school. Every single one of my six classes is in a different location. Portola Junior High is roughly the size of seven Camps Bay Primaries put together. It's my third day and I still get lost trying to find my classes.

"You! Baby! Turn aroun'!"

The hallways are clearing as the six-minute passing period ticks to a close. A good proportion of those who remain pause to take in the unfolding theatrics. I scan the faces around me anxiously. They are, to a last one, untarnished by empathy. Not a single face is familiar. No one to stand up for me. It would be impossible to know everybody here, or even a tenth of everybody. Who ever dreamed of putting two thousand kids into one school?

The bell rings, ear-splittingly loud. Drilling into my brain, sealing my mortification.

"You! Yeah, you in the red shirt!"

I can no longer make pretense to anonymity. I stop, and then turn, millimeter by painful millimeter, until I am facing my persecutor. He is Mexican, wearing those bizarre baggy pants. Mexicans are still new to me. As are Asians, Persians, and a whole host of other identities I'd never even heard of. But nonetheless I have a good idea of what's to come. As I suspected, he's not alone.

"Hey baby, my frien' here, he in love with you!"

I look at his friend. He is doubled over in mirth, incoherent, making spastic, scarlet-faced gestures of protest.

"He wanna make love with you," continues the first, straight-faced, drawing out the word *love* until it sounds like its own event. Like a circus, replete with spandex-clad acrobats and fire-eaters. He watches me innocently, waiting. He is pudgy, brown, studded with acne. I glare at them both with a fury that sears me with its purity. What insolence. If this was South Africa he'd know how to treat me. Perhaps lightning will course from the clear sky to annihilate them both on the spot. Then people will know my power, and my afflictions will be over. I pray briefly, fervently, for their speedy demise.

"He wanna have sex with you," resumes my tormentor, unsatisfied with my lack of response. He makes an O with the forefinger and thumb of his left hand, and pokes his right middle finger through it. "Like this, baby, like this."

Do these people even have parents? Who lets them act like this? Where are the teachers? At Camps Bay Primary, we didn't talk unless we were spoken to. We roved the halls in neat, silent lines, hands behind our backs. Until recently, discipline for the boys included being whacked on the bum with a paddle.

"Yeah, like this, he wanna do it to you..." His tongue starts roaming his upper lip like a distended slug, coating it with a glistening layer. His eyes are droopy and yellow and they burn into mine as if those fried-sausage fingers are actually—actually—touching me—*sis* man—

"Stuff off!" I yelp out helplessly. "Just stuff off!" I take my right hand off my hip and wield it in front of me, making the worst sign I know. "Up yours!"

They collapse in hysterics, the fat one literally falling to the ground in paroxysms, his friend leaping around in unmitigated delirium. "Baby he love you!" howls the first. "I love you," concedes his sidekick, baying with laughter, graciously resigning himself to destiny.

It takes me a few more days to learn that the middle finger is the dirty sign here. What I was giving them, in this country, was the peace sign backwards.

The Valley

Leaving South Africa was the hardest thing I'd ever done by far. My beloved teacher, Mr. Pearson, planned a wonderful surprise party and *braai* to send me off, which went magnificently until I got hit in the face with a ball and collapsed into a brief bout of tears. Astounded at my great luck in moving to Los Angeles, my peers promptly elevated me to an abrupt and heavenly popularity. At the final assembly of the week we left, after leading us in singing "Die Stem" and "All Things Bright and Beautiful," the principal announced his regret at our departure. "I'm very sorry you're leaving South Africa, Mariza," he intoned from the podium in his thick Afrikaner accent. Peering down at the neat lines of uniformed children striping the hall, blinking from behind glasses that rivaled mine in magnitude. I burst into tears and was attended to by a gaggle of newly solicitous friends. "Three cheers for Marisa!" screeched Felicia courageously at the close of the day, and the class cheered dutifully as I began weeping.

I bid a tearful goodbye to Dinki, my budgie, who did indeed follow me wherever I went when he was uncaged and who had mastered phrases in English, Afrikaans, and Xhosa. I hugged my cousin Richard tightly. "I'll be back," I said without conviction as he cried. Back to share Shabbat and Rosh Hashanah dinners with his family, the two of us giggling uncontrollably at the children's table as the adults droned through the prayers. Back to confirm that we were still in complete agreement on everything under the sun.

I kissed my grandmother on her cool, prickly-soft cheek, then drew back and studied her, straining to memorize every etching on the face I adored.

I watched as strangers entered our house and packed up everything we owned into a huge truck. And then I said good-bye to Maureen, squeezing her so tightly she could barely breathe, crying as she laughed and wept and didn't complain.

"I'll miss you, Maureenaz."

"You be a good girl, Mimi, good to Mommy and Daddy, okay?"

"Okay."

"And remember Maureen loves you so much, so so so so much."

"I love you too, Mau. I love you even more."

"No my baby, not possible."

And then we were in the airport, just the five of us. Somber and anxious. October 28, 1988. The day we'd been longing for. The day we'd been dreading.

"Frank Handler!" booms a voice over the loudspeaker. My father jumps in a panic. We have told the South African government we are leaving temporarily, going on a long trip. "Mr. Handler, please come to the South African Airlines office immediately." But it is only Mr. Pearson, come to the airport laden with gifts for our family. For my father, the dark chocolate he loves. For me, a journal, and a pen with my name inscribed on it.

Then we are on a plane, soaring over toy mountains, dollhouse gardens, vast bowls of heavy-cream cloud.

Then Heathrow, where we have a five-hour layover. I listen to the posh English accents and gaze at the chocolates behind glass in the bookstore. Same chocolates, different labels.

Then Dulles airport. "Welcome to Washington, D.C.," I tell my doll Nadine. She appears unimpressed. We are herded into an immigration line, then into a stuffy office where a man with a hook instead of a hand is drilling a German woman. We settle into our plastic chairs and I gawk at him in terror. This is the man who can give or take away our future. He's a real American, I can tell from his accent. Do all the immigration officers have hooks for hands?

Behind us is a large colored photo of The President. I like him instantly. He looks very kind, like someone who couldn't help but give me sweets whenever I asked. "Welcome to America, Marisa," I can hear him saying with his twanging TV accent, smile stretching even broader. "Welcome to the Land of the Free." Next to the photo is pinned a huge pastel map of our new country.

"Look, that's where we're going," I say in great excitement, having located Los Angeles on the map. "Shut up, Marisa," whispers my mother fiercely. Our sponsor, a rabbi, lives in Pennsylvania, and our papers say that my mother will be teaching Hebrew school in Pottsville. I sink into my seat, horrified at my stupidity. If we have to go back it'll be all my fault.

But the man with the hook lets us through. We emerge to the crisp air and raging colors of a northeastern fall. "We're in Amerrrica, folks!" says my dad, and we cannot stop laughing, relief bounding hot-breathed among us. That becomes the phrase to sum it all up — the many anomalies, delights, and puzzles of our new home: This is Amerrrica, folks. We visit the Lincoln Memorial, examine the Capitol and the White House from behind their fences, marvel at the size of everything from the top of the Washington Memorial. Stuff is bigger here. This is Amerrrica, folks. We go to the National Air and Space Museum, where I try to envision sleeping standing up in a rocket ship and can't stop chortling over the tube astronauts have to use to pee. This is Amerrrica, folks. We fly to LA and settle into an apartment in a gated community in Tarzana. It is tiny, cramped, and drab after our well-appointed quarters in Camps Bay.

My dad inspects our new home, characteristic enthusiasm hammered down a few notches. I wait. "Well, this is Amerrrica, folks."

Our first Thanksgiving: we are mentored by close friends, also expatriates. We gorge on the huge bird that sits brashly in the middle of the table. Not at all like ostrich meat, definitely closer to chicken. Then each of us takes our turn saying what we are grateful for, rolling this new tradition delicately across our tongues.

My mother, firm: "I'm grateful that we made it here, where we can live with a clear conscience. And that we're among friends." Looking about her warmly.

My father, eyes moist: "I want to give thanks for the whole family pulling together like we have. I'm very proud of all of us for working so hard to make this move a success." He meets my eyes and jerks his eyebrows up and down manically until I giggle.

My sister: "I'm grateful that we get to wear normal clothes to school instead of stupid uniforms. And *ja*, of course for arriving here safe and sound, getting out of South Africa, blah-blah-blah."

My little brother, pointed: "I'm grateful that we're all here, but mostly I'm grateful that it's my birthday in six days and that I'm going to get a remote-control car."

Me, suddenly blisteringly shy and on the verge of tears: "I—I think we should thank God for bringing us here and taking care of us." Then I am crying again as my sister rolls her eyes and sighs lustily, and my brother pesters my dad about remote-control cars. "She's very sensitive," mouths my mother to the table as I bury my face in her shoulder.

Our first earthquake, three weeks after our arrival: my parents are away. I am sitting at the table in our kitchen, writing an essay on George Washington (thanking my lucky stars that history harbors something novel after years of the Dutch East India Company, the Hottentots, and the Boer War). Dishes and other loose objects begin to rattle. My pencil skates across the page in an inelegant line. I am clutching it so hard it breaks. Then the floor starts rolling: the entire world is suddenly afoot and jogging toward what I know with absolute clarity will be total annihilation. "M-maybe someone's jumping on the roof," my sister proffers hopefully from the couch, clinging to an armrest. Pardon me? "This is an earthquake, you flipping idiot!" I rise shakily, sprint to our bedroom, huddle under a desk, and begin praying. "Please forgive me for all my sins, I'm so sorry, I'm trying really hard to be good and did I remember to thank you for my new school bag and also I never really meant to hit Marc he's just so annoying and if you only let me live I promise I'll never tease him again and also I'll never nag Mom and Dad again for anything ever again in my whole entire life I swear dear God and yes I know it wasn't nice to just call Gabi a flipping idiot but—"

In hindsight, I was a pretty easy target for your average schoolyard sadist. I wasn't used to wearing "civvies"— civilian clothes—to school, and my fashion sense was, well, unhoned. I tucked my sweaters into my jeans. I was one of approximately three people who actually did the school spirit day assignments, like dressing backwards on Yad Sdrawkcab, or wearing my school's hat and T-shirt on Fridays. Coolness was an entirely new concept to me, one that took a good couple of years to get the hang of. Instead of falling in lacquered waves, liberated from its Camps Bay Primary–mandated ponytail, my curly hair — which I continued to blowdry and brush out — assumed impressive proportions. And then of course there were my glasses. And the way I spoke. And what I said.

"Excuse me, can I borrow a rubber, please?" Turning politely to the boy sitting behind me.

"Oh my God! Marisa just asked me for a condom!" The entire class erupts on cue. Mental note: eraser, eraser, *eraser*, for God's sake.

Or:

"I really like your braces." (Translation: suspenders.)

Blank look. "What?"

"*Ja* hey, they're really nice."

"You like my braces? What is, like, wrong with you, anyway?"

"Er, nothing. So do you wear them for fashion or to keep your pants up?"

Somehow I remained relentlessly optimistic as I scuffled ineptly through the pitfalls of this foreign culture — a culture, I soon realized, comprised almost entirely of media and consumer culture. Coming from censored South Africa, with its single television channel and few hours of programming each day — half in Afrikaans, the other half divided between British and American shows — I discovered I was dangerously ignorant. My standard two hours of TV a week was wholly inadequate when it came to keeping up with lunchtime conversations at Portola Junior High. Mysteries abounded. Who were the new kids, and upon which block might they be located? What was so gosh-darn lovable about Lucy, anyway? Was Star Wars a game show or a restaurant chain? I learned that maintaining my dignity entailed keeping my mouth rigorously shut until I knew what my peers were going on about. At least I was familiar with some of the code: the Bill Cosby show, for reasons that continue to mystify me, was aired weekly in apartheid South Africa.

Along with catching up on algebra and Spanish, I issued myself an ongoing customized homework assignment: watch television. Lots of it. With particular emphasis upon the commercials. Commercials were perhaps my greatest teachers. They enlightened me to the sources of countless inside jokes. I learned to sing along with the jingles. I made friends with Ronald McDonald, the Pillsbury Dough Boy, the benevolently smiling M&M cartoons. I learned that Snickers Really Satisfies, Beef Is What's for Dinner, Milk Does a Body Good, and that when I was confused about something the superior response was to Just Do It. Most importantly, commercials instructed me on what I was supposed to want. Not that my parents were remotely sympathetic: having sunk all their resources into immigrating, they were deaf to my requests. But I knew what I was supposed to want, which was what really counted when it came to fitting in. In a culture meticulously constructed around the constant cultivation of desire, I was learning to play the consumer.

Yet I missed South Africa viciously. The malls and unremitting suburbs of the San Fernando Valley were little match for Cape Town. My friends in South Africa had told me I'd be running into Madonna and Michael Jackson on the street, but so far the only famous person any of us had met was Tony Danza. My sister was jogging in Balboa Park when she spotted him. When she told him we watched his show in South Africa, he smiled blankly and offered to sign his autograph.

Despite the assorted snags, Amerrrica is two fingers from paradise to our shining eyes. We are finally living in A Democracy. Unlike my classmates, I recite the Pledge of Allegiance with great fervor, hand firm over my heart. I feel a fierce love for my new country, a clarion gratitude for the beautiful vision laid out in its Constitution. Don't these people understand what they have here? Blacks in this country are lawyers, doctors, teachers. They're even in commercials. And there are some white people who clean homes! Compared to South Africa, this is racial nirvana. I make a black friend in school, Annette, and am inordinately proud of myself and attentive with her.

"You're friends with that girl?" says Michelle, another new friend, eyeing Annette from where we are sitting eating our lunch. Michelle has glasses like me and long permed brown hair, and I am very pleased to be the recent recipient of a glitter-pink invitation to her bat mitzvah.

"Yes. That's Annette. She's really nice." Annette is talking to another black friend, but she feels my gaze and looks back and smiles warmly at me. I can't wait to get home and tell my mother how much I like her.

"But doesn't the way she smells bother you?"

"Pardon?"

"The way she smells. Black people smell funny, haven't you noticed? Kind of greasy. They don't wash enough, you know."

I am openmouthed, too dumbfounded to even respond as Michelle shifts blithely to another topic and continues chattering away.

Everything here feels too big. "King-sized," rumble the voices on commercials. It's as if even the buildings know they have a lot of room in this sprawling country, so they stretch themselves out accordingly. And everything is "All New." (What's wrong with just plain "new"? asks my dad of a native with genuine curiosity.) Plus there's a lot of it all: reams and oodles and neatly stacked masses of the King-sized and the All New.

Going grocery shopping here is an adventure, a bold sally into the brightly packaged unknown. I drive with my mother to Lucky's. We locate a spot in the vast terrain of parking lot, and then make for the door. We stand just inside with our cart, trying to look as purposeful as the other women who look past us. Generally people are very friendly here. So friendly that we mock them at home, saying, "That's awesome!" and "You're very welcome!" with teeth bared in garish grins and eyebrows suspended millimeters below our hairlines. When they hear our accents, Americans smile widely and ask us where we're from. I've discovered I can say almost anything and these people will believe it. Half the time they refer to me as being from South America anyway. At school yesterday I told the girl copying my English homework that we wore nothing but grass skirts and rode on lions to school, which was in a big hut. She stared at me wide-eyed. "That's so cool," she said, and it was too late to fix it. People are friendly here, but I'm starting to see that it's mostly just when they're supposed to be. Like when I ask someone a question or they're ringing up our purchases. The rest of the time they look past each other. It makes me feel lonely even when I'm somewhere as busy as Lucky's.

My mother pulls her shopping list out of her purse. "Okay, Mims, let's find some raisin bran."

We begin with what would appear a simple assignment. I leave my mother at the miniature jungle that is the plant section and tear across the breadth of the supermarket and back.

"Cereal's on aisle five. Let's go."

We have direction. Off we charge, my mother examining her list as I try to steer the unruly cart. "Well..." she begins uncertainly, when we reach aisle five. It yawns before us like a carnivorous tropical flower, rainbow palate panting waves of recycled air. For a minute we stand in the blast of shimmering color and fluorescent light, overwhelmed.

"Come on, Mom." I pull her hand and we advance undaunted, me tugging the cart like a wayward goat behind us. I have never seen this much cereal in my whole life. Who could eat so much cereal? How would you ever learn to choose? Later, this face-off with excess will glow lurid in my memory, an early warning sign of a society severely off-kilter. But for now I am bowled over. Odd-shaped creatures beam dazzling from the boxes. Unequivocal block letters extol each item's many health benefits. I am familiar with some of the cereals from my stints in front of the television, and I note them as we pass, puzzling out their branding like code. And then I cannot help myself, I am temporarily distracted, mesmerized, Odysseus in the thrall of the Sirens. I slow my pace, eyes spinning with snippets of color and print as the cart thrusts at me like a bull hooking its inept matador. Yet Providence has not forgotten us: my mother remains clear-headed and rigorously on task.

"Raisin bran!" She has spied the grail where it rests unobtrusively at the very end of the aisle. She is running now, arms uplifted in triumph as the women around us turn and stare. "Look, Mimi, it's raisin bran!" And I am racing after her, shrieking with joy as she clutches it to her chest and gently closes her eyes with the unmistakable savor of victory. *Yes*, my mother is thinking, *I can do this. We can do this. We were right to leave and we're going to make it work.*

I always feel a bit of an oddball, but I come to love my new homeland. Or at least the idea of it. Democracy, justice, equality: it is love at first sight with these, and even though I soon begin to see how the actual society fails to measure up, I am too far gone to backpedal. I love the idealism upon which this nation is based, the goodness of the intentions behind it. And I love the distinctly American nature of the constant struggle to fulfill those intentions. Six years after our arrival, I get "naturalized" into U.S. citizenship. I stand in the hall during the ceremony, a lone white face among a sea of Latinos and Asians, and with a full heart pledge my loyalty to the country that has come to feel like home.

But that's years down the line.

In the beginning, much of Amerrrica is strange to me. Some of my peers, like my new best friend Allie, have enough stuff to outfit a medium-sized village. Allie's parents are never home and we amuse ourselves with her huge-screen cable TV, video games, and "pigging out" on the sweets — "candy" — my parents refuse to buy. Play is different here: while I still draw and write stories to amuse myself, my new friends either mock me when I suggest it or grow rapidly bored. What's "cool," I learn, is what falls within the bubblegum borders of pop culture. Exercising our own imaginations? Decidedly uncool. No one reads books here. Instead we rent videos or choreograph dance moves to Madonna. Allie introduces me to pornography, which was illegal in South Africa. She pinches her father's *Playboy* magazines and we study the centerfolds with awe, lamenting our own stubbornly flat chests. She reads the articles aloud with relish as I shudder in horror and covert pleasure.

My classmates seem very sophisticated. When we study sex ed in health class, no one even laughs when the teacher says "penis" and "vagina." I meanwhile give vent to a fit of snorts trying to stifle my hysterics. Standard 4P would have been up in arms. No doubt: sex ed is definitely a good swap for religious studies, when the four Jews in the class got shuttled off with *Morah* Rivka while the rest of Standard 4P stayed behind to pay their respects to the Father Son and Holy Ghost. But other than the occasional subdued bout of boredom, the classes here in general strike me as utter anarchy after Camps Bay Primary. This must be part of living in A Democracy, I reflect. I pity the teachers who are treated so rudely by my peers. "Thanks for sticking it out," I say to one substitute teacher who is obviously swallowing back tears at the close of math class. "It must have been hard, with this bunch." She gapes at me like I have a halo and manages to whimper out a thank-you.

But somehow, despite our best efforts and gutbuckets of good intentions, we are always misfits, my family.

We have to ask for a "glass of water" three times in restaurants before the bemused waitress understands us.

My parents throw around phrases in Yiddish and Afrikaans and South African English slang to such an extent that when I invite a friend to supper—"Huh? You mean dinner?"—I have to actually translate.

Nearly a year after immigrating, we move into a house in a gated community in Woodland Hills. "Will you go with me?" asks my latest crush, as we cavort in the community pool. He is pedaling water, eyes fixed ardently upon mine. "Go where?" I inquire ingenuously, and he splashes away in embarrassment. My astounding good luck dawns on me and I dog-paddle madly after him, crying "Yes! Yes, Carl, yes! Anywhere you want!"

We get packages of money in the mail. It is our own money that the South African government won't let us take out, and that a friend converts into multiple currencies in order not to arouse suspicion. It arrives in fat envelopes, a rainbow of stiff bills: yen, pesos, pounds. Still, despite this incontrovertible evidence of great riches, my parents won't buy us anything but the essentials. I start babysitting for two dollars an hour to fund the bicycle I want. At fifteen I get my first real job, at Hot Dog on a Stick at the Fallbrook mall. I don the colorful tank top and hat with pride, and proceed to fry up corn dogs and "stomp" lemonade with a vengeance. We are mostly teenage girls working there, and invariably we have a small fan-club of hormonal adolescent boys. My biweekly paycheck equals a measure of independence. By this point I'm no longer playing a part—I really *do* want the clothes, the music, the makeup. And now I have the power to buy whatever I want. From fifteen on I manage my own finances entirely.

My family never assimilates, but I do get better at suppressing the evidence of our difference. I adopt the flat intonations of a Valley accent (*like, gag me with a spoon*). I try desperately to be cool. In high school, I grow my hair long, discover hair products, get contact lenses, and am nonetheless largely ignored as I hover hopefully at the fringes of the popular crowd with my similarly ambitious friends. Academically I am an overachiever, and not above lording my successes or publicly correcting my teachers (it doesn't take me terribly long to get in the chaotic swing of things in the classroom). A couple of intrepid boys ask me out, but these ventures are short-lived: I am simultaneously bored and dreadfully shy, and far too innocent to hazard the murky provinces beyond kissing. Like most everyone around me — although I fall for their masks, and hope they fall for mine — I am ravaged by insecurities, convinced I am not pretty enough, not cool enough, not good enough. While I do have my small circle of friends, I can't help feeling there must be more to life than nail polish, acid-washed jeans, and boys. Not to put too fine a point upon it, but essentially high school sucks.

Salvation comes in the form of Habonim Dror: a worldwide Socialist Zionist youth movement. Where the counselors collect the campers' candy on the first day and redistribute it at parties. Where every session the junior counselors stage "Revolution" and kick the counselors out for an entire day of jubilant mayhem. Where each Friday we hold Hyde Park and anyone who wants, age eight to Methuselah, can step up on the soapbox to give feedback on any aspect of camp they desire. My parents had been involved in Habonim as youth in South Africa, and they are delighted at this opportunity for our happy indoctrination. In terms of locating Jewish community, we have largely floundered since immigration. Services here often feel like fashion shows; bar and bat mitzvahs in general strike us as absurdly extravagant and ostentatious. I am sixteen, a junior counselor, for my first summer at a Habonim *machaneh* in rural Pennsylvania, and it feels like nothing less than a generous slice of heaven. My friendships at *machaneh* are much richer than the thin sustenance I eke out of the arid terrain of my high school. We share ideals! We are building community! United by a cause! And of course when these get old there are still boys, clothes swapping, and clandestine cigarette rendezvous in the wilds beyond the pool.

Finally, I am being presented with a philosophy based on larger issues, on concern for the world, and it is of my own tradition. Judaism, Zionism, Socialism, Social Justice, and Self-Actualization: these are the five pillars of Habonim Dror, and the activities we plan always include one of them as a furtive — or bald-facedly overt — educational goal. "No, Joe, don't you understand? We all win when we *pool* our M&Ms and *share* them. That way everyone gets four. Otherwise you only get two and plus you're lonely and nobody will want to share with you the next round." We also learn about the occupation of Palestinian lands, and the vast political divide between orthodox and secular Israeli society. While relatively far on the left of the Israeli political spectrum, Habonim makes no bones about steeping us in the glorious lore of Zionist mythology. I learn about the waves of Jewish settlers working the desert (and deserted) land under a blazing sun, the Eden-like kibbutzim that sprang up within their muscled embrace. Like a mail-order bride, I dutifully fall head over heels in love with an Israel I've never seen. I also join *Chug Nashim,* the women's group. The two counselors who run it do not shave their legs or underarms, and they counsel us on the evils of media representations of women and on subverting the patriarchy. I am smitten.

At camp, I realize that our society's current modus operandi is not inevitable. I discover that alternatives exist, that these alternatives are beautiful, and that they can be lived. I learn what community means. Like my great-grandfather and my parents before me, I begin to conceive of other possibilities. I return to El Camino Real High School for my senior year ready and armed to just say no. I have stopped shaving my legs — a mere year-and-something after my mother let me start in the first place. I have become militant in my egalitarian employment of gender pronouns. I approach my favorite teacher and ask her to sponsor a new club. And then I launch Womyn Aloud, merrily inviting all and sundry to its first meeting over the PA system — and am completely bowled over by the fallout.

"You're a dyke!" accuses my friend Justin, who later makes half-hearted stabs at initiating a men's club. "No I'm not!" I screech back tearfully. "Not that there's anything wrong with it anyway!" The head of the Student Council tells me I obviously hate men. One teacher accuses me — *me!* — of being sexist for excluding men. "Men are welcome,"

I inform him coolly. "You're cordially invited." He regretfully declines. Another teacher tells me I am stirring up trouble for no good reason. They simmer down, however, after a teacher is put on probation when we send a letter to both him and the assistant principal, protesting his repeated harassment of female students.

No, I proclaim with great bravado, to the school, to the Valley, to the mindless narcissistic vacuity of it all. *No.* My voice loud, this time, and shrill with defiance. *No* and *no* and *did you hear me?* I said *NO! Shove it up your ass!* At this point I've lost whatever remote chance of fitting in I'd ever had. It is too late to say yes. But I discover, to my wonder, that I have a hardy band of compadres willing to turn *no* into a chorus.

Today, I still count Womyn Aloud as one of the best things I've been a part of creating. This posse of young women and a couple of brave young men coalesces in a way that blurs the boundary between political action committee and support group. We are honest, sensitive to each other, and unabashedly radical. We celebrate women's right to choose, scoff at supermodels, and study the text of Title IX. We listen quietly as each of us shares our experiences of harassment, abuse, even molestation. And we are not above swooning over John Travolta in *Saturday Night Fever* and *Grease.* Womyn Aloud even has a car in the homecoming parade, and I maintain with complete impartiality that by this point our reception is more cheers than heckling.

Habonim Dror had shown me the possibilities of life beyond the Valley, and returning felt about as comfortable as donning a hair shirt. But in this bleached-out terrain of silicone and strip malls, it was Womyn Aloud that helped preserve my sanity. Womyn Aloud showed me, often painfully, the consequences of saying no. But it also showed me that I could survive the fallout, that ultimately it made me stronger. And most importantly, that saying no out loud fortified others who were muttering it under their breath. Four years later, when I was a senior at U.C. Berkeley, a girl approached me on campus and asked if I had gone to El Camino Real High School. "You're the one who started Womyn Aloud, aren't you?" she asked, and I nodded, amazed. "I was a freshman at the time," she told me. "All I knew was that the world was a mess and everyone was trying to pretend like it wasn't. But Fridays at lunchtime I could speak my mind, and listen to other women speak theirs." She thanked me and told me that the club was still active and had grown. I stood there as she walked away, tears prickling, marveling over it all—it seemed like such a small effort in the scheme of things, but it continued to ripple out in ways I hadn't imagined. Womyn Aloud taught me that I could not just choose, but could actually build an alternative.

Not that I wasn't hell-bent on getting out of the Valley.

Three:

Jerusalem

I have been living in Jerusalem for over nine months before I venture into its other half. I've thought about visiting East Jerusalem, but no one in my program has done so thus far. We have been warned against it. My year in Israel is approaching its close when a new friend, Gillian, suggests it. Gillian is from Montreal. She is tiny, with long ropes of hair and a brand of defiance that is at once familiar and a little daunting. Most of the time I can't decide whether I want to follow her or argue with her.

"Let's go into East Jerusalem," she says to me one day. We are sitting on a bench just outside Hebrew University's Rothberg International School, where most of our classes are held. It is a glorious day, the sky an azure-glazed bowl. Students flow around our bench and out to lunch in an ebbing tide, enveloping us in a menagerie of clanging American accents. I resent that I spend most of my time in Israel surrounded by other North Americans. Without fail, on weekends I flee the campus.

"Okay." I am dubious. "Do you think it's safe?" This is 1997, my junior year of college. Suicide bombers have yet to appear, like grisly couriers from the lower circles of hell. But there are bombings. The previous week I happened upon an entire block of Ben Yehuda Street in downtown Jerusalem taped off due to an ownerless backpack. The bomb squad arrived, and I waited at the corner with a small crowd, watching the indifferent faces around me with incredulity as the bomb was detonated with an ear-splitting thud. But even I have gotten used to the military presence here, to the young soldiers riding the buses with their AK-47s perched against the windows as they snore. During my first couple of months in Israel, while on *ulpan* in Haifa, I had an American boyfriend who was a paratrooper in the Israeli army. When he came to visit me on weekends he would stow his rifle under my bed, which was where I kept my dirty laundry. Every time I tossed a pair of socks down there I cringed.

"Of course it's safe. We'll be fine." Gillian watches me intently. She is waiting for me to back down, ready to pounce, and I won't have any of it.

"How do we get there?"

"Do you realize where we are? We just keep walking once we get off campus. It's about ten minutes from here."

Navigation has never been my forte. Hebrew University is on Mount Scopus, or Har Hatzofim, a tenacious island of West Jerusalem in the otherwise foreign terrain of East Jerusalem. The Romans camped on Mount Scopus in A.D. 70, ruminating on their final attack as they pored over the besieged and smoldering city. In 1949, at the close of the Israeli War of Independence, cease-fire lines left Israeli defenders in control of Hebrew University and Hadassah Hospital, both squarely in the midst of what was then Jordanian East Jerusalem. Over the next nineteen years these outposts were supplied and maintained, while the institutions were transferred into West Jerusalem proper. During the Six-Day War of 1967, along with capturing the Gaza Strip and Sinai from Egypt and the Golan Heights from Syria, Israel commandeered the West Bank — including East Jerusalem — from Jordan. Mount Scopus was thereafter reinstated as the main campus of the Hebrew University. In 1980 Israel passed the Jerusalem Law, which formally declared East and West Jerusalem — "whole and united" — to be the capital of Israel. In response the U.N. Security Council, with the abstention of the U.S., unanimously adopted Resolution 478, pronouncing the annexation a violation of international law.

It's amazing how quickly one can get used to living in half a city. Close to 60 percent of Jerusalem's residents live in East Jerusalem. About 55 percent of these are Arabs. There are some places I know: technically the Arab Quarter of the Old City is part of East Jerusalem, and I visit its bustling markets whenever I get the chance. But from where I stand, most of East Jerusalem looks like the small, rickety shacks descending Mount Scopus, impoverished tenants quartered a safe distance from the sprawling white manor of the university. Off-limits, our administrators warn us. I think of the townships around Cape Town; of Langa, Guguletu, Khayalitsha. Except here Guguletu is on my doorstep.

My parents didn't want me to spend my third year of college in Israel. "It's a dangerous country, Mimi," my mother pleaded. "There are bombs going off on the buses. Why don't you just visit for a couple of weeks?" But I was bound and determined. Thanks to Habonim Dror, I had been immersed in Israel every summer for the past four years. I wanted to get to know the country I'd been courting from afar. Not just the postcard version, but the reality. Besides, my parents also hadn't wanted me to go to Berkeley. They'd thought I should go to UCLA, to be close to home. But Berkeley had been the best thing that could possibly have happened to me. Berkeley had been my white knight, my rescuer from the cultural gulag of the Valley. I met remarkable people, formed enduring friendships, enrolled gleefully in feminist theory and art history and European literature. After living under my parents' strict supervision, Berkeley meant independence, freedom, hedonism. I'd entered university intending to graduate in three years and go straight to law school. I left aspiring to be a musician. What an education! And every hour of it, thanks to a chancellor's scholarship, on the university's tab—including one whole year abroad in the country of my choosing. There was no doubt in my mind which country that would be.

Habonim Dror had educated me to some of the complexities of Israeli politics, but I arrive starry-eyed and indisputably naive nonetheless. I step off the El Al airplane and onto Israeli soil and I pause, motionless among the rushing Israelis and clamorous Americans. This is it. This is the dream held by innumerable Jews from myriad places across the globe for the past two millennia. I am living it. I am in her chambers, looking directly into her eyes, exulting in her arms. I resist the urge to kneel and kiss the concrete. I pick up my bag and keep walking. For the rest of the day, I am in a trance. The sun is setting as we approach Jerusalem in our bus: red fire pooled over white stone, and every square inch of the bald hills is shining, sacred, singing to me. We are taken to the Kotel, the holiest place in Judaism, the retaining wall left by the Romans when the Second Temple was destroyed.

"Can you believe that?" breathes my friend Nicole.

"No."

We are looking down upon it from an elevated courtyard. The wall is massive, forged from huge white blocks of Jerusalem stone. Behind it the gold dome of Al-Aqsa mosque gleams dully in the slipping light. Arabic surges around us in urgent staccato: the muezzin is calling the faithful to worship. Below us, hundreds of orthodox Jews are gathering to pray. They draw toward the wall like bees to a hive, focused, rapt, ancient chains of words rising in a muted drone. Two religions, their sacred places flanking each other, their people praying to the same god. Yet here, in the nimbus of faith, is where the bloodshed begins. We descend the steps slowly, heading toward the women's section of the wall. "We're so lucky," says a friend, as we pause at the margins of the swarm. "Thousands of Jews worldwide aspire to be here. Just think how many Jews have prayed over the centuries to be where we are now."

"L'shanah ha'ba-ah b'Yerushalayim," I murmur. Next year in Jerusalem: words recited at the close of every Passover seder, when the redemption of the Jews from bondage in Egypt is celebrated through elaborate ritual. After the ten plagues, after Moses parted the Red Sea, after its waters closed over the luckless Egyptian troops, the Jews wandered in the desert for forty years. They learned not to worship false idols. They learned the true nature of God. Only then were they led into the Promised Land.

I plunge in. Around me, women are bobbing in prayer, *siddurim* clasped to their breasts. Many are weeping, eyes locked tight in rapture as they recite, lips molding to well-worn patterns. I wonder what it is they are feeling. How can they look at the world around them, at the injustice and the carnage, and still believe? I move toward the wall, raise my hand to touch the smooth stone. Next to me a woman clutches her infant, holding a tiny hand up to the wall as she dips and weaves in prayer. There are bushes sprouting from fissures between the blocks, and they bear white blooms. When I look closer I see that the lower blossoms are shreds of fabric and paper: the flowers of a multitude of sun-starved hopes and terrors, reverently sown in this holiest of soil. The lower cracks in the wall are crammed with tightly folded wads of paper, a flotilla of many-colored notes bearing the miniature print of fraught petitions. I lean my forehead to the stone, and for the first time in many months, I try to pray.

"Let me bless you."

A hand is tugging at my shoulder.

"What?" I turn. She is very old, her face deeply furrowed, tufts of white hair poking out from under her headscarf. She grins at me, displaying a generous swath of gum and four eroding teeth. "Let me bless you." Taking my hand into hers. I feel the cold knobs of knuckle, the folds of skin tough as rhinoceros hide.

"B'seder." All right. We move back from the front lines to a calmer patch. She holds out her other hand. "Three shekels."

I dig in my pocket. She accepts the coins with a nod of approval, knots them into one end of the shawl around her shoulders. Closes her eyes and begins intoning, pitching and muttering as I stare. After a minute or two she draws to an abrupt close, pulls a string out of one of the pouches in her dress, and proceeds to tie it around my wrist.

"What did you bless me with?"

She looks at me solemnly, sparking black eyes probing into mine. Doubting, I sense, my good judgment. "I blessed you with what every upright Jewish woman deserves. I prayed for you to have a good marriage and at least thirteen, fourteen children."

It is July of 1996 when I step off the plane. Eight months earlier, during a giant peace rally, Prime Minister Yitzhak Rabin had been assassinated by right-wing religious settler fanatic Yigal Amir. This proved a catastrophic close to the most hopeful period in decades, and heralded the initiation of a bloody disintegration of the peace process. Ultraorthodox Jews had viewed Rabin as a traitor for his willingness to give away a part of Israel for the sake of peace. Religious settlers define Israel as the land God gave Abraham and his descendants in "everlasting covenant"; this includes the ancient nations of Judea and Samaria, known today as the West Bank, along with Jordan, Lebanon, and a sizable chunk of Syria and Egypt to boot. Rabbis in the West Bank sermonized that Rabin was a persecutor of the Jews, comparable to members of the S.S. A group of ultraorthodox rabbis gave religious sanction to his murder, reviving the obsolete *halachic* precepts of *din rodef*—the duty to kill a Jew who jeopardizes the life or property of another Jew—and *din moser,* the duty to get rid of a Jew who intends to turn another Jew over to non-Jewish authorities. The settlers heralded Rabin's death as a miracle comparable to the parting of the Red Sea and held Amir as their savior.

I attend a peace rally on the first anniversary of Rabin's assassination, in the renamed Kikar Rabin in Tel Aviv. Tens of thousands of people pack the square and surrounding streets. Security is high, as Islamic Jihad has been issuing threats recently. Garbed in black, Rabin's widow Leah speaks. I watch as around me Israelis of all colors and ages weep openly, leaning on each other for support. The night is luminous with thousands of candles, sharp-scented from the countless wreaths lining the square. Some of the mourners carry signs: "Peace will avenge his blood" and "*Chaver* [friend], I remember." The wall where Rabin was shot is covered in graffiti. "Save the Peace," I read, and "Shalom, *Chaver*": slashes of black and red and blue, eloquent captions to the mural of Rabin above. There is a palpable rage, too. What singes the edges of this grief is no less than hatred, a hard, glinting loathing for the ultraorthodox and all they represent. Among the dregs of peace lie the seeds of a cultural civil war that may prove more destructive to Israel than any external enemy.

Kol od balevav p'nimah
Nefesh Yehudi homiyah...

Israel's national anthem, *Hatikvah,* "The Hope," wings through the gathering. I have been singing this beautiful song as long as I can remember. It courses through my limbs like my own blood; it is our history, our longing, our despair, our gritty survival. I sway with my friends as we sing, our arms around each other. The whole crowd is rocking in serpentine currents of grief, and we are caught up now, twisting and wailing. The words wrenching as out of one being. We are a flayed beast gasping for air, every cell stoically intoning its coding, deaf to competing anthems: "The hope of two thousand years"—

rising, floating, dissipating in the heavy-handed Tel Aviv night—"to be a free people in our own land." I realize my face is wet with tears. We have been dreaming this dream for so long that some of us refuse to wake up. Our own land is not enough. We have been victims so long that victimhood is branded into our psyche, and we have lost the faculty to recognize our own ability to persecute. Yet in our zeal to prove we will not let ourselves be victimized, we become the bullies, defending an occupation that denies the Palestinians the very same dream to which we have clung for millennia.

Our program is based in Haifa for our first two months in Israel. We spend the weekdays doing *ulpan,* intensive Hebrew studies. On weekends, we are carted all over Israel, being introduced to the various wonders and predicaments of life in the Holy Land. We visit Tzvat, a sacred city that has historically been a center of Jewish philosophy and mysticism, on Tu B'Av, the Day of Love, and watch as the black-clad ultraorthodox men celebrate with delirious abandon and dance raucous through the streets. We marvel over the magnificent, obstinately enduring Roman ruins at Caesarea. We hike along the breathtakingly lush Yehudia falls in the Golan Heights, and then tour Israel's borders with Syria and Lebanon, visiting a Syrian bunker from the Six-Day War. Our guide points out the town of Kiryat Shmonah, adjacent to the border with Lebanon. It was hit with Katyusha missiles by the Hezbollah months before our visit. The desert terrain along the borders is littered with tank monuments. I stare at the faded behemoths, rusting in rigor mortis, and the naked actuality of Israel's microscopic size and vulnerability penetrates with a resounding thud.

While the orthodox bear piles of offspring and take care never to reveal an ankle, the rest of Israel feels like a night out at a particularly racy club. It is skintight or nothing for the young women here. In Berkeley, I was a hippie. I went with my friends to Grateful Dead shows, wore corduroys and embroidered peasant blouses. I arrive abysmally ill-equipped to hold my own among the hipsters peopling Israel's nightly panorama. Nicole and I decide we are each in severe need of a new pair of pants. We head to Tel Aviv's Dizengoff Street on a shopping mission.

"How's my ass look?"

"Great. Like it was molded out of polyester. Mine?"

"Magnificent. Let's go."

It's amazing what a pair of hip-huggers can do: as if I've been magically transformed, suddenly detectable by their radar, Israeli men start paying attention.

"Allo baby. I take you out tonight."

"You have boyfriend?" Automatic, albeit untruthful, yes. "No problem. I'm better man, guaranteed."

"You American?" I nod. Sometimes I tell people I am South African. It depends on the day, my mood. He looks at me quizzically, lovingly fingering a thick gold chain buried in a lush nest of chest hair. "Have you tried Israeli man yet?"

Early on, when I have been in Haifa only a week, I accept an invitation from an Israeli studying engineering at the Technion. He takes me out to a bang-up dinner at a spanking new restaurant and will not hear of splitting the bill. At some point the conversation veers into the illicit.

"Drugs? Terrible. I was offered grass once, but oh no. No no." He shakes his handsome buzz-cut head, and eyes me warily. "You've tried it?"

"Uh…" I picture the numerous bowls circulated among friends on Wheeler Beach, the sunny green patch next to Berkeley's English building. Then there was 4/20, practically a calendar holiday on campus. And the nightly toke I shared with friends following the dutiful completion of our reading. "Well, maybe once or twice."

"How it was?"

"Yeah, okay, you know. Kind of like beer. So… what do you think of American music? A lot of what makes it here is really rather awful." It takes about five minutes to convey this sentiment, between my stammering stabs at Hebrew and his broken English.

"Oh, pop music! Yes, American music. Yes yes, I'm big fan. I love Bon Jovi and Michael Jackson. I have each album."

"I see."

He leans in. "Yeah I'm wanted." Beat. "Dead or alive." He sings with bona fide emotion, wielding his knife as a makeshift microphone.

"Uh-huh, that one. I remember it well. So... How's your dinner? Would you like to try some of my food?" I proffer a forkful of spaghetti.

"No thanks."

"Are you sure?" I'm getting desperate. "It's quite delicious. Here, have a taste."

"Marisa, I'm not shy guy." A vein pops out on his forehead. It is throbbing, I note with awe, in precise time to the monotonous thump of the trance music pumping through the speakers. He glares at me. "Israeli men not shy. When I want, I help myself."

"Gotcha." Two spoonfuls of Womyn Aloud, please, then call me in the morning. "So, nearly ready for dessert?"

When Israelis realize I am American, they treat me differently. For one, they insist on speaking English. "Not here," I respond firmly. "When you come to America I'll speak English," and continue in Hebrew. They also assume I am weak and can be pushed around. At the *shuk,* I get quoted absurd prices. I rapidly adopt what I think of as an authentic Israeli accent, which seems to work fine for me, although it is well into the year before an Israeli friend informs me that I sound like a French ultraorthodox mother.

Decades of living in a state of near-constant warfare have saturated the culture, and assimilating — or even getting by — requires adopting a veneer of toughness. I learn to push madly to get on a bus. I learn that in order to garner the respect of the average Israeli, I need to be mercilessly assertive, even aggressive. "What, four shekels for these carrots?" Pawing them disdainfully. "Are you mad? I'll give you two. That's it, no more discussion." But beneath the crusty exteriors, I discover, Israelis bear a thorough goodwill. "*B'seder,* two shekels. And for you, I'll throw in a persimmon too." Slowly I adapt, and gradually begin to love the reality that is Israel.

Having been part of a minority all my life, it is gratifying to live among an extended community of my own. Despite different nationalities, there is a shared cultural heritage among Jews, and being in Israel feels a little like showing up at an impromptu family gathering, especially as my Hebrew improves. Israelis may kvetch, but they are unfailingly hospitable and generous. The toughness unveils itself as the kind of familial intimacy that doesn't require polite manners. Conversations with strangers begin at the point I would have reached a week into a friendship in the U.S. Terrorist bombs are a constant threat, but within Israel we feel safe enough to hitchhike.

In a way that runs deep as blood, Israel starts to feel like home.

In September, our *ulpan* completed, the University of California program migrates from Haifa to Jerusalem. Days after our arrival in this holiest of holy cities, everyone I know promptly abandons ship to visit Greece and Turkey, summer destinations of choice. I examine my scholarship-allocated budget and decide to stay and explore my new city. The next day, Prime Minister Benjamin Netanyahu approves the opening of an ancient tunnel in the Old City to archaeological excavation. The Hasmonean tunnel lies right next to the foundations of Al-Aqsa mosque, the third-holiest shrine in Islam after Mecca and Medina. Opening it is equivalent to sacrilege. This comes on the heels of Netanyahu's reneging on a string of political promises. Predictably, the Palestinians riot. "Don't leave campus," instructs Chana, the administrator of our program. "They're throwing stones. It's dangerous out there." I huddle in the deserted dorms. I don't have access to a television, can't pick up the BBC on my radio, can't comprehend enough of the Hebrew radio and newspapers to get a sense of the situation, and only get enraged reading the reactionary, albeit English-language, *Jerusalem Post*. My family and friends in the U.S. are probably far better informed than I, despite the fact that people are getting killed half a mile from my sunny little dorm room. But I understand enough to glean that seventy Palestinians and twelve Israeli soldiers die in the violence that ensues. "You can leave now," Chana informs me a couple of days later, and I step tentatively out of the dorms to explore the sanctioned half of my new home.

The Arab Quarter of the Old City is without a doubt my favorite part of Jerusalem: it is a place where I can lose myself, and I am just beginning to understand the value of this. I wander its narrow alleys sniffing heady spices, fondling silk scarves, bargaining playfully with the vendors over henna or sandals. My interactions with Israeli Arabs — or Palestinians, depending on how they identify themselves to me — are generally very positive. But I find the relations between Israeli Jews and Arabs to be pungently, disturbingly reminiscent of apartheid South Africa.

Soon after arriving in Jerusalem I work for a brief stint as a waitress at a restaurant on busy Ben Yehuda Street. There are two other waitresses: Shlomit and Nitsan. Both are beautiful and popular with the customers. In the back are Mohammed and Hassan, the Arab dishwashers and food preparers. We have contact with them only through a small window used for passing dishes. Watching Shlomit and Nitsan feels like participating in a clinical observation of the mood-swings of two bipolar patients.

"*Betakh,* of course, one cappuccino, two lattes, one Greek salad, one Caesar, one penne with pesto." Shlomit smiles beatifically, pencil tapping away at her notepad as the three businessmen ogle her ample chest greedily. "I'll be right back." She moves through the restaurant like a gracious empress indulging her subjects, dipping to check on beverage levels or smile at a child. When she reaches the corridor leading toward the kitchen, her entire demeanor shifts visibly. The smile curdles. Her brow tightens, neck sinks, shoulders draw forward. The easy gait quickens to a restrained sprint. She approaches the window and barks the order through. "And I said now! *Etmol, chik-chuk!* Did you hear me?"

Mohammed is bending down to peer through the window, nodding rapidly. "Yes, Shlomit, it's coming right up." His voice is carefully edgeless, tone dry as sawdust.

"And where in the hell is the pizza order I handed you three hours ago? Are you both complete idiots? Fucking Arabs. Lazy bastards. If that pizza isn't out in one minute, then I'm going to tell Yitzchak to fire both of your asses, and you'll have to figure out some other way to feed your nine brats in goddamn Ramallah."

She pauses, realizing I am standing two feet away, staring at her, thunderstruck.

"What are you looking at?" Something faintly related to shame momentarily clouds her features, then is gone. "If you don't get moving, there's no way you'll keep this job." She picks some lint off her blouse, and both of us automatically move aside as Nitsan comes rushing through. "Hassan! What in God's name did you do with the side salad—"

I follow Shlomit into the seating area. At the threshold she pauses, smoothes her hair, removes the notepad and pencil from her back pocket. Her entire body language transforms as she steps out: back straightens, hips roll, breasts bounce. From behind, I imagine her lips spreading into a wide smile, the kind of smile that makes you feel seen, that makes you want to order a chocolate croissant and a latte when all you came in for was a decaf.

The racism toward Arabs here is endemic and, like the whites in apartheid South Africa, most Israeli Jews appear to feel it's natural. In contrast, when I visit Egypt and Jordan, I tell taxi drivers and waiters that I am American; if the topic of Israel somehow crops up, all and sundry are invariably subjected to a volley of virulent anti-Semitism. The Jews are responsible for all the evil in the world, I am told. Israel is a plague to be wiped off the face of the planet. I am horrified and scared by such vitriol. Yet while I do not hesitate to argue with the Egyptian taxi drivers, I recognize where my efforts are best applied— if indeed there is any tiny difference I can make in this daunting conflict. I am a Jew. Israel is, by definition, my homeland. As a citizen of Israel, I too am responsible for her actions. When it comes to Palestine, it is my people doing the oppressing. Just as the Palestinians need their leaders to push for nonviolent resolution, so the Jews need their own insistent and committed voices calling for an end to the Occupation. That, I resolve, is my role.

But I remain unclear about how to exercise my convictions. No one around me seems to care very much. I am disappointed by the almost complete indifference toward politics on the part of my peers in the foreign school, who far prefer guzzling bottles of Goldstar to deliberating the intricacies of waging peace. Many are unthinkingly conservative on the issue, standing resolutely behind Netanyahu's decisions out of what strikes me as blind tribal loyalty. Here, when I say no, I am either ignored or called a fool.

Israel hardens me. It takes my idealism and turns it into a punching bag, belting away until I am exhausted from trying to prop it up. Over the course of the year, I stop calling myself a Zionist. And I move consciously away from Judaism. Where one stands within the religious spectrum of Israeli civil society, I learn, is generally a reliable indicator of one's political views: the more religious, the more reactionary. After attending a couple of Shabbat dinners at the homes of orthodox Jews — those extending their hospitality with the explicit purpose of returning prodigal secular Jews to the fold — I stay away. These families are unfailingly gracious and kind to my friends and me. But I invariably lose my appetite; the white tablecloth and silver candlesticks are defiled by my hosts' unobstructed loathing of Arabs. Religious observance becomes indissolubly tied, in my mind, to a set of sociopolitical views I find repugnant. What is the value in a religion that discounts one life in favor of another, that consigns women to glorified domestic serfdom, that gauges one people as inherently of higher worth than all others? What kind of spiritual truth manifests in such warped forms as to legitimate another's murder? While sworn enemies, the ultra-orthodox Jews and the fundamentalist Muslims, I conclude, are nonetheless locked in an arctic embrace: both want all the land, neither is sincerely interested in peace, and each incites the other to further extremes in an escalating war dance of ever-bloodier proportions. I am appointed the Rothberg School representative to Ofek, the student Labor Party, and I try, by handing out flyers and sitting on organizing committees, to assuage my tugging conscience.

"Ready?" Gillian is set to go, small body strung about with bags and backpack and water bottle. She looks suitably outfitted for a bracing week in the Himalayas.

"Are you sure you have everything?"

"Well, I thought about bringing a cooler, but I figured the cheese would keep."

It is early afternoon on one of those spring days that reduces all productive mental activity to the singular longing to be horizontal in a field. The sky is polished spotless, the air about us frenetic with parachuting seeds and waltzing motes of dust. I battle the urge to sink down right here on the path and take a nap. Gillian eyes me askance. *"Y'allah nu,"* she pronounces firmly. "Off we go then."

We head south on one of the narrow paths winding across Mount Scopus, leaving Hebrew University behind and heading toward the adjacent Mount of Olives. The Mount of Olives, the traditional burial site for Jews, holds an estimated 150,000 gravesites. Stretching east of the Mount of Olives is Ma'aleh Adumim, the largest Israeli settlement in the West Bank, home to thirty thousand Jewish settlers. Planned expansion of the settlement will close off East Jerusalem and divide the West Bank in two, which poses a serious threat to the viability of a two-state solution to the Israeli-Palestinian conflict.

But we are blissfully ignorant of the barbed political future of the terrain across which we roam. According to our (admittedly limited) research, the top and eastern sides of the Mount of Olives are filled with Palestinian homes and shops, and so we advance in that direction. Our path—scored out of the long grasses by myriad feet over several millennia, no doubt—eventually broadens into a dirt road. We crest a dry hillock and find ourselves at the threshold of a sparse and seemingly desolate village. Haltingly, we walk into it, staring about for clues.

"Where is everyone?" Gillian is whispering.

"I don't know. Do they have siestas?"

It is eerily still. Ramshackle homes lean into the day at odd angles, windows gaping scraps of darkness. A sudden movement sends my chest lurching, but it is only a tattered curtain. Wordless, we both pick up the pace.

"Allo! Allo!" On cue, we turn. Two Palestinian boys are running up to us from behind. Where did they come from? How long have they been watching us? They slow down as they approach, panting.

"You Israelis?" They are both young, maybe thirteen. One of them diminutive and skinny, too shy to meet my eyes. The other tall, already thickly muscled. He has a long, angular face, impudent nose, square chin languidly sown with delicate, wispy stalks. He speaks for the both of them, watching us intently. As if we are overindulged rats in his home laboratory, it occurs to me. The experimental group.

"No. American and Canadian." If this tidbit surprises them, it certainly doesn't register visibly. "Do you live here?"

"Yes." He is wearing an ancient red T-shirt, dotted with the vanishing outlines of now-illegible Hebrew lettering. A vivid rectangle on his chest where a pocket used to be.

"Where?"

"Over there." He gestures vaguely behind us. Upon the horizon, apparently. We turn to look. Nothing but more deserted village.

"You want to see a church? Very beautiful. Just over that way." He points to our left, behind a sprawling building resembling a barn. I could recognize him as an Arab with my eyes closed; his Hebrew is densely layered, the r's rolling bumpily instead of streaming out in guttural tugs. "It's very special. Not to be missed."

Gillian's eyes snap to mine. "What do you think?" she asks in English.

"Why not?" I look back at the boys. "*B'seder,* show us."

They dart off instantly, and we have to trot to keep them in sight. We wind around the building and pause when we reach the rear.

Later, counting my blessings that we emerged still clothed and with no bones broken, I will remember this moment. This is when we should have turned and run. Instead, we peer about us, baffled.

They have vanished.

"Where are those boys?" says Gillian finally. Her voice is rickety.

"And where's the church?" Before us stretches a large square of red dirt. Beyond that, more grass. "I didn't know they had pagans here." Gillian laughs weakly.

And then they are upon us. Out of nowhere, out of the fragile, seething spring air. A hand on each of my breasts, clinging. Gillian is leaping up and down, batting at him ineffectually, screeching in incoherent blasts of fury. The smaller one hangs back, cowering, torn, but his friend is unmoving. Finally words come to me and I say what I know will wield the most impact. "Police! Police!" I am screaming through sacking rammed down my throat, clawing at eyelids that will not open, running on legs of concrete, stuck. Stuck. Stuck. "Police! I'll send the Israeli police here!" His fingers ply my breasts like clay.

Press, knead, pull. Ready for the firing. I am pushing at chest, shoulders, face. I am staring into pitiless wells of eyes as my mouth keeps shaping sounds into neat syllables, hardheaded packaging. I scream for the police. Shock reducing my vocabulary to a single word, a solitary regimented salvation. One well-armed hope. *Mishtara.* Police. Police. Dirty Arab, I am thinking, fucking Arabs, as he watches me from an immobile face while his hands work my flesh like it is his own. Like he walked onto it and made it his own.

Four:

Nepal

The women of Pathan are washing their laundry.

Dip, smear with soap, scrub, dip, swish, knead. Dip, smear, scrub, dip, swish, knead. Then a muscular wring and reach behind, to a growing mound. And ahead, to an eroding knoll. Dip, smear, scrub. Barefoot, squatting in bright *salwar kameez* above tin tubs. Dip, swish, knead. Working quietly, breaking rhythm only to borrow a neighbor's clay-colored soap ball, or tender a lean limb of conversation. Dip, smear, scrub. The washing place is a sunken stone courtyard adjacent to a temple. Centuries of gentling by water and feet have worn its rocks smooth. Dip, swish, knead. A stream gushes from the side of the temple into a trough in the square, giving way instantly to extravagant suds, iridescent pinks and purples glistening voluptuous in the early evening light. Dip, smear, scrub. Occupying the center of this courtyard—as with most—is a shrine, a small cement replica of the temple, surrounded by oil candles and festooned with the vivid litter of devotion: smears of *tikka* red, plucky yellow marigolds. Dip, swish, knead, wring, reach—

"Look! See child!"

I am so startled that I jump, nearly falling off the wall where I sit cross-legged above the square. Before me stands a tiny Nepali woman, holding a girl who looks too big to be carried. She is at least five, her forehead marked with the *tikka* thumbprint of devotion.

"*Namaste,*" I say, bowing my head slightly, smiling.

"*Namaste,*" responds the woman, grinning broadly. She looks to her daughter. "No, she no talk." Responding to a query that had yet to surface. She laughs at me as I watch the girl, rocks her on a plush hip garbed in swaths of flowered burgundy. The child is slack, folded into her body. I reach forward to touch her hand and she whimpers; the hand lifts, drops, then opens to mine. Her mother laughs, sets her down on the wall beside me. The girl's rolling eyes meet my gaze for a second, holding it before knocking off like pinballs. I am confused, emotionally adrift and clutching. In the United States, this child would be pitied, as would her mother. Without warning, she releases the child. Her spine buckles instantly and I jerk forward breathless with horror, but her mother is quicker. She holds the impassive girl gently and throws her head back, laughing and laughing at me, at the absurdity of my reactions. Eventually I join in. The child's gaze drifts languid back to mine. A drop slides from slipshod lips, idles down her chin. Together her mother and I laugh, bells pealing incandescent through the slithering light of dusk. The women are leaving the square now, filing out in a leisurely rosary. They tap the shrine as they pass, ascend the stairs in loose constellations. The low hum of leave-taking; the wide sweep of hips lilting the day's labor home.

I return to the U.S. from Israel in the fall of 1997 for my final year at Berkeley. I decide to write my Interdisciplinary Studies thesis on the status of the West Bank as an illegally occupied territory. This topic will fuel me with sufficient energy, I explain half-jokingly, to power eighty pages of material. I construct a historical argument, maintaining that while the occupation of the West Bank is inimical to peace, nonetheless the expansion of Jewish settlements within it has been actively encouraged or covertly permitted since 1967 by both right- and left-leaning governments. I struggle to remain objective in the writing of this, not to allow my analysis of the settler movement to stray into the arena of condemnation. One of my thesis advisors is a Palestinian professor. He gives me an A and requests that I meet with him. "Your work is good, Marisa," he says. "But you fail to take this to its obvious conclusions. If you want to get it published, you need to close your argument. For any kind of lasting peace, the Occupation has to end." I nod. "And Palestinians must win the right to return." I am silent. If all the Palestinians who once lived in Israel proper chose to return, they would outnumber Jews. Israel as a Jewish homeland would cease to exist. I cannot, in good conscience, take this step. "But this is an academic text," I finally respond. "It's not a polemic. I've tried very hard not to take sides." "You can't avoid it when it comes to this issue, my dear," he tells me, speaking slowly, deliberately. "You are a Jew. You have come this far. There is no such thing as neutrality."

No such thing as neutrality? But the two sides on this issue are miles apart. How will they ever meet if there is no middle way? I decide that I'm not ready to pick a side. I'll take my A, thank you, and forgo the publishing.

Thesis completed, I graduate from Berkeley in May of 1998. I stride out of its green patinaed gates and wait with bated breath for the next dazzling thing to fall into my lap. Why would I expect otherwise? In school, I knocked down awards and A's like flies. But life after university proves rather a strain on my ego. I have been studying voice, and I decide I want to sing. I want to sing, and I will support my musical career by working at a nonprofit. Where I will save starving children/the whales/the planet.

The only glitch is that the nonprofits, to my amazement, aren't clamoring for me. I finally settle for a job as the coordinator of a program for teenagers at the Jewish Community Center—not quite the platform I had envisioned for realizing my hazy dreams of saving, or stunning, the world. After this job I work as an associate producer at a kids' media company, then as a counselor with severely emotionally disturbed adolescents. Yet while I learn a lot in these roles, none of them fits quite right. I feel aimless, frustrated. I want to give more to the world, but remain unclear about how and where to best apply my energies. While I am performing with some regularity as a singer-songwriter, my gigs earn me roughly enough to buy a burrito. This can't be it, can it? There has to be more to life than cubicles, art compressed to the margins, the desperate respite of weekends. There has to be more.

I am twenty-four when I decide I want to go to India and Nepal. I can't explain why. The region intrigues me. And I need a journey. I need to prove my mettle. If life isn't going to provide me with suitable stimulus, I'll just have to go off and create my own. Over the past couple of years I have also begun freelancing as a writer for local newspapers, which I enjoy immensely. I want to write, and I want to travel, and I want to do it by myself. I tell Eric, my boyfriend of a year, that I need my freedom.

"Why?" He is hurt. "What are you running away from?"

"Nothing," I say unhappily. Am I running away from something? Am I running away from him? Reality? "I'm running toward... something... I think."

He pulls back, away from me. "What about me?"

"You'll be with me." I'm suddenly unsure. Do I really want to do this, really want to risk losing him? I reach my hands up to cradle his face, looking at him imploringly. "I just—I just—have to do this. On my own. Without any strings or crutches." I know I sound cold, but commitment feels like a shackle right now. What I crave is adventure, the bliss and thrill of honeymoon piled upon honeymoon. I scrape up my savings. I buy a three-month round-trip ticket to Delhi (which I later extend). I quit my job, apply for visas, get my shots. But I'm panicky and suffused with doubt. Why am I doing this?

Life since college has been a disorienting and generally bumpy ride. A year into working at the kids' media company, I realized I loathed my job but lacked the volition to leave it. At some point it dawned on me that I was depressed, and I started seeing a therapist. When the tech bubble burst, I was laid off. Vastly relieved, I set about trying to arrange my life in line with my values. But unemployment and the subsequent structurelessness of part-time work and freelance writing left me anxious, and I found myself neurotically constructing an iron scaffolding of assignments from which to drape my patch-work of a life. I proved a far more grueling taskmaster than any of my bosses; my expectations were sky-high, I tried to do everything, and I ended up exhausted and dismayed at any dropped stitches. Romantically, it took me half a year to extricate myself from my first boyfriend, and of late I have been fixating obsessively on Eric and a couple of other men who keep circling. I need to go cold turkey on men, even Eric.

In the murky haze that is my life right now, I've been having real trouble separating what I want from what others want of me. It may not be a particularly rational or sensible choice, but I feel that this trip will bring clarity, a stronger sense of who I am. Still, I can't help but suspect there's something gravely amiss with me. Everyone else seems content to figure out who they are without flinging themselves across the planet. Not to mention that so far my only experience traveling alone has been a five-day trip to Portland, at a friend's suggestion that I "try it out." Sure, that was great. But that was Portland, for crying out loud. South Asia? Alone? Am I certifiable?

Three weeks before my departure date, planes crash into the World Trade Center and the Pentagon. The world shifts on its axis. Out of the ashes and grief shrills the strident war-hawking of the Bush administration. "Marisa, you can't go now," my mother tells me over the telephone. "It's just not safe." My parents are baffled by my desire to go in the first place. Every time I visit them in Southern California, my father grills me on my plans for the future. When am I going to fulfill all that potential? Grow up and get a doctorate? "I'm still going, Mom," I say. Moreover, I now have a mission: to write about sociopolitics in the region. The mainstream media's coverage of political developments following 9/11 largely strikes me as biased rhetoric, thinly veiled support for Bush's warmongering over Afghanistan. Afghanistan shares borders with Pakistan, which is itself adjacent to India. There is very little reporting coming from the area, but I know that Washington's newfound chumminess with Pakistan bodes ill for perennially tense Indo-Pakistani relations. Here is an opportunity for me to put the skills I have accumulated writing for local papers to good use. U.S. foreign policy affects millions of people around the world, but very few of those people appear in the mainstream U.S. press. I want to amplify their voices. I pitch myself as a freelance stringer to the foreign news editor at the *San Francisco Chronicle,* and he is interested. I'll be reporting on how ordinary people view the global political forces that shape their lives, and whatever other intriguing stories I may stumble upon along the way.

First stop: Taiwan. A weeklong stopover en route to India proves a wonderful introduction to traveling solo. I am lucky enough to meet people with whom I immediately connect, and realize with some relief that traveling alone can also be a highly sociable affair. I spend the week traversing the island with new friends Sigal from Israel and Sean from Canada (who lugs around a bag full of miniature Canadian flags and pins and distributes them liberally, educating locals and fellow travelers alike about his motherland's distinctive geography and politics). We are reclining on Chichi beach, a palm-bedecked, unpopulated paradise on Taiwan's east coast, when we get the news.

It is a warm night. A colossal yellow moon is slowly disrobing from the clouds quilting the horizon. Surf pummels sand with soothing insistence. We are drinking Taiwan beer and engaging in an early variation on a discourse with which I will become all too familiar: the Backpacker Dialogues.

"I mean, you have to be seeking something. No one just ups and leaves their country for months without, you know, some kind of deep need propelling them." Sean is adamant, eager to share.

"Sure. I guess. Well, like, I want to figure out who I am, you know. How to speak my truth, whatever that is. Stuff like that." I am cagey, waiting to see how much he's willing to reveal. "You?"

"I want balance. I need to figure out how to live a more balanced life, so I figured removing myself from normality altogether would be a good start."

"Sigal?"

Sigal is belly-down on the sand, playing with her cell phone again. Israelis and their *pelefons*. It's an enduring love affair. "Basically I needed to escape the reality of living in Israel." She looks up, dragging deeply on her cigarette. "The army, the bombs, the terrorists, all that shit. I just can't deal anymore." Silence. We nod sympathetically, look elsewhere. I stare at the chalk line where the waves break, thinking of my time in Israel. Shlomit, Mohammed, the Kotel. Tanks in the desert. A nameless Arab boy whose eyes still blaze into mine.

"Well, I'm learning a lot already." Sean is back on track like a bloodhound. "I mean, these people, they just live more simply. You can see it in their eyes, they're peaceful, they don't have to figure out how to—"

"Oh my God!" Sigal is staring at her cell phone. "Oh my God. You're not going to believe this. You are not going to believe this, Marisa."

"What?" I am at her side, reaching for the phone. "What?"

"It's from my mother." She hands it to me. "Afghanistan, you know?"

I nod. The message is in capitals, incontrovertible black blocks straddling the wan lime screen.

HI HONEY, it reads. THE WAR HAS STARTED.

And so my journey begins. I spend the next five months switching between two very different identities. Not that this feels new: immigration left me well versed in the subtleties of rapid adaptation and with an ambidextrous knack for carrying incongruous vantage points simultaneously. For weeks at a stretch I am a backpacker, straying in and out of a tribe of the grungy like-minded. Yielding to my lust for adventure, savoring the redolent pleasures of solitary exploration, indulging in the fruitful narcissism of self-examination. India and Nepal are ripe grounds for all of this: theirs is a compendium of cultures that contrasts sharply with my own, and I am fascinated by the differences. By a mother who neither resents nor pities her disabled child. By the surfeit of faith—Hindu, Buddhist, Muslim—that greets me wherever I turn. Alongside the grinding poverty, with its trusty henchmen—disease, child labor, urban filth—there is also crushing beauty: the sumptuous hues of saris and streetfoods, the ornate, fragranced innards of temples, the smiling overtures of children and vendors. I take it all in, revel in the delights, rise—albeit shakily —to the challenges, and record the details lovingly in my journal. And then every few weeks I pause, retreat to my three-dollar hotel room, scrabble about in my backpack for its least-wrinkled contents, and emerge a Journalist, Not to Be Taken Lightly. I do research using the ancient and frustratingly slow computers in cybercafes. I interview street vendors and muckety-mucks alike with humorless pragmatism. I compose my articles in cybercafes, ramming plugs into my ears and shushing overenthusiastic email-checkers. And then I click send, praying that my drafts reach my editor.

I am in India for only two and a half weeks before I fly to Nepal. It is a relief after my hectic introduction to the subcontinent. India's graces have yet to sway me: I have been cursing the dirt and bony cows (and omnipresent cowshit), appalled by the poverty, hounded by the endless crowds shoving through the streets. "I don't like that," I say in Hindi to the diminutive Indian men who stare me down. Whereupon their eyes shift elsewhere for two tenths of a second before flicking back to me. I am a western woman traveling alone: an object of endless intrigue. I fume quietly beneath the weight of their collective gaze, occasionally pulling a face to see if they react. This evokes nothing but further fascination on the part of my groupies. Finally I wise up and buy some *salwar kameez,* the dress-over-pants worn by modern Indian women, which helps a little.

In contrast, when I reach Nepal in late October, it feels heavenly: it is slower, cleaner, quieter, and far less populated. My first stop is Kathmandu, and I am at once besotted with its narrow cobbled streets and elaborate temples, with the Himalayas arrayed about the city like a sleeping army. Kathmandu is also a backpackers' paradise, and I partake liberally of the western cuisine and handwoven wares.

Yet I soon discover that there are two Nepals: they trundle along next to each other, but they virtually never touch. Most places have a twin: there is the glossy variety offered to tourists, and there is the gritty fare of locals. But in Nepal the contrast is particularly striking. One morning in late November, I am hiking a popular mountain trail near Pokhara, a central Nepali city that rests in the lap of the Annapurna range of the Himalayas. The vista is sumptuous. Below, Lake Phewa glints turquoise. Behind, the white shark-tooth of Machhapuchhare peak slices into a cobalt sky. I am with friends and we wend our way up the narrow paths and through the small villages that dot the mountain. When we reach the summit, there are soldiers everywhere. "What's going on?" I ask one. He motions me to the captain, standing nearby. I approach him.

"Can you tell me what's happening?"

"Nothing, nothing." He is contemptuous of my curiosity, dismissive, eyes half-visible beneath his khaki cap. "Normal procedure."

His disdain and his uniform intimidate me. I study the ground, waiting until I am sure my voice will be steady. Reminding myself I am a Journalist, Not to Be Taken Lightly.

"It's normal procedure to have fifty armed soldiers on the top of a mountain at ten in the morning?" I pull my notepad out of my bag. I am morphing slowly but surely into my alter ego.

"Normal." He waves me away. "Go be tourist. Everything normal."

"I guess that depends on what normal is. Can I have your name, please? I'm a journalist."

He refuses.

On the way down the mountain, I stop locals we pass to ask them what happened. They too are evasive. Finally one man, a prosperous-looking Nepali who is visiting Pokhara from Kathmandu, fills me in. "There was a massacre here last night. Fourteen people killed. The Maoists, you know."

"What? Last night?" I struggle to digest this. In these tranquil villages, on this dew-laced summit?

"Yes. The Maoists and the government, at each other's throats again. And who gets killed?" He gestures angrily ahead of us, to where two children are coming up the path, barefoot and laughing. "Civilians. Peasants. The same people they both say they're representing."

Nepal was an absolute monarchy until 1990, when King Birendra conceded to calls for reform by creating a parliamentary monarchy. But he retained control over the army and police. In 1996 the Communist Party of Nepal called for an overthrow of the monarchy, and Maoist insurgents began waging civil war in the countryside. Nepal is one of the poorest nations on earth, and tourism is a crucial industry for its economy. So there is an unwritten covenant governing the violence that sears the countryside: leave the tourists out. Terror may reign among the locals by night, but by day a veneer of normalcy is scrupulously enforced.

On June 1, 2001, only five months before I arrived in Nepal, eight members of the royal family were massacred. King Birendra, much loved by the Nepalis, was among those slain. The Palace released little information, but the story that eventually emerged was that Birendra's son, the Crown Prince Dipendra, had shot his father, mother, sister, brother, five other relatives, and himself in a drugged rage over his parents' refusal to allow him to marry his girlfriend. In any event, that's the version I read while still in the United States.

Despite the statements of eyewitnesses that Dipendra committed the crime, I discover while in Nepal that no one believes the official story. Most believe the massacre was contrived by Gyanendra, Birendra's brother, who subsequently took his place as king. On the night of the massacre, Gyanendra was in Pokhara, 120 miles away. But his son, Paras, a royal thug implicated in three separate cases of manslaughter (and unprosecuted thanks to royal immunity), was present. He escaped unscathed. Many of the Nepalis I talk with think that Paras, now the crown prince, was somehow responsible. Neither Gyanendra nor Paras are popular in Nepal. Nepali journalists who print stories challenging the official version are arrested for treason. Maoist revolutionaries exploit the conspiracy theories in an effort to mobilize resentment against the monarchy.

Believing that Nepalis should not fight each other, Birendra had refused to use the military to combat the Maoists. Gyanendra, however, has no such qualms. Following his succession to the throne, discussions between the government and the Communist Party of Nepal disintegrate. The country begins lapsing into disorder. On November 23 the Maoists unilaterally withdraw from peace talks with the government. They launch a series of attacks on the military and other targets, killing over a hundred people in four days. On November 26, the day before I go hiking near Pokhara, Gyanendra declares a nationwide state of emergency, suspending a host of civil liberties and authorizing deployment of the army. Nearly ten thousand of the twelve thousand slain in this war have died since November 2001.

I pitch to my editor at the *Chronicle* to cover the royal massacre and ensuing events, and he gives me the go-ahead. But the story proves a thorny one to write. Nepalis are loath to discuss the matter with a foreigner. Those who will talk to me invariably refuse to go on record. Officials decline to speak with me or return my calls. It is in Pokhara, after a frustrating afternoon of abortive interviews, that a shopkeeper mentions he has a journalist friend. Would I like to meet him? Why yes, I would. My head is killing me and I'm fed up with being shunned for trying to write this story. For the love of god, yes. He takes me to an apartment building just off Simalchaur Street and introduces me to Kiran.

"A pleasure," says Kiran, shaking my hand and flashing a dazzling grin. He is young, sympathetic, easy to talk to. I unload my litany of woes upon him. "Yes, this is an article that must be written," he declares with great resolution. "The whole world believes Gyanendra's story. I am happy to help. You must only tell me who you need to speak with." I almost weep with relief, and thank him profusely. "Of course, of course, it is nothing. Would you like to have dinner tonight?"

"I'd love to. Can I bring a friend?"

"Certainly. I'll cook *dal baat.*"

I head over that evening with Amanda. I met Amanda in Chitwan National Park a couple of weeks earlier. We get along wonderfully, and have decided to trek the Annapurna range together once I file my story. She is a New Zealander, irreverent and side-splittingly funny. I warn her to tone it down for dinner.

We arrive armed with chocolates. "Welcome, welcome," says Kiran, ushering us into the steaming kitchen. He lives with his mother and sister, who appear to be helping him with dinner. Both receive us politely and then make a swift exit. The kitchen is tiny. On the wall hangs an outdated calendar depicting Shiva, trident militantly upright, locks flowing. Kiran gestures to the rug in the middle of the room. "Please, sit. Dinner is ready." He begins dishing up steaming plates of *dal baat* with *naan* and *aloo gobi*. We arrange ourselves on the floor. "How cozy," says Amanda drily, inspecting the rug with great interest. I glare at her.

"Take, please take." Kiran hands us the plates. "It's my special. Would you like spoons?" I decline, preferring to practice eating with my hand. "Very good," he graciously fibs, observing my technique.

"It's delicious. Where did you learn to cook?" I swat discreetly at a stray chunk of potato on my chin.

"Mostly from my big mother."

"Did you just call your mother 'big'?" Amanda is alarmed. "My mother'd put me over her knee and give me a good hiding. It'd be an icy day in hell before she let me get away with that."

"Oh no," Kiran laughs. "You misunderstand. My big mother is my father's first wife. We are very close. My own mother is my father's third wife. She was his love marriage."

"Ah, I see," says Amanda. "Indeed. That makes perfect sense."

"Yes," Kiran continues genially. "My mothers are happy. In the west you have so much suffering over love. It is the result of too much freedom."

"Too much freedom?" Amanda's voice is shrill. "You think the freedom to be able to choose who you marry is too much freedom?" Her temperature is rising in visible degrees, a flush creeping from her pale chest right up to the roots of her red hair. "Stop," I mouth angrily. But she's oblivious. "What about the so-called freedom to have three wives? Seems to me like freedom here depends on being male and that's the end—"

She catches my eye.

There follows an awkward silence during which all present stare avidly at the closest inanimate object. In my case, the rug. Faded, threadbare in places. But certainly an attractive pattern, I muse. An altogether suitable dinner rug.

Eventually, Kiran resumes. "Women deserve respect," he says haltingly. "On that I believe we agree. For example, I myself have had three girlfriends. All of them I have respected. I have not tried to kiss even one."

"But how can you know there's chemistry if you haven't even tried kissing?" I am genuinely curious.

"Chemistry?"

"You know, if there's a spark, if your bodies, uh, enjoy each other."

"You mean sex?"

"Well, not necessarily. But I suppose that could include sex."

"Women who have sex before marriage are cheapened." This isn't news to me. At Chitwan, a drunken Nepali finally just came out and said it: *All western women are whores,* he told me, features twisted with contempt. He pointed his finger in my face, leaned in hot-breathed. *I can see just by looking at you that you are not pure.* "Anyway," Kiran continues, "Nepali women do not enjoy sex. It is considered a duty."

"Now that is tragic." Amanda rejoins the conversation, notably subdued. I nod. "That's terrible, Kiran. What a huge loss for both women and men. Sex can be such a beautiful thing if both partners are enjoying it." Good lord. Someone rein me in.

"How can a woman enjoy sex?"

"Um. Well. She just naturally does, I suppose. If you take the time to find out what she likes."

"How would I do that?"

Am I seriously speaking to a grown, educated man here? "You could just ask her. But also you need to listen to her. Listen to her body. If you're paying attention you'll be able to tell what makes her happy." Ladies and Gentlemen of the Venerated Kingdom of Nepal. Meet yours truly: Scruffy Backpacker, Journalist (Not to Be Taken Lightly), and Doctor Ruth Without Borders. At your service.

"I see." Kiran is looking at me rather intensely. "I will definitely listen to my wife to find out what is making her happy." He gets up and begins collecting the dishes. Amanda stares pointedly at me. "He wants to root you," she mouths as soon as he turns his back. "No he does not," I mouth in adamant response. "Root you," she mouths with a wicked grin, and begins twitching her pelvis lewdly and jerking her elbows back and forth. I can't help myself. I erupt into hysterical giggles.

"What's going on?" Kiran turns from the sink, smiling like an indulgent father. Amanda looks up at him, eyes wide, pure as driven snow.

"Nothing, dearie. Just girl talk."

Kiran makes the article. He knows the people I should talk with and how to get them to talk to me. He escorts me patiently around to neighbors and officials, introducing me formally as his friend the journalist from California. Together we interview individual after individual who challenges the official story.

"If the prince was so drugged that he needed four men to help get him to his bedroom, how could he kill the whole royal family in a palace full of guards?" a shop proprietor asks me. An "official" committee of four appointed by Gyanendra recently concluded that Dipendra was guilty of the massacre, and that he acted alone. "How could he kill eight people in different rooms using different weapons?" demands the proprietor. I shake my head, scribbling away, suppressing the urge to voice my sympathy. That's been a hard one for me to master as a journalist. Particularly when I agree with the person I'm interviewing.

"Princess Prekshya's death was no accident," a librarian tells me emphatically. Prekshya was the estranged wife of Direndra, Gyanendra's younger brother, who was also killed on June 1. She was one of the few eyewitnesses to the massacre. On November 12 she was killed in a helicopter crash. "It's just too convenient," says the librarian.

Another eyewitness cited in the report is Gorakh Samser Rana, husband to Birendra's daughter Sruti, who was also killed. Rana survived three bullet wounds. "He's lying," Aakash, a journalist, tells me.

"Everyone knows he's lying. He saw his wife and family killed. He's afraid."

"Why no autopsy?" Kiran challenges. "Why is the Palace refusing to release any forensic evidence?" I have no answers. When I ask people to explain the events of the night of June 1, I hear not a single theory that holds water. How do you account for the eyewitnesses who say Dipendra did it? I ask. Witchcraft, an old woman tells me. Paras stole Dipendra's soul, says another. Paras was wearing a very convincing mask, offers a vendor.

I am mystified. Has grief driven these people half-mad?

Kiran takes me to interview Prasad Kumar Koirala, a political science professor at a leading Nepali university. Koirala is a member of the Raj Parishad, the royal council that formally proclaims each new king. "The members of the Raj Parishad are quite powerful," Kiran tells me. We are walking toward Koirala's apartment, having caught a bus to this markedly more affluent suburb of Pokhara. The streets are clean and the apartments stacked in neat, freshly painted blocks. "The King turns to them for unofficial counsel. And Koirala is a Brahmin. That is the highest caste, you know, the priestly caste."

I ask Kiran which caste he belongs to.

"I am Chhetri, or Kshatriya, the warrior caste." He delivers this with some pride, tweaking at a near-invisible crease on his immaculate pink button-down shirt.

"Cool. So, I've been wondering. Where would a non-Hindu rank in the caste system? Where would I fit in?"

"Well, that depends on several things. For example, have you eaten cow meat?"

"Beef? Yes, I have."

"I see." He looks fixedly ahead. Obviously that doesn't bode well for me. I ask him if that means I am a Sudra, the fourth and lowest caste. Members of the Sudra caste traditionally occupy positions of menial labor.

"Not exactly." Kiran is reluctant, avoiding my eyes. His walk turns into a restrained jog and I have to scurry to keep up.

"What then? Am I a Dalit?"

An untouchable. From the Sanskrit *dal*, meaning "broken." Considered outside the caste system altogether, the Dalits are leather-workers, beggars, subsistence farmers. In some traditional villages in rural India, Dalits are still required to sweep the ground where they walk in order to prevent "contamination."

"You are not a Dalit."

"So what am I?" I'm astonished at the shrillness of my voice, at how much I suddenly care.

"You are..." Kiran's voice trails off. He stops abruptly, turns to me. "Marisa, for eating cow meat, I am afraid you are even below the Dalits." He lets this drop gently, watching my face with great concern.

"Oh." And you, I regret to inform, are a goy, while I am a kosher-certified member of the chosen people. I do not say this, of course. Instead I pat his arm, assure him it's okay. I ask him why it is that every religion has to convince its followers that its way of organizing the world is the best way, that it alone was chosen by God.

Kiran is unhesitating. "Because we are terrified of what we do not know and cannot control."

We walk the rest of the way in companionable silence, each lost in our own private musings.

The professor, unsurprisingly, is the only person I interview who defends the official story. "Dipendra did it," he says. "He killed because of love. The rumor about Paras is propaganda circulated by the Maoists." Koirala is tall, dignified, bespectacled. We are sitting on an overstuffed couch in his comfortable living room, drinking chai.

"How do you explain Dipendra managing to kill eight people in different rooms with different weapons if he was so drugged that he had to be carried to bed?"

"I have consulted with people close to the palace," says Koirala. "My brother-in-law was Dipendra's bodyguard, and he believes he did it. Even Dipendra's maternal grandmother blames him." He uncrosses and crosses his legs, takes a sip of chai. Behind him an elaborately carved, gleaming grandfather clock burps out a subdued chime. I watch its brass pendulum swinging from side to side at a measured gait. This is not easy for me. As a child in a hyperdisciplined environment, I was thoroughly instilled with a respect for authority figures.

And society has taught me, as a woman, to pacify, to avoid offending at all costs. I respect Koirala and am grateful for his time and hospitality. I want him to like me.

The silence is growing heavy. I clear my throat, reminding myself where my obligation lies. Reaching for the nerve to say no. *No, Koirala, that's not enough.* I watch him until his eyes meet mine.

"I understand that they believe the story. But I'm asking you to explain to me *how* he did it."

Pause. Koirala will not hold my gaze. He contemplates the brown leather of his expensive-looking loafers.

Finally: "Dipendra did it. He killed his family."

There is a new edge to his voice. I am officially out of favor. But now that I've crossed the line, it gets easier. I ask him why the palace initially called it an accident.

He answers quickly. "As you can imagine, there was great confusion at first."

He's hedging. Protecting a man who may have killed his own brother, thrown his entire nation into unrest. I feel a surge of righteous anger.

"I'm sure you're aware that most Nepalis do not believe Dipendra did it—or at least not alone. Many are suspicious of Paras, who will one day be king himself." I'm on a roll now. I've scented the prey and I'm stalking it raptly. "There are a number of details that point to the Palace attempting a cover-up, not the least of which is the fact that journalists who challenged the official story were charged with treason." Breaking out of the bushes. Going in for the kill. "Tell me, why no autopsy?"

"Listen, my dear." Koirala removes his glasses and leans forward, looking me straight in the eyes. "Dipendra committed the massacre. It was a terrible tragedy, and Birendra is deeply missed. But Gyanendra is king now."

He doesn't believe it. It's as clear as day to me, although I also see that he'll never admit it. He can't admit it. But if he believed the official story, he'd be making more of an effort. My anger sputters, awash in a wave of sympathy for this man, for what must be a difficult position. Yet I am also frustrated that I will not get to the bottom of this, resentful that he refuses to bow before Truth, Justice, History, et al. We watch each other in silence as the great clock ticks. Then Koirala looks down at his teacup, replaces it delicately in its saucer on the coffee table. "The kingship is not an individual," he pronounces with finality. "It is an institution that we need. Rajas come and go. Gradually, people will be in favor of Paras."

We thank him for his time, and head back into town.

The next day I interview Putali Khadka, the grandmother of a close friend of Kiran's, in her bedroom. "Putali will tell you exactly what she thinks," Kiran assures me. "And what she believes, the people of Nepal believe." Putali is eighty-six and lives with her daughter's family. She is in bed when we arrive, but eases herself up creakily to greet us. White-haired and shriveled, she gives me a warm, gummy smile, and takes my hand into her own. She does not speak English, so Kiran serves as translator.

I ask her if she believes Dipendra killed his family.

"No." She is unequivocal. "Gyanendra did it." She fixes me with a beady stare while Kiran translates. I sense that she sees more of me than I would choose to exhibit.

"But Gyanendra was here in Pokhara. How did he do it?"

"Through Paras. I do not know how, but I know they did it. They killed Birendra." She looks behind her, to two ornately framed photographs hanging above her bed. They are of Birendra and Aiswarya, the slain queen. "Gyanendra killed our beloved father and mother." When she looks back at me her cheeks are wet. She pulls out a handkerchief and trumpets loudly into it.

I don't want to keep asking questions. I want to end the interview and give her a hug, make her some tea. But I am still missing a crucial piece of the puzzle. A piece I know Putali holds. I press on.

"Putali, nearly all of the Nepalis I speak with do not believe the official story. Why don't the people of Nepal do something about it? Technically this country is a democracy. What about protesting? Removing Gyanendra from the throne?"

"No, my dear. Nepal needs a king." She smiles at my naivete as Kiran translates. "The king, you know, is an incarnation of Vishnu."

One of the three principal Hindu divinities (Brahma and Shiva are the other two), Vishnu is worshiped as the protector and preserver of the universe.

I ask her if she really believes that a man she has labeled a murderer is an incarnation of Vishnu.

"We cannot understand the workings of the deities." She raises her eyes heavenward, shaking her head at the unfathomable antics of those tricksters populating the divine realm. "We need a king, or there will be a civil war. Gyanendra killed his own brother—it was a matter of the palace. God will punish him." Satisfaction settles briefly over her features at this thought. She folds her hands deliberately in her lap, waits for Kiran to finish translating. "But we need a king."

I never thought the concept of democracy was anything other than crystal clear. Either you have a democracy or you do not. And if you do not, you want one. Apartheid South Africa was not a democracy. One man, one vote, cried the black population. *Amandla, awethu!* Power to the people! There were external boycotts, internal riots. De Klerk stepped down. Mandela stepped up. South Africa became a democracy. When you don't have a democracy, the goal is to create one, right? "Democracy is a child in Nepal," Aakash the journalist tells me. "We have a constitution, but the Nepalis are not well educated. We don't know our rights. The police are the same people who were in place before democracy. The system has changed, but not the minds of the people." As I discover in Nepal, it isn't only the monarchy that believes in the need for a monarchy. The people also believe. Not everyone: generally, the younger the Nepali, the more ardent the embrace of democracy. "But the minds," I respond to Aakash, "are changing." "That is true," he says. "But your ideas are too simplistic. The people must be ready, or there will only be chaos."

And if some of the people are ready and some are not—what then? Chaos.

If the king clings to power while faith in the monarchy erodes? Chaos.

If the only available options are an autocrat or a violent revolution?

Chaos.

The situation in Nepal today?

The Maoist insurgents control roughly 70 percent of the country. Thousands of people, most of them wanting nothing to do with power, wanting little more than to live in peace, have been killed in a civil war that exalts their name. Chaos.

My story appears in the Nation & World section of the *Chronicle* on December 13, although I don't see it in print until I return months later. It has been edited liberally. Sentences I crafted with care have been coldly chopped up into news-speak — a language, to my editor's frustration, that I am still mastering. But it is my article, the fruit of my labors, and I swagger about for a day or two feeling terribly proud and professional. I am also gratified that the other side of the story is being heard — somewhere, at least, if not in Nepal. Still, I wonder what difference this article will make in the grand scheme of things.

Certainly it helps convince my parents that there is some merit to my harebrained journey. Finally, some serious ammunition with which to face the burbling parents of all those lawyers- and doctors-to-be. *We're so proud,* my mother gushes in an email. *Such an interesting story, and on the front page of the section too!*

I can see my father smiling, his brow clearing, thinking, *Maybe she's going to make something of herself after all.*

The community of Boudhanath is walking *kora.*

The devout circumnavigate the holy dome in a steady clockwise or-bit, accumulating merit as they meditate in unhurried strides. The faces — old, young, eastern and western — are tranquil, near beatific in the half-light. The sun has just set, and the world remains briefly, strangely bright, as if our local star paused to reconsider just below the horizon. As if it did a double take. This is an apt time for the ex-pression of devotion: faith in the unseen but nonetheless present.

I am sitting on steps beside the whitewashed hemisphere of Boudha, the massive Buddhist stupa just east of Kathmandu. Historians estimate that Boudha, the largest of these holy sites in Nepal, dates back to the fifth century. Each segment in the ascending structure of this sacred mound of earth and plaster corresponds to one of the five elements: earth, water, fire, air, and space. Atop the dome, red-rimmed blue Buddha eyes survey each of the four cardinal directions. Between the eyes, painted in Nepali script: the number one, representing universal unity and interdependence.

Unity. What a beautiful dream, I think. Reality, on the other hand, is by all indications galloping madly in the opposite direction. I think of Kiran, Koirala, Putali, Aakash. Of George Bush and Osama Bin Laden. Nuance, I muse. That's the key. Life is endlessly nuanced, and growth implies an unfolding to ever-greater degrees of subtlety. I dig my journal and pen out of my bag.

Nuance. I have my ideas. I love my ideas. I bask in them, cling to them, noisily impose them. And then I move beyond my bubble and they get wrecked. I grieve them. They really were beautiful, in their oblivious idealism, in their purity. Later I am grateful: I see that the intention behind them was good, the intention remains — but it has been stretched in its applications. It's a little humbler, a wee bit more generous. Life, it seems, pushes me ever wider, deeper, in an ongoing struggle to accommodate things I never imagined existed.

In the prayer area, devotees are prostrating themselves. Rising, kneeling, lying down, rising. Monks in their billowing saffron robes, laypeople in their shawls and caps. These rituals feel so foreign to me. Yet the intention behind them is no different from that behind the lighting of candles on Shabbat. Or kneeling in a church. Ritual, I think, is a reminder of what matters. It carves out a space in which to exercise our sense of connection with the divine. I glance up, and the colorful peace flags ringing the stupa catch my eye. They quiver in the breeze, and I have a sudden impression of Boudha as a living being, a place so thoroughly suffused with devotion that it breathes. I lean back, back, until I see only peace flags against the sky.

Faith is simply a home for love. Faith is a place to express our love. It gathers love, aims it at a higher power, and opens us to receive in turn. In the face of the unknown, as Kiran pointed out, faith lends us security, a sense of meaning. But all too often faith boxes us in. It dictates who and how and what we should love. In defining the unknown, it confines the unknown, circumscribes the mystery. And then it narrows who we are. It limits our love, even distorts it. And I am more and more convinced that the fundamental nature of our being is love. I can't explain this. I just know it in the deepest, quietest part of me. As a solo traveler, I meet this truth on the road every day. I encounter amazing people, know them for a few hours, a week, and then move on. More amazing people turn up. Guaranteed. Just about every face I come across holds goodness, and I am slowly learning how to recognize this essence. There are times when I lack the courage to meet it. There are times when it is too deeply buried to discern, and then I snap closed. But when two people are open, it doesn't matter where they come from or what they worship. Yes, the world is a bewilderingly complex place. But in that moment, it is all simultaneously piercingly simple.

Five:

India

A boy of about eight is riding an adult-sized women's bicycle. The seat is far too high for him, so he hovers as he rides, bottom angled out over the left side of the bike. His left foot works the left pedal while his right leg extends between the bars to push the right pedal. I watch from the garden where I sit, on an agricultural ashram I am visiting several miles outside of Bangalore. The dirt road he travels becomes a bridge of sorts, a mud dike elevated between two shallow bodies of water. The sun is behind him, and I squint watching his silhouette framed and reframed against the unforgiving midday light. I am holding my breath, convinced he will topple at any second. But this lopsided contraption, boy and bike in baffling harmony, perseveres. It shouldn't work. He is heavily weighted on the left side, and his arms barely reach the handles. But somehow it does. As he approaches, strains of a hugely popular Bollywood hit waft toward me over the heat's assault. He is whistling.

India. Nothing in this subcontinent of over a billion seems to work. Buses break down with near-clockwork regularity, trains leave dependably late or occasionally early. Post offices lack stamps. Gas stations run out of gas. You pay for one thing and get something else entirely—and invariably delivered with great pride. Tradition tussles with modernity, democracy wrestles with caste, Indian-produced Thumbs-Up dukes it out with global goliath Coca-Cola. The Hindus despise or endure the Muslims. The Muslims—a largely moderate minority of 130 million—struggle at coexistence. Meanwhile Sikhs, Buddhists, Jains, Christians, and even a few Jews busily carve out their own customized niches.

India. This is the country that gave the world Gandhi's enduring legacy of nonviolent *satyagraha,* yet that today possesses an array of nuclear weapons. A nation where subsistence farmers drink pesticide in protest against Monsanto's onslaught of genetically modified crops. Where a gay pride movement takes its halting first steps—in Mumbai men dance together bare-chested at India's first gay club, in Calcutta they march—while sodomy remains a crime punishable by life imprisonment. Where some of the most visionary thinkers of the global justice movement bump up against some of the most foul-mouthed nationalists on the planet. Where millennia of ayurvedic wisdom rubs shoulders with generic HIV drugs. Where infanticide is illegal but the aborting of female fetuses and the killing of female newborns have only worsened over the past two decades—and consistently go unprosecuted. Child brides, tech moguls, lepers, Bollywood stars, untouchables, wandering ascetics: all call India home.

Somehow, despite the vast contradictions, despite corruption, entrenched religious and caste divides, and antidemocratic transnational corporate colonialism—despite, in short, that it really shouldn't work, India works. Often badly, and invariably in the least efficient, most unpredictable way possible, but it works. The world's biggest democracy endures. The lopsided contraption trundles on, every part of it occupied by a veritable sea of humanity—hanging from the spokes, hammering at the handlebars, jogging atop the wheels, upside-down on the seat, hollering at the driver... and whistling all the while.

I've never seen a place like this. India defies both my sensibilities and my common sense at almost every turn. India unsettles countless notions that I hadn't even realized were notions, that I had simply assumed to be givens of the human condition. Wrong, I learn, and wrong again. Take privacy, for example. I'd always assumed privacy was a natural right, falling somewhere in the broad vicinity of the pursuit of happiness. But not in India. In India, five people share a single room and seem content. After four months in India I still am not used to it. I still get peeved over late buses, staring men, the heat and pollution. But I also am still amazed and delighted. After South

Africa, the U.S., and Israel, I fall for India, and somewhere inside me
it too becomes home.

At the end of November 2001, I take a bus from Nepal through to
Haridwar in the northern Indian province of Uttaranchal. Haridwar
is a sacred city, a major pilgrimage destination for Hindus, and the
promise of exotic ritual and devotion draws me. It is while on the bus,
watching the bedlam that is India unfold anew before my eyes, that I
start to ease into it. There is a stumbling buoyancy to the chaos on
the streets and in the markets, a giddiness to the devotion that infil-
trates every aspect of life, with its Shiva-brand toothpastes and Ganesh
crockery. From behind my ramparts, I hold up a small white flag. I
give in to India. I stop battling her and begin moving with her, hanging on to her hips as she gyrates and wheels.

Haridwar: literally, "Gateway to God." According to Hindus,
Haridwar is one of the seven holiest places in India, and it squats on
the banks of that most holy of holy rivers, the Ganges. Along with
300,000 ardent pilgrims, I unwittingly arrive just in time for Kartik
Purnima, Haridwar's biggest annual festival. All of the $2 hotel rooms
are filled. The only room I can find, after my thirty-one-hour bus
journey, costs $6.50, double anywhere I've stayed thus far. But it does
have a television. I have been away from home going on two months,
and am missing everyone and everything. I watch *Top Gun* and *Dirty
Dancing* on Indian cable and indulge in a tearful bout of nostalgia.
Generally, what I miss of the U.S. lies at its margins: at the unmani-
cured edges of a society of such wealth and relative freedom blossom
the radical visions of alternative communities and underground cultures. I miss the progressive politics and enthusiastic cultural miscel-
lany of San Francisco. I miss reading poetry in cafés, cooking dinner
with friends, making music, dancing outdoors at festivals. But now
even the nails-on-chalkboard American commercial voice-overs make
me cry. Eventually I drag myself out of bed to observe the festivities.

Hindus believe that bathing in the Ganges at Haridwar washes
away a soul's sins and gains one entry to heaven. On Kartik Purnima
the ritual is even more sacred, as it commemorates the day that Shiva

destroyed the insidious demon Tripura-Sur and made the world safe again. Conveniently, it also celebrates the birthday of Guru Nanak, founder of Sikhism. I step out of my hotel to a scene of utter pandemonium. Alongside the river are a number of ghats, or stairways leading down to a landing. Har Ki Pairi ghat, just beyond my hotel, marks the point where the Ganges leaves the Himalayas. Vishnu's footprint is set into one of the stones in its walls, and it is believed that the Ganges flows in its purest form here. Har Ki Pairi is the focal point of the revelry in Haridwar. I watch with awe from the top of the stairs, too intimidated to descend. Hordes of people line the river as far as I can see. They mill about in an unhurried anarchy that appears to possess its own mysterious order. At the edge of the Ganges, women in petticoats and *salwar kameez* dunk underwater, giggling at each other and avoiding male eyes. The men venture in further. Dressed only in their underwear, they are holding hands, splashing about, bellowing to each other in delight. Directly below me, a family is offering *puja* on the steps. The women are arranging marigold heads and lighting incense, laying out small sweet oranges and nuts. One of the men, a child in his arms, glances up and catches sight of me.

"Come down!" he yells, beckoning energetically. I smile at him, shaking my head slightly. The entire circle around him looks up to the source of this new diversion.

"Join us!" calls one of the women. "You must come down!" orders another. They all begin shouting encouragement to me. I am outnumbered. I step slowly down the stairs. As if through some greater design, the masses part fluidly to let me and the other descenders pass. Most of them ignore me, intent upon the day's demands. But some of the men break off as if struck dumb at the sight, fixing me with The Stare. I scowl back menacingly. When I reach the family at the bottom of the stairs, they greet me like a long-lost cousin. "Please, please, welcome to India," says the man, shoving his child into my arms in a no-holds-barred gesture of goodwill. "Welcome to our wonderful country, welcome to Haridwar." He has a swath of gray scarf wrapped around his head and shoulders, a struggling suggestion of mustache, and buckteeth that look about ready to take off.

"Thank you, thank you so much." I struggle to settle the wriggling child on my hip. She beams up at me from kohl-rimmed eyes.

"What is your good name?"

"Oh. I'm Marisa. Nice to meet you."

"Welcome, Marisha, welcome." He takes my hand and shakes it vigorously. The women smile at me and resume preparing *puja*, leaving him in charge of formalities.

"Which country is suffering from the loss of you?"

"America." I don't always say America. Anti-U.S. sentiment is on the rise here. I met an Australian woman who told me a Swedish backpacker was attacked at a railway station for being an American. Blond hair and blue eyes spoke louder than his passport, apparently.

"Ah, America. America great country." He smiles indulgently, then frowns thoughtfully, shakes a finger at me. "But too much power America. Now going to war in Afghanistan. India, we must be restraint. We have terrorism for fifty years, but we do not attack Pakistan. But America gets one taste, runs to war." I am alternately nodding and shaking my head through this fiery monologue.

"Well, certainly war is not—"

"Are you traveling alone?" He is looking behind me now, up the steps of the ghat, searching for a partner.

"Yes." At this all the women look up. The entire circle stares at me in kindly distress.

"No husband?"

"No." Now the faces have transformed to total incomprehension. "Well, um, what I mean is—" They are hanging on my every word, so anxious to relate that I can't resist. This is one mammoth cultural rift that I'm simply not up to crossing right now. "What I mean to say is no husband right now. My husband is coming. He's meeting me later."

The faces collapse into smiles. "Oh, yes, yes." They are laughing with relief, loving me again, offering me syrupy *gulab jamun* in pink tupperware.

Haridwar lies off the backpackers' circuit, and I do not come across another westerner all day. I spend the afternoon wandering through the frenzy, photographing it, basking in it. I come across a child receiving his first ritual head-shaving; he bawls inconsolably as his mother holds him down and the barber drags the razor doggedly across his scalp. I come across Shivaite *sadhus,* dreadlocked ascetics sitting cross-legged and glowering, clad only in loincloths and smeared in ash. They are abundantly armed with *charas,* or hashish, and zealously bless each bowl in the name of Shiva before imbibing. I come across a man with no arms, using felt pens clutched between his toes to produce elaborate and stylized depictions of the river-haired goddess of the Ganges. And I come across beggars and lepers and snake charmers and cripples and more beggars.

The devout and the mercenary: both find a home at Har Ki Pairi. While some come to earn points in heaven, others show up to reap the harvest of the point-earners' piety. I have seen beggars so far, but never this many. Here, there is an elongated line of them, a jagged, yawning queue of the importuning and beseeching.

"One rupee! Madam, one rupee!"

A dish is thrust at me, knocks against my wrist. I look down to eyes that are accusatory, that prey righteously upon my guilt. *You have so much,* say those eyes, in a face engraved and congealed by a life I can barely guess at. *I have nothing. Ease your conscience.* When I give it is so often motivated by guilt, and received out of a mercenary foreknowledge of that guilt. I am left feeling guiltier—for not giving more, for giving to one and not others, for giving when it is guilt, not compassion, that prompts me. For the life with which I have somehow been blessed. An old and familiar guilt, this one, tenacious as white roots in the black loam of Africa. Who am I, anyway, to judge, or to choose, or to allocate? I am suddenly furious with myself and with her. I hand her five rupees and the entire line begins clamoring stridently. Children with faultlessly cast expressions of woe, lepers wielding fingerless hands, the ancient and the emaciated, cripples pointing to their missing leg, eyes, arm. I quell the urge to scream or run. I have seen poverty: in rural Zimbabwe the children's bellies were swollen with hunger, the mothers indolent with despair, eyes glazed over and impenetrably bleak. But poverty in India assumes its unique proportions through the physical distortion of so many of its victims. Poverty here is frequently grotesque. Initially I find it unbearable. I toss some coins and look away. Later, I get used to it. Warped limbs and faces settle into the commonplace amid the bright wash of chattering Hindi, the reassurance of sunlight. And at some point I realize, with no little astonishment, that the beggars here are not necessarily miserable. In the U.S. the very poor are generally unhappy. There is an abiding sense of shame aligned with poverty, an implicit assignment of blame. Here the poor accept their poverty with the equanimity of those to whom karma has doled out certain apportionments. Not the best, maybe, but who can guess at divine will? Who to challenge the diktat of the universe?

"One rupee, one rupee," they clamor. I cannot give to all of them, so I give to a few. The others eye me savagely and grumble, but ten seconds later they are chatting companionably with their neighbor, sucking vigorously at their betel leaf *paan* and whiling away the day in wait for the next possible benefactor.

Karma, I am frequently instructed. Our choices and actions in past lives determine our circumstances today. Complaining is senseless: all plagues — and blessings — are attributed to karma. Karma, however, mysteriously shifts in application when it comes to political and communal tensions. "Pakistanis are selfish and proud," Umesh, a young man I meet in Delhi, tells me. "I hate them so much." Excuse me, and what of karma? Isn't it possible that Pakistanis are Pakistanis only because the universe assigned them to a chunk of land further north? Won't karma take care of it all? No, I am told. They are Muslims. And "Muslims want to make the world Muslim. They create terrorism." That, apparently, is the karma of Muslims.

"Muslims are uneducated and fanatic," says Manoj, owner of a handicrafts shop in Jaipur. "Now they all think Bin Laden is God." Many of the Hindus I speak with are in vociferous agreement. "Muslims have a lifestyle of their own," Krishna, a retired engineer from Delhi, informs me. "They'll never give it up. Their leaders want them to fight, so they tell them Islam is in danger and they all follow like idiots." I am stunned at the prejudice I encounter among even the most educated Hindus when the topic turns to Muslims. In every social and economic survey, India's Muslims rank just above the Dalits.

In 1995 a series of urban bombings in Mumbai, far and away India's most westernized and metropolitan city, was presumed the work of Islamic fundamentalists. Enraged gangs of Hindus responded by rampaging through Mumbai's Muslim neighborhoods, killing and looting at random — with the police purportedly turning a blind eye.

Tensions between India's Hindus and Muslims have been at a rolling boil since the partition of India and Pakistan in 1947. In what was the largest migration in human history, an estimated thirteen to seventeen million refugees crossed borders in the hope of locating safety within their religious communities. Massive communal violence on both sides of the border killed half a million. The famously indecisive king of Kashmir vacillated up until the last minute, but finally decided that despite its majority Muslim population, the mythically lovely territory should go to India. Roughly thirty thousand lives have since been lost over Kashmir. Pakistan maintains that Kashmir, due to its Muslim majority, should be part of Pakistan. India will have nothing of that. Meanwhile, Islamic fundamentalist terrorism — funded by Islamabad, the Indian government insists, while Pakistan claims its support is only moral — erupts with regularity along the Line of Control dividing Kashmir. For India's Hindus, embittered by the climbing death toll, there is little difference between the Taliban and Islamabad. Or, for that matter, between a Pakistani and an Indian Muslim. A Muslim is a Muslim is a Muslim. "In their inner circle, every Muslim agrees with Bin Laden," says Krishna.

Among Hindus, there is the sense that 9/11 at last forced the U.S. to face facts. "I'm happy that Osama bombed America," says Ravi, a bookstore owner from Pushkar. "It opened the world's eyes to terror." But as the U.S. brawls in Afghanistan and cozies up to Pakistan, all the while urging restraint on the part of India, resentment mounts among Indians over the implicit hypocrisy of a "global war against terror." "The American government is controlling the whole world," says Manoj. "It's not fair. They have a war against terror, but they are being selfish. Why can't we solve our problem? Why does India need American permission?" If the U.S. can bomb the nation that houses the perpetrators of its terror, runs this line of logic, then why can't India do the same? In the months following 9/11, Islamic fundamentalists wage a string of guerrilla attacks in Kashmir. India responds by hammering Pakistani army positions along the Line of Control with artillery fire. "[T]here is a limit to the patience of the people of India," warns Prime Minister Vajpayee in a letter to Bush. Because Pakistan is providing the U.S. with access to its military bases, the U.S. will not censure Pakistan's support for Kashmiri separatist groups, which maddens India. On December 13, a group of gunmen attacks the Indian parliament in Delhi, killing twelve and injuring twenty-two. While Pakistan denies involvement, India is not convinced. Over the next few weeks, India deploys half of its army of one million along the border with Pakistan, as well as nuclear-capable ballistic missiles.

During my time in India, I write a series of articles focusing on the connections between the U.S. war in Afghanistan, Indo-Pakistani relations, and Hindu-Muslim tensions within India. At the end of December, I am in Ahmedabad, working on a piece on Hindu-Muslim relations. Ahmedabad is not a major tourist destination. It is large, congested, and noxiously polluted; I am there mostly for the article, and because I want to visit Gandhi's ashram, Sabarmati. But Ahmedabad wins me over. The largest city in the northwestern province of Gujarat, which was conquered in 1299 by invading Muslims, Ahmedabad is home to numerous beautiful old mosques. The city retains its distinctly Muslim flavor, even though only 14 percent of its residents are Muslim. Ahmedabad was also home to Gandhi and *satyagraha*, the nonviolent resistance movement that swept India and eventually won it independence.

I meet Abdul Bakr while I am wandering as unobtrusively as possible through a residential neighborhood in the old city. It is an unmistakably middle-class locale, with tidy apartment blocks and tiny plots of yard sporting shrubbery and the odd swing set. As soon as Bakr spies me, he scurries over to introduce himself.

"Hello, hello! How are you?" He holds out a hand, smiling warmly. I like him instantly. The man exudes goodwill from each pore.

"May I introduce myself? Abdul Bakr, civil servant in the bumbling bureaucracy of the great state of Gujarat." He shakes my hand robustly, his smile stretching impossibly wider. "And what might be your good name?"

"Marisa Handler, itinerant journalist, at your service."

"A journalist! Very exciting indeed! What, if I may be so bold, are you writing about?" Bakr is rangy and slightly hunched. He wears a pressed, button-down striped shirt. His hair is thick, neatly combed; his ears veer out into the world at right angles, as if striving to heed the wisdom of children and the more diminutive species.

"By all means, be bold. I'm writing right now about Hindu-Muslim relations in India."

"Indeed, this is a worthy topic." Bakr's smile retracts suddenly. I think of a snail, of the way its sensitive antennae venture out delicately, then draw back abruptly. "Certainly Hindus and Muslims have a difficult history here. This no one can deny." He sighs, moved now, brow furrowed and eyes liquid, and I wait, fascinated by the streaming play of emotions on this lucid face. "Let us sit and talk." He gestures to a bench in a scrupulously neat yard behind me, then to the building adjacent to it. "This is where I live." He takes my elbow and escorts me over. "Please, sit." I ask his permission to record our conversation for my article. "But of course, of course." I pull out my notebook and a pen, and wait for him to resume.

"Well, I am a Muslim." He smiles, a little wistful. "Indian first, I say, Muslim second. Although many Hindus do not consider us real Indians." The smile evaporates. "To my great sadness, we are often treated like second-class citizens. There are times, even, when I do not feel safe." Now he looks away, and I do too, for the pain on his face is so transparent that it pierces me, stirring something deep, something kin. "But in this neighborhood" — his eyes back to me, now, sparking up — "we live together jointly and happily." The smile reappears, unvanquished. "Ravi!" He calls eagerly, beckoning to someone behind me. I turn as a plump, bespectacled man approaches us from the apartment building.

"Ravi Parasha, my good neighbor, I am delighted to present Miss Marisha Handler, my journalist friend." Ravi smiles until his eyes vanish altogether, shakes my hand. "Tell me, Ravi," resumes Bakr, "are you not a Hindu?"

"Yes, I am Hindu."

"And I am Muslim, correct?"

"You are a Muslim."

"Are we friends?"

"Of course." Ravi's bald head bobs energetically from side to side in the Indian version of a nod. "We are dear friends."

"That, precisely, is my point. You see, Marisha"—turning to face me, finger raised instructively—"we have lived together as neighbors for eight years. When I was in Delhi and my child Nazima broke her wrist, Ravi went with Nazima and my wife to the hospital. Tell me, are we not living proof that Hindus and Muslims can get along?" He looks to Ravi and to me, daring us to challenge him. We both nod vigorously. "Thank you, Ravi." Ravi shakes my hand again and heads off, dismissed.

"So you see, my friend," Bakr continues triumphant, "I worship Allah, I go by the words of Muhammad, and I believe that truly practicing my Islam means practicing its teachings with every person I know, no matter whether Muslim or Hindu."

"I understand." I keep my eyes down, on my notepad, so that he will not see the tears welling up. I have happened upon a kindred spirit. I want to drop my pen, laugh, tell him that he is an inspiration to me. I do not want to push this sensitive man. I want to ask him why different people have such different versions of God. I want to talk philosophy and metaphysics, tell him what I believe. But I remind myself that I have a job to do here. My role right now is not to speak—or rather, it is to speak only insofar as to engage the voices of others. My role here is to listen. To render those voices as faithfully as I can, so that readers will know what it means when they choose to speak. So that I will know, when I speak. So instead I ask Bakr if he thinks there is going to be a war with Pakistan.

He shakes his head decisively. "We don't believe in war in India." This is a sentiment I hear from everyone I talk with. Hindus often follow it up with *but we have been pushed to the limit and have no choice.*

I point out that half the army and a handful of nuclear weapons are marshaled along the border.

"We don't have proof that these attacks were ordered by Pakistan. We don't know that Pakistan was directly involved." Now Bakr is tired, flat out of patience with these callow chiefs and their reckless games. "War is a last resort. The leaders should sit at a table and talk." His rejoinder is typical of the Muslim response to the standoff with Pakistan. Krishna, the engineer from Delhi, told me that Hindus are pacifists by nature, Muslims militant fundamentalists. But in my interviews, it is generally the Muslims who provide the closest thing to a united—albeit largely ignored—voice of dissent against war.

"Perhaps it is simply an excuse." Bakr is thoughtful now, one elongated forefinger massaging his hairline. "Kashmir. Pakistan. All of it. Simply an excuse to let out our frustration, our loathing. Tension between Hindus and Muslims goes back a long time, you know, even before Partition. It is old, a comfortable hatred. Most Indians are very poor, living lives that are often brutal." He shakes his head, face flaccid with distress. "Who better to blame than the people your grandparents blamed? And theirs before them?"

I think of South Africa and Jerusalem, of how ordinary hatred can be. How routine and habitual, until enough people say no. Or else until it explodes.

When the interview is over Bakr takes me into his home, introduces me to his wife Iman and to Nazima, who is pigtailed and hides behind her mother, shy and saucer-eyed. We drink chai and make small talk. When I leave they press sweets upon me and tell me that I must come back someday to visit them with my family.

I go to Sabarmati, Gandhi's ashram, Bakr's words ringing in my head. Gandhi was opposed to Partition, to division along religious lines. After India declared independence, as communal tensions flared into mass slaughter, Gandhi dropped politics altogether to focus entirely on Hindu-Muslim relations, devoting body and soul to the pursuit of unity. He went to Calcutta and Delhi, fasting until the riots subsided. In Delhi, twelve days after peace settled over the city, Nathuram Godse stepped in front of Gandhi and fired three shots. The Mahatma, the great soul, was assassinated by a Hindu extremist enraged at his "appeasement" of the Muslims. An old hatred exploded, and the world grieved.

I walk about the grounds of the ashram, marveling over the life of this extraordinary man. Gandhi needed no arms to free his country; his primary weapon was his steadfast faith in the essential goodness of human nature. This is a faith I have come to share, but it tends to fall flat every time I pick up a newspaper. I wonder at this, at the tremendous power carried by a conviction most of our politicians—most everybody—would laugh off as naive. Gandhi wrote his *Satyagraha Leaflet No. 13* in 1919, five years after returning to India from South Africa, where apartheid had provided fertile ground for the seedlings of nonviolent resistance. The struggle for Indian independence was taking its first shaky steps. "Victory attained by violence is tantamount to a defeat," wrote the Mahatma, "for it is momentary."

En route to my hotel in downtown Ahmedabad I take a detour into one of the city's many mosques. It is early afternoon, and the place is virtually deserted. I wander around, thumbing through my guidebook, absentmindedly admiring the ornately carved domes and ceilings. In the sanctuary I pause. Only one man is praying. He sits cross-legged on a mat, clad entirely in white, his back to me. From the elaborately wrought latticework above, shafts of light cascade directly onto the small plot he has staked out. For a minute I am motionless, transfixed at the sight. He is silent, head nodding in staccato rhythms of devotion. I think of Bakr and his Islam. I imagine the room filled, emptying, filling again, as reliable a cycle as the moon tugging at the tides, over and over through the centuries. How many men, how many times, what inconceivable range of grievances, petitions, joys? What cumulative force of the heart? I think of the Kotel, Boudhanath, Notre-Dame, the magnificent viscera of dozens of Hindu temples I have visited—of the clasped hands and closed eyes, the clutched texts and tokens, the lips moving with all the will of a marionette—of every bit I have devoured, greedily, like a connoisseur of zeal, like a practiced pickpocket of the believing. What does he know that I do not? What does this air, what do these walls know? And suddenly I see him turning, and looking at me, with ferocious concentration. For a breath's eon those startlingly green eyes bore into mine, and something is exchanged. I have been pilfering, hoping no one would notice, but now he sees, accepts, hands it to me, and I am dizzy with the measure of it. *Take*, say those eyes. *There is no need to steal from your own garden.*

I am in Rishikesh when I decide it's well-nigh time to tend that garden.

Traveling alone in the subcontinent has taught me a great deal. I have learned that fear doesn't have to stop me. It is often with me — yapping shrilly, nipping at my heels — but what lies beyond it is more profound, and I can choose to listen to that. I am still not sure what I am seeking here. Truth, I think, of some kind. But while my course may be meandering and often confused, it somehow seems to be bearing fruit. I realize at some point along the way that I am happy. Traveling alone gives me confidence, the confidence to discover and listen to what I really want. What I have at times thought I wanted, what most other Americans seem to want, always left me feeling barren and groundless. India teaches me that striking out on my own is fertile. And still I sense there is more.

Rishikesh is a thriving hub for seekers. The Beatles came here to study transcendental meditation with the Maharishi, and throngs of the questing hopeful have since followed. The town is crawling with shaven, saffron-robed westerners, and it is aclutter with western delights — specifically of the gastronomical variety — in which I indulge voraciously after long weeks of curry. Rishikesh is a haven for expatriates, and, like other such havens, it strikes me as awash in irony. Refugees of western society — with its grinding materialism, its ambition and consumerism — come here to live out their fantasy alternative lifestyles. Yet it is the same unjust global socioeconomic system they typically despise that enables them to live out their ideals here — on the backs of a brown underclass. And moreover (familiar guilt kicking in my chest) that enables me to travel for rhapsodic months at a stretch.

Philosophical concerns aside, I am grateful when I reach Rishikesh. I am in desperate need of a reprieve. In the past couple of weeks, I have begun to feel that things are happening around me, rather than to me. They are happening around me in a gummy glaze of hammering pandemonium. Lately, India has stuffed my senses and then some.

I check into one of Rishikesh's many ashrams and head out to locate a meditation retreat. Before leaving for Nepal, I did my first full day of meditation at Spirit Rock, a Buddhist insight meditation center north of San Francisco. The day proved to be roughly a hand's breadth from hell. Every "sit" I was positively trampled by some new horror: rage, grief, and fear each flooded me in merciless succession. Meanwhile those around me, to all appearances, passed the day in blissful tranquility. I seethed with loathing, plotted petty vengeances. It was a torturous experience, but it alerted me that I was onto something. Since then I have been meditating intermittently. I come to Rishikesh hoping to find myself a retreat.

But everything here is yoga, yoga, yoga. Hatha, Kundalini, Tantra, Bhakti, Raja, pranayama, asanas. Yoga this, yoga that, yoga here, yoga there. I like yoga, but I need something rather more intensive to penetrate this fog. I come across a single flyer for an ongoing insight meditation retreat, which sounds about right, but there's no phone number. Just an address: Phoolchatty ashram, a few miles north of Rishikesh. Well then. It doesn't take much to defeat me right now. I return somewhat dejectedly to my ashram.

Over the next couple of days I dabble in the local recreational opportunities. I chant "Shiva om" and "Hari rama" with an energetic circle of the dreadlocked, pierced, and tribal-tattooed in our ashram's temple. I attend a yoga class and can't stop giggling as the muscled teacher proudly removes his shirt to demonstrate something impossible, as the Australian girl next to me farts away shamelessly, as we close the session with a meditation and I realize that the notion of me trying to stop thinking is in itself hysterical. I go for a lengthy stroll along the banks of the Ganges with a Spanish friend, and we happen upon the hut of a *sadhu*. We are invited to enter, and we sit in the dim space sharing a chillum of *charas* with a convivial circle of loin-clothed ascetics. We discuss Rumi, the Internet, the nature of life and death, and each of them takes a turn trying on my oversized black sunglasses.

I am soaking up the sun in the ashram garden one afternoon, recovering from the strenuous exertions of backpacker life—sleep, eat, loll about, yoga, eat some more, loll—when I overhear an English guy talking about the retreat at Phoolchatty. He has his backpack on and is about to head over there. I perk up. Really? Does he know more details?

"Yes, I went up to visit. The teachers seem to know what they're on about, and it's a beautiful place, really peaceful. You should go."

"Is there a format? I mean, what are they *doing*?"

"It's your typical silent retreat. Sitting meditation, walking meditation, interviews with teachers."

"Silent?"

"Yes, most of the time."

"I see." Days of silence with complete strangers? Actually I don't see, can hardly imagine that at all, am aghast at the very idea. But the "peaceful" part lures. I pack my bag, bid adieu to the yogis, and hunt down a taxi.

I spend ten days at Phoolchatty, and these ten days change my life. For months I have had recurring dreams of massive tidal waves. In my dreams I keep running, panicking, running. At Phoolchatty I become still, and the waves break over me in relentless succession. I sit in the meditation hall and I watch my breath and I watch myself and I am astounded at all I see. For many years I have wondered what to believe in, whether there is anything to believe in. Ten days of silence, practicing awareness, and I somehow relocate what I always knew. The unmanageable love for my classmates in Standard 4P. For the strangers, now, sitting next to me. The bursting wonder at the world around me, at the sky, the river, the intricately patterned minutiae of any given patch of earth. The exotic foreignness and the intimate familiarity of it all: a new face, a rose, my own breath, my hands, my thoughts. My heart. It is a wrenching time, as well, because I see heinous chunks of myself which I have thus far kept hidden. I see how hard I drive myself—to be good, to achieve, to win attention, to figure things out. I see how I am constantly judging and punishing myself for perceived failures. I sit on a rock at the edge of the Ganges and howl. "Give it all space," says Jaya, one of the teachers. "Be very gentle." Later, much to my astonishment, I glimpse what I can only call my fundamental goodness. Except it isn't mine. It belongs, as I had suspected, to all of us. Indeed it is bigger than all of us.

I sit on the sandy shore of the river and meditate on the sinewy currents, on the constant pummel and give of the water, and every now and then I release, for a rapturous blink, enough to feel it. And then I know, although I will spend most of my time forgetting: there is no such thing as separation.

I have been rambling about the world looking for something I couldn't identify. Something more. And here it is. Within, without, with all.

"All humanity is one undivided and indivisible family," said Gandhi, the Mahatma, the great soul, "and each one of us is responsible for the misdeeds of all the others. I cannot detach myself from the wickedest soul." The meaning of our interconnection, I see at Phoolchatty, leads directly to ethical action. It dawns on me that social justice work is not simply a compassionate response; it is a logical response, a natural response—the only response, really. In harming each other we hurt ourselves. And in running from the ways we are hurt, we harm others. "As human beings," said Gandhi, "our greatness lies not so much in being able to remake the world—that is the myth of the atomic age—as in being able to remake ourselves." Yes, I think. That's it. As the Mahatma maintained, remaking ourselves— our views, choices, actions—is how we remake the world. In that case, I wonder, what should I *do*? Should I sit in meditation until I remotely embody my ideals, or should I work, flawed as I am, to ease the suffering of others?

As usual, I chew over this with angst while continuing on my way, hoping life will answer what I cannot intellectually resolve. My time at Phoolchatty does, however, show me that change is possible. In holding everything that comes up during my meditations with gentle awareness, as much as I am capable, I start to see a shift in myself, subtle transformations in how I perceive and react to the world. Old patterns begin to release their grip on me, rusted gears creaking apart just a few millimeters.

But this doesn't come cheap. Holding some of the fear, grief, and anger that I've spent a goodly proportion of my life running from— and that I have thus, in many ways, allowed to govern me—is perhaps the hardest thing I've ever done. No wonder we believe it is easier to push away what we do not want to see in ourselves. Perhaps that's why we construct systems that divide us, I think, as I sit on the ashram's rooftop one evening near the end of my stay at Phoolchatty. I am surveying the valley beneath as the sun sets, suffusing all with an apocalyptic blush. We project the undesirable within us outward, onto an "other"; we build walls, put the "other" behind them, aim our arsenals over them. Yet this kind of security, like any material security, is an illusion. I can still step out my front door and get run over by a bus. Moreover, it is an illusion that breeds further fragmentation. In separating ourselves from the "other," we not only sow conflict, we also cut ourselves off from what lies within—and close ourselves to the possibility that this may teach and even transform us.

While I am discovering what the world's wisdom traditions have maintained for millennia—that separation is ultimately not real, that it is fueled by our own fear—the planet continues to fracture further into discord. The U.S. is rapidly isolating itself, busily striving to remake the world according to its ends. And Gandhi's beloved India is watching with envy and resentment from the sidelines, watching as the earth shifts beneath it, and an old fissure, an old hatred, ruptures anew.

I am in Delhi at the beginning of March 2002, about to catch a plane out of India, when all hell breaks loose in Gujarat. Since January, India and Pakistan have taken small, steady steps away from the precipice, but Hindu-Muslim tensions within India have been amply stoked by the conflict. The violence is rooted in Ayodhya, a small town in the northern province of Uttar Pradesh. From 1528 until 1992, Ayodhya was home to the Babri mosque. This mosque was situated on the same spot that some Hindus maintain was the birthplace of Ram, one of their most revered deities, and thus it became a flashpoint for Hindu-Muslim tensions. In 1984 Hindu nationalist extremists formed a committee to "liberate" the site by building a temple where the mosque stood. On December 6, 1992, as the police looked on, a crowd of Hindus demolished the Babri mosque using whatever they could—shovels, pickaxes, their bare hands. Anti-Muslim riots followed, which prompted violence all across India. Over the following days, two thousand people were killed, most of them Muslims.

In 1998 the Hindu nationalist Bharatiya Janata Party (BJP) rose to power as the dominant force in India's coalition government. Prominent leaders vowed to build a Ram temple on the disputed site. In February 2002 hundreds of Hindu volunteers headed to Ayodhya to begin construction of the temple. On February 27 a train filled with Hindu activists returning from Ayodhya to Gujarat was set on fire, allegedly by Muslim insurgents (an official forensic investigation would later reveal that the fire was started inside the train, not outside where a Muslim mob had gathered). Fifty-eight were killed. On February 28 Hindu gangs began wreaking their revenge.

Over the next few days, two thousand Muslims were slaughtered, mostly in Ahmedabad. Shouting *Jai Shri Ram,* Praise Lord Ram, hundreds of young men rampaged through the streets, pouring kerosene on Muslims and burning them alive. Children were not spared. Women were stripped and gang-raped, then hacked and burned to death. Muslim homes and shops were looted and burned down. One hundred eighty mosques were destroyed. According to eyewitness accounts, the police either turned their backs or actively facilitated the carnage, directing rioters to Muslim homes and businesses and even joining them. An estimated thirty thousand were left homeless and seriously injured in Ahmedabad alone.

The official response, when it finally came, was abysmally inadequate. According to all independent reports, the government either stood by as the nightmare unfolded or actively colluded in it. Gujarati Chief Minister Narendra Modi, a nationalist extremist, called the riots a "natural response" to the train incident and praised Gujarat's fifty million Hindus for their "remarkable restraint in the face of grave provocation." Later, both Muslims and Hindus would accuse the BJP state and national governments of exploiting the violence for political advantage.

I am sitting in the courtyard of my hotel in Delhi when I first read the headlines. It is March 3, the morning of my last day in India. I am eating yogurt with granola and honey and musing blissfully over all those beloved to me whose faces I cannot wait to see. It is a comfortable hotel; on my last days, I have finally conceded to pay an astronomical five dollars for a room. The walls of the courtyard are lined with potted plants and tourist posters. Parakeets twitter sociably from a spacious cage. Backpackers are laughing and talking in an assortment of languages, a harmonious medley of accents. "Can you believe it? In the middle of a busy intersection, two cows, and everyone bloody well driving around them, barely even a hoot..." I pick up the *Times of India* from the newspaper table.

Riots. Bloodshed. Gujarat.

"And then he says, 'Listen, I like you, but I met this girl in Dharamsala and we kind of decided to meet up again in Delhi.' And it's not like I was really even into him, but—"

Rape. Mutilation. The death toll at four hundred and rising.

"I was thinking I'd get my mother one of those tapestry things, you know the kind with the hand-sewn beadwork, but I've already collected so much, and as for trusting the Indian postal system—"

Hindu gangs. Jai Shri Ram. Kerosene.

Muslims. Burned alive. Ahmedabad.

Muslims. Ahmedabad.

Ahmedabad.

Abdul Bakr is sitting across from me now, talking to me about his Islam. About his country and his neighbor Ravi and old hatred. His hands are moving gracefully as he speaks, not fast enough to follow his expressions, though, not fast enough to trace the fluid topography of his face. Nazima is next to him, hanging on to his knee, staring up, just beginning to be scared. Iman has her back to me. She is bustling, busy with the food, the chai, the washing. I watch them as I cry, softly, into my breakfast. Now they are leaving me, but still Iman keeps working, Nazima keeps staring, mouth slowly dropping open, and Bakr keeps talking, face alight with an abrupt joy and ears bent to the ground, to the ground.

Six:

Anytown, USA

"Water! Water over here, please." I dash over with a water bottle, hold it up to Tom's mouth as he swallows. "Enough?" He produces a grunt that sounds more like a yes than a no, so I pull the bottle back.

"Thanks." He grins up at me briefly, then returns to the work at hand, brow folding, jaw working: "Occupation is a crime, Israel out of Palestine! Occupation is a crime..."

There are around a hundred of us, chanting vigorously. "Security for Israel requires Justice for Palestine" reads one sign. "A Jewish Voice for Peace" reads another. I am happy to see these folks here. And bobbing about on the edges: "Occupation Is Apartheid." My friend Carwil is manning the microphone, airy afro abounce as he squires the masses, placid as ever amid the chaos. Our action is targeting the U.S. government, so we chose the Oakland Federal Building as our site. Its atrium is a massive, rounded, glassed-in affair, and the acoustics prove little less than deafening. Across the circle, Kate, one of the media spokespeople, is giving an interview to local radio station KPFA. She yells into the microphone as the interviewer nods intently, pressing her earphones closer to her ears. Beside me, Drew is getting a massage, emitting the odd groan in pleasure. One lockbox over, Lauren feeds Steve a spring roll, wiping his chin with a napkin and catching the shreds of sprouts and carrot that don't quite make it. It's lunchtime. All around the circle, those on "support" are gently plying with food those who have opted to risk arrest.

Fifteen brave souls chose to lock down. They are seated in a circle around two of the massive pillars in the atrium, arms linked inside bright yellow cylinders stenciled with "Unlock Palestine" and "No

Guns to Israel." People in suits and ties give us a wide berth, gaping at those doing civil disobedience, fending off proffered flyers with irritation, hurrying, scurrying to their meetings and appointments. Later, the police will have to saw through the PVC tubing to remove and arrest the activists, whose wrists are tied to steel bolts on the inside. They will be charged with trespassing. Outside the building, a massive yellow banner reading "No U.S. Guns for Israel's Occupation" hangs suspended between two lampposts. David and Jene used ropes to scale the lampposts to hang it. They bob fifteen feet above the ground on makeshift rope seats for the duration of the four hours we occupy the building.

"Marisa!" It's Carwil, handing me the microphone. Without his sturdy monotone at the helm, the chanting is starting to ebb. "Ready? Go for it." I'm nervous as all-get-out. This is the part where I'm supposed to sing the song I wrote—my small attempt to cobble some meaning out of so much senseless death and destruction, some beauty out of my own outrage and pain. How to sing, when I can barely even inhale? But then this isn't about me. I take the microphone and the song comes.

> *Jenin*
> *tell me what your soil has seen*
> *tell me what your broken have gleaned*
> *tell me that the rain will wash clean*
> *this nightmare into a dream*
> *of peace*

It is May 7, 2002. In April the Jenin refugee camp—home to over twenty of the suicide bombers who have recently battered Israel—was invaded by the Israeli Defense Force. Initial reports from the camp are of a full-scale massacre. These reports cannot be confirmed because Israel refuses to allow the international press to enter the refugee camp for a full two weeks following the invasion. Later investigations find no evidence to support claims of a massacre, although there is evidence of willful killings, summary executions, and the use of Palestinians as "human shields." More than fifty Palestinians are killed during the invasion, an undetermined number of them civilians. Homes are bulldozed, neighborhoods wrecked. While some kind of response to the waves of suicide bombings is obviously required, Israel's heavy-handed reaction stuns and dismays me. Isn't it obvious that actions like this only lay the breeding ground for more hatred, more terrorists? Israel also pays an immediate and heartbreaking toll: twenty-three Israeli soldiers are killed during the invasion. I know these men — these boys, rather; I sat next to them on countless bus rides between Jerusalem and Tel Aviv, argued politics with them, flirted with them.

As a Jew and an American, I feel doubly compelled to voice my conscience. It is U.S. political support for Israel that enables it to act in violation of international law. And U.S. economic support of Israel — over six billion dollars a year — too often ends up feeding U.S. arms manufacturers. We occupy the Oakland Federal Building with a set of three demands on the U.S. government: stop sending military dollars to Israel, apply real pressure on Israel to end the Occupation, and support just international solutions to the conflict — including compliance with international law. We insist on speaking to someone from the State Department in a position to negotiate these demands.

Eventually someone official-looking in a suit and tie arrives. He glances about apprehensively, obviously unsettled by this rowdy bunch of radicals. Wishing, no doubt, he was back in his cubicle with coffee and donuts at hand. He introduces himself as the "Assistant Special Agent in charge of the San Francisco Diplomatic Security Service." He is duly thanked for showing up. Can he negotiate our demands with us?

"Sorry, no."

Can he call someone in the State Department to discuss the situation in the occupied territories?

"Uh, no, I'm afraid not."

All right then. In that case, no need to unlock.

By the time I leave — rushing to my much-needed job as a Hebrew school teacher, where I proceed to embroil myself in furious debates with the other teachers — I am exhausted. My voice is hoarse. But I am utterly exhilarated. In India, I listened. I listened to other voices and to my own. I stumbled again into the cataclysm of suffering that we wreak upon each other, but I also began to grasp why, and — at long last—what might be done to staunch the bloodletting. Today, we walked through the streets of downtown Oakland and made them our own. We walked in the footsteps of Gandhi, of Martin Luther King, of the thousands of nonviolent protestors who have changed the world in small, steady increments. As Israeli Prime Minister Ariel Sharon met with George Bush, as another suicide bomber blew himself to gory bits, we walked into the Oakland Federal Building and dedicated it to peace. For a single day, our action carved out a space for justice—a space to remind people, in the midst of their busy lives, that there is a larger canvas. That the Palestinians are suffering. That our tax dollars are fueling an occupation.

And people on the streets listen. Bystanders take our flyers. Supporters honk their horns as they pass. Journalists record our words. Priests and officials come to speak. The police try to negotiate. We make the evening news. I spend the day high on adrenaline, charged with victory, every new development in the unfolding drama searing into my brain in electric relief. I am amazed and inspired by my new activist friends, by their dedication and resourcefulness. I feel joined to them in a bond that runs deeper than camaraderie: we share a vision, a commitment to put ourselves on the line for our principles. Together we are exercising our First Amendment rights under an administration that is determined to clamp down on these basic liberties. What a visceral sense of relief to find these people. What a visceral sense of relief to finally accomplish something concrete.

It is singing that gets me into all of this in the first place.

I come back from India and sit in my beloved cafés and walk through my favorite neighborhoods. The streets of San Francisco feel empty, muted, lifeless. The people around me, lonely and afraid. We are all of us trying so hard to avoid each other's eyes. Doesn't everyone else notice? How could I have missed this? I feel it in myself: a sense of fear that arises with each passerby. Do I meet his eyes or not? Can I risk a smile? It nearly overwhelms me, the amount of effort we put into avoiding each other. What is this society we live in? How fragmented have we become, when the most basic connection with a stranger—a greeting, a smile—can feel like a near-insurmountable hurdle?

I also come back from India wondering what to do with myself. I am, however, convinced that I want to do *more*. For the past few years, I've mostly watched from the sidelines: watched as corporations commandeer and gobble up our natural resources, as the environment is wrecked and the imbalance in wealth worsens, as the U.S. ignores genocide in Rwanda and later starts its own wars, as Israel perseveres with the Occupation and the Palestinians erupt in intifada. I've read the papers and listened to the radio with grief and anger, shaking my head, shaking my fists, and feeling powerless. What can I do? I can email my representatives, sure. I can check the right box come election time. I can volunteer for a worthy cause, write the odd article. But it has become clear to me that humanity is on a course to annihilation—if not of each other, then of the planet—and that avoiding this fate requires changing the entire system. Checking the right box strikes me as little more than ornamental. My anger regularly sinks, with a nauseating squelch, into despair. I feel horribly guilty, when I let myself think about it, because I'm not doing more. And I feel frustrated, because I don't know what I can do that will be of any real help. So mostly I just rant, and my friends, bless their hearts, listen patiently.

But during my time in South Asia something shifts. In the rest of the world, people are suffering because of the political choices and economic "freedoms" of my adopted homeland. How many Americans recognize the link between Indo-Pakistani war games and the war in Afghanistan? How many Americans see that our levels of consumption depend on the existence of a global underclass, on the appropriation of natural resources that belong to others? In India, I realized the significance of ethical action, and of *satyagraha*, nonviolence, as the path to change. I left Phoolchatty understanding, through my own experience, that change is possible, and in ways that are barely conscious this knowledge invigorates me. I come back wanting to craft action out of my convictions. I am ready to contribute in a bigger way. I am ready to speak. Yet saying no is no longer enough. Things are dire. The clock is ticking. It is time, I declare—feeling like a second-rate college basketball coach psyching up the shivering benchwarmer—it is time to *be* the *no*. Yes, friends and benefactors, it is time for me to walk the talk. Okay then.

Caryn, one of my closest friends from college, invites me to a meeting. Caryn is officially an activist: she works at the San Francisco non-profit Global Exchange, coordinating their travel program to Cuba.

"Come with me to a meeting at Art and Revolution," she says, smiling alluringly. Art and Revolution is a local arts-activism collective.

"What for?" I am suspicious. Caryn is eternally trying to drag me into stuff. When she isn't busy haranguing me on U.S. policy toward Cuba, that is.

"We're working on a pageant for this year's Radical Performance Festival. It's called 'Alice in Oil-Land.' Or maybe 'Oil-less in Wonderland.' The Caterpillar is high off oil fumes, and the Cheshire Cat is played by Dick Cheney. It'll be fun. You can sing."

She's got me there. One thing I know I can contribute is my voice. This, at least, I am convinced I can provide without risking too much. I accept, with reservations. Caryn's friends always make me want to argue. They wield their radicalism with a holier-than-thou attitude that makes me feel inadequate—as if I could never be that slavishly self-effacing, that dedicated—and also uncomfortably conservative, as if my realism is no match for their wanton idealism. But I go to the meeting and get sucked into taking on a minor part—Tank Girl—in the world debut of "Alice in Oil-Land." It is the art that pulls me in. I get sufficiently absorbed in the singing and painting to lose myself a little, to let go of my doubts and begin to get to know some of these folks who seem to care so much.

The performance is a blast: we caper and cavort for all we're worth, and by the time we get to the grand finale—"A Better World Is Possible"—the audience is giving us a standing ovation. Next I am asked if I want to be part of a performance at an action protesting the Bechtel corporation. Bechtel is suing the city of Cochabamba, Bolivia, for $25 million—roughly equal to the revenues Bechtel earns in half a day—for breach of contract. With 64 percent of its population living below the poverty line, Bolivia is the poorest country in South America. After Bechtel took over Cochabamba's water contract, rates doubled, and even tripled in some neighborhoods. In response, an organized citizens' movement of Cochabambinos rose up and pushed Bechtel out.

Next thing I know, I'm singing into a bullhorn outside Bechtel headquarters as my compatriots leap and twist in front of me, as the crowd hoots its approval. Then comes the action at the Oakland Federal Building. At this point I'm gaining confidence, actually starting to like these scruffy radicals. And the Occupation is an issue about which I have cared deeply since my time in Israel; now I see a way to act on my beliefs. I go to the first planning meeting at the Berkeley Cannabis Club and sing the song I wrote about Jenin. To my own mild alarm, I also volunteer to organize the program and write and teach the chants. So that's how, two months back from India, I wake up one sunny spring day to find myself leading a crowd of chanting dissidents through the streets of downtown Oakland.

Of course there is also the delicate matter of earning a living. With so many worthy causes, who has time for a job? But I do need to eat (which proves mortifyingly expensive after India). I'm not quite ready for grad school, and I break out in hives when I think about a nine-to-five cubicle job. I decide to continue freelance writing and singing, and cast about for a part-time job to tide me over the grim months. Then my friend Nancy calls.

"You're not going to believe it. I found you the perfect job."

"Really." I can't wait to hear this. I have no clue what the perfect job for me would be. So far only the only appealing positions are those for which I am not remotely qualified: senior editor for *National Geographic*, associate director of Amnesty International, that kind of thing.

"Listen. I cut it out of the back of the *Guardian*." She reads it to me: "'The Tikkun Community seeks a full-time National Organizer. The job will involve building a national campus network of students supporting a progressive middle path to peace in Israel and Palestine, as well as growing our national noncampus community. You will be traveling and speaking across the country, and expected to work more than forty hours a week. This job requires abundant energy, the ability to speak publicly on difficult and contentious issues, excellent organizational skills, and passionate dedication.'" She pauses. "Am I right? It's totally you."

Well, this wasn't exactly the grand plan, but I like the parts about traveling and public speaking. Lord knows I've been lugging my own soapbox around when it comes to Israel and Palestine. Energy and passion I have in profusion. Could this be it? My big chance to make a difference? I indulge in visions of jetting across the country, setting vast audiences afire with my words. I try to envision peace in the Middle East, an end to the bloodshed and hatred. All of a sudden I'm practically aching to give of myself.

I apply, go in to interview, and, to my delight and terror, end up getting the job. Days later I am ensconced in my own tiny office. It doubles as the kitchen, and I bump into the microwave whenever I stand up. I sit at my desk staring at the books and files I've been given to review, wondering how I'll ever get through all the work I now have before me, wondering whether I am more anxious that I will or will not lose myself to this job.

DIE JEWISH TRAITOR WITH THE BLOOD OF YOUR FELLOW JEWS ON YOUR HANDS. I KNOW WHERE YOU LIVE.

I stare at the screen. "Can you come see this?" I holler out to Liz, who sits in the next office. She appears in my doorway, scans the email, and laughs. "Yeah, we get stuff like that all the time. Sometimes even death threats. Last week we got a used tampon in the mail. Once we had to call in Poison Control about this weird white powder in an envelope. It's the ultraorthodox Jews. They hate us."

"Oh."

"But don't let it get to you. Their bark is worse than their bite."

"Okay."

"They don't really know where you live."

"Uh-huh."

Death threats against members of an organization dedicated to peace? What confounds me is the intensity of faith the ultraorthodox seem to possess. I have my own newly refurbished spirituality, which rests in a vision of interconnection, of love, and which nonetheless gets shaken—or vanishes altogether—with disquieting regularity. How can these people have so much faith? How can they have so much faith in something so different, something I believe is very wrong? How did we get so far apart, considering we are of the same heritage? And how, in the face of such unshakable belief, can I have any conviction that my way is right? Ironically, I think it comes down to my faith, to the entirely nonrational underpinnings of my choices. We are all of us operating on faith. My faith is simply that we are here to be love, and that every one of us is equally deserving, regardless of race or creed. I may never understand how they can believe what they believe, but perhaps I can accept it. To build peace in the face of these differences, I reason, I must love, regardless of what people believe—even, or perhaps especially, those whom I'd on instinct abhor. This is the conclusion I arrive at intellectually. Putting it into practice proves another matter altogether.

I start at Tikkun in June and spend most of the summer working with a team of interns to construct the foundation for a campus network. Pro-Palestine and pro-Israel student groups have been clashing stridently and occasionally violently on campuses across the nation. The Tikkun Campus Network advocates a "middle path" to peace: we call for an end to the Occupation and an end to the terror against Israel, reparations for Palestinian refugees, and real security for Israel. In late August, I hit the road on Grand Speaking Tour Number One.

The plan is ten cities in two weeks. My first date is Macalester College in St. Paul, Minnesota.

"Welcome to the Midwest," says the professor who has been my contact, pumping my hand like I am his long-lost twin. I smile so hard my teeth ache. The campus organizers have come through. There are at least a hundred and fifty people in the circular, sunny auditorium. I head to the podium and stand weak-kneed behind it, gawking like a simpleton. They may as well be ten thousand. I am shaking with nerves. Sure, I was sufficiently geeky to be president of my high school speech and debate team, but that was eons ago. And I've sung in front of a lot of people, but that's different. Even when my songs are political, the audience can write me off as an artist. And the direct actions—well, in those cases I'm among comrades.

I lean heavily on the podium, smile feebly, clear my throat. Which slams through the microphone like an 8.9 on the Richter scale. Everyone jumps. An administrator scurries up, smiles apologetically, moves the instrument delicately away from my mouth.

Oh. Shit. Oh. Shit.

Who am I again, and why are these decent people taking time out of their day to hear me? I can see it now: two minutes into my speech they'll be rising in flocks, sprinting for the door, barely bothering to lower their voices as they cleave me limb from limb—

Breathe. Breathe, Marisa, breathe.

I focus on the faces in front of me: the students looking to be inspired; the professors, exhausted by the weight of history, hungry for a morsel of hope. I can give them this. I can. I know I can.

"Thank you so much for coming—" My voice emerges at the same pitch as a rat's, and I abruptly drop it by about an octave. "It's really inspiring to see all of you. As you know, I am here today to speak about a different path to peace in Israel and Palestine, a genuine path to peace..."

I'm doing it. I'm doing it. Praises be. They are listening, and they're nodding, and, at one point, they interrupt to applaud. At first I stick to my notes. Later, emboldened, I veer off the page, dive into the buoyant current of their attention. I know what I need to say. It moves through me at its own pace, with its own rhythms and imperatives. There is a truth here for which I am more or less a vessel—a leaky one, as it happens, with an immoderate throttle and a slanting mast, but a vessel nonetheless. Violence will never create lasting peace. Hate cannot end hate, as Martin Luther King said. Only love can do that.

At Phoolchatty, I sat on the ashram roof one night and asked a question of the stillness, of the glimmering immensity unclothed by dark:

How can I serve?

The answer was both immediate and, at the time, cryptic:

Through your voice.

As an organizer for Tikkun, I find myself preaching compassion: compassion for the suffering of both Palestinians and Israelis, compassion for the dueling histories, compassion for the blindness of each to the other's truth. Tikkun's message is essentially a spiritual one. I was drawn to the job by the opportunity to work for social change, yet now that I am here—as I realize with a start in the middle of a speech—I am speaking a vision that is fundamentally spiritual, that is a startlingly good match for my own beliefs. Indeed, this vision is my own, for in speaking it, I voice it as I conceive it to be. In my activism thus far, I have not been brave enough to speak it, because addressing politics and economics is much easier than talking about consciousness or spirituality. It is far more socially acceptable to rage against a new policy or an oppressive government than to speak, as King did, of "the love that does justice." But now it is my job to speak of it. I had thought, previously, that activism and spirituality were separate realms. While they would, of necessity, inform each other, I had not conceived it possible for them to merge. Now, I watch with no little wonder as they move into fluid alignment through my work.

"When my family lived in South Africa, we thought apartheid would never end peacefully. My parents left because they saw no future, only a bloody civil war. But apartheid did end. There was the Truth and Reconciliation Commission, in which people came forward and confessed, in public, to horrendous crimes: murder, rape, arson. In return, they were offered amnesty. The country took an honest look at its own history, at all the pain, and opened to it, together. This allowed its people to begin to heal, to move forward. Change is not only possible, it is inevitable."

I am a preacher, preaching love. I speak what the best part of me believes, even when I don't believe it. I am so dogged that I convince myself. I discover that people are desperate to believe in the possibility of kindness. They are ravenous for affirmation that change is possible, that they are capable of making a difference. They want to be convinced.

I am a salesman, peddling hope. I travel with my carpetbag and papers, confident of the indisputable superiority of my product. With fanfare I present the goodies, the pamphlets and magazines. With grave assurance I cite evidence: statistics, memorable quotes. After I speak I ask interested people to stick around to discuss how to organize a campus group. There are always those who stay—sometimes three, sometimes twenty. I train them, deliver the goods, go on my way.

I am a nomad, hopping merrily about the country. After the first tour, I am home for a week, then back on the road for another two. Columbus, Cincinnati, Cleveland, New Haven, Ann Arbor, Ithaca, Denver, Princeton, Brattleboro, Rochester, Syracuse, D.C., Providence. I shuttle about in various rental cars, poring over maps, constantly getting lost (I have no sense of direction, none at all). I mosey in and out of the homes of kind people who want to help. I stay in their guest bedrooms, join them for dinner, talk Israel-Palestine until I'm ready to consign both to the sea. I try not to impose.

"Er, excuse me, is this cereal up for grabs?"

"Yes, of course. Help yourself to anything."

"Great, thanks. Also, I've been totally craving a burrito. Does Rochester have a Mexican restaurant, by any chance?"

"Syracuse. We're in Syracuse."

"Right. That's what I meant."

Early in my second tour I am scheduled to speak at Boston College. My contact is a sophomore named Luke. As we walk together to the auditorium, he tells me about the student body: it's big on football, not particularly politically active.

About twenty-five people show up. I smile winningly, welcome them, and launch into my shtick. At this point I pretty much have things down. Or so I think.

"It's vital for us to recognize that there will not be peace until both sides acknowledge that each has a valid claim, that Palestine —"

"Why you call it Palestine? There is no Palestine. There is no country Palestine." He is thickset, heavy in the jowls. An Israeli. Looking to brawl.

"Excuse me, sir, would you mind holding your questions till the Q&A?" He is sitting in the second row with his wife and child, whom I presume is a student.

"I have question now. You call it Palestine, but what is Palestine? This Palestine is a myth. An idea." He spits out "idea" like a prize-fighter ejecting a tooth. "There was no Palestine before there was Israel. What about all the Arabs? Look how much land they have. They cry for their Arab brothers but they close their doors —"

"Please, sir, there will be time for discussion later." My voice is annoyingly shaky. I take a deep breath, glance around for allies. Other than Luke, who is literally wringing his hands, everyone looks more or less indifferent. A girl in the front row picks at her split ends. Three guys in football shirts in the back are whispering to each other about something obviously unrelated. Like the girl in the front row.

"So, as I was saying, until the Occupation—"

"What occupation? What is this bullshit you are talking?" He is shouting now, up out of his chair, stabbing his finger my way. His wife and child both glare at me with the kind of vicious fury I imagine only my blood would sate. "These Arabs started the wars, and Israel defends herself. You are a child, an idiot. You live your protected life here and know nothing of reality."

"It's true I do not live with the suicide bombings, but I am Jewish, and actually I spent a year—"

"I cannot listen anymore." He dismisses me with a flip of his hand and stomps out, wife and child scampering in his wake, loyally shooting back a few murderous parting glances.

The audience, now effectively awake, stares at me in silence.

"Well. Um. Let's see now. Where was I?"

Silent stares. Even the football players appear mildly interested in my mortification. Somewhere in another universe a bell rings, drilling faintly through the suffocating mire that is my brain.

"The Occupation?" Luke proffers solicitously.

"Of course. So, until the Occupation ends, there will not be peace..." The girl in the front row returns to her split ends, methodically sorting and plucking.

Somehow I make it through to the close. Then comes the Q&A.

"Miss Handler, thank you very much for coming today. No doubt you've given us all a lot to think about." His tone is laden, dry. As if he's laughing at himself laughing at me. He is obviously a professor: he has cultivated a look that pronounces, in duly modulated tones, "intelligent." Behold, all ye undereducated plebes: my IQ is roughly equivalent to the highest prime number you mortals can think of. Squared.

He sniffs delicately, fondles his sparse goatee. "Now tell me, my dear, do you really think the Arabs are interested in peace? After all, at Camp David, Barak and Clinton offered them everything they claimed they wanted. Ninety percent of the West Bank and Gaza. And Arafat walked away."

I eye him beadily. I'm in no mood for this. Has the man no soul?

"Actually, Camp David didn't allow for contiguous access to Jerusalem, a deal-breaker in itself." I line up my stats like those little knives in kung fu movies. "And we should keep in mind that that 90 percent — or 87 or 92 percent, we don't know how much exactly because it was never written down — is still only 90 percent of the 22 percent of pre-1948 Palestine." Take that, dude. "But more importantly, Camp David didn't address the 3 to 4 million Palestinian refugees. No Palestinian leader could have gotten away with signing an agreement that didn't even mention them." Check. "And then later it was Barak who cancelled the Taba talks, right before the Israeli elections." Checkmate.

"I'm sure we could argue all night about these details, Miss Handler, so even though I have good reason to challenge you, I'm going to let this slide." Why thank you, Your Brilliance. I'm confident what I'm saying is true, but I'm relieved he doesn't challenge me here. When it comes to debating facts, stalemate inevitably results. What I have learned from this job is that the different sides have different stories. History is malleable. Even very recent history.

"But, Miss Handler —" he is back up, index finger noodling at his goatee, "what I am curious to know is this: are you saying you support the right to return?"

I think of my thesis advisor, of the fantasy of neutrality. Of the plodding journey from one side into the vast no-man's-land conjoining it to the other.

"No, I'm not. I support reparations. And I think Arafat should have taken what he was offered at Camp David, and then continued negotiating. But what I'm saying is that it's possible to understand, if we make the effort, why he didn't. Just like it should be possible for people to understand why Jews want a Jewish homeland, given that six million of us were slaughtered not all that long ago. Moving toward resolution of this conflict requires compassion for both sides."

"So you're telling me we should treat terrorists with compassion? That we should show compassion to people who plan to blow themselves up in the middle of Jerusalem on a Friday morning?" He is smug now, waiting for me to stroll starry-eyed into reality.

"I'm not saying there shouldn't be consequences. Terrorists should be removed from society, obviously."

"I'd be ever so grateful to know how you plan on doing that with your precious compassion. How?—when the Palestinians are teaching their children that Jews are the devil, that they must grow up to wipe Israel off the face of the earth."

"I'm just saying that nothing will be resolved by reacting to violence with more violence. Bulldozing homes and killing civilians only breeds more hatred." Suddenly I am exhausted. "Compassion. I'm saying have compassion. For Israelis living with the horror of suicide bombings. And for Palestinians suffering so much that they're desperate enough to blow themselves up."

"Well, honestly, I don't feel like I'm getting a single solid answer out of you, Miss Handler." He looks around to the other members of the audience—most of whom, thankfully, appear bored. "I must say I'm rather disappointed. I was hoping to hear something new, not just the same soppy bleeding-heart rhetoric. Compassion, you say. Compassion? Compassion for the jihadis, for the suicide bombers, the martyrs with their virgins?"

He is sneering. I am a child, an idiot. I know nothing of reality. I hate you, I think. I hate hate hate hate you.

"Yes," I say. "Compassion."

My audiences are often largely Jewish. Most places I speak I am challenged, frequently angrily, and generally by other Jews. Occasionally, when they come to my talks, by Arabs. I understand the anger: this issue is painful on both sides. When I debate with Jews who have more conservative positions, the frustration I experienced in Jerusalem returns. I am infuriated by what feels like willful blindness on their part, like cold indifference toward the unrelenting poverty and violence of daily life in the occupied territories. I understand, of course, that it's not this simple. I too grew up in the shadow of the Holocaust. Yet in a sense, because we are community, because our community largely shares progressive values, I expect more from other Jews. We are less patient with our own family. When I speak with radical pro-Palestinians, I encounter a wall of a different kind: a near-total indifference to Jewish history, which is equally maddening.

But I see that indifference is a response to pain, an attempt to numb oneself against further pain. It is, moreover, an attempt to render into black and white what will stubbornly endure in shades of gray. So I work hard at practicing what I am preaching. For those who come to my talks knowing that they disagree with me before I open my mouth — and there are quite a number — I am a walking, talking opportunity to unload gutbuckets of pent-up frustration. I come to know the billows and edges of my own anger. I learn to think clearly despite it. But it is still there, and I often walk away from these charged debates superficially tranquil while blistering on the inside.

Then *The New York Times* article comes out.

I am in Cambridge when I buy the paper. I sit on the curb outside a grocery store, rifling through the sections until I get to Arts and Ideas.

"Oh my God! That's me!"

"What?" An elderly man passing by pauses. "Sorry, what did you say?"

"Look! It's me! I'm in the paper!"

He lays aside his cane and hunches down next to me, looks from the paper to my face, back to the paper. His face lights up. "It is you! And you look fabulous!"

We sit on the curb and laugh and laugh.

Given recent clashes between pro-Israel and pro-Palestine campus groups, the formation of the Tikkun Campus Network makes for a timely story. A reporter and a photographer came to my talk at the New School University in Manhattan. I knew there would be an article, but I didn't realize that I'd be plastered across the front page of the section. Is my nose really that large? Vanity aside, the piece is overwhelmingly favorable.

A day later, I am standing in line at the airport, about to board a plane back to New York for the founding conference of the TCN, when my cell phone rings.

"Miss Handler? This is David Cohen. I'm a freelance journalist, and Nurit from the Tikkun office gave me your number."

In that case he must be legit. I ask him who he writes for, and he names a couple of papers I've never heard of. I tell him I only have a few minutes to talk.

"Great. So I saw the piece in *The New York Times,* of course. Very sympathetic article. You must be happy with it."

"Yes, we are."

"And I was reading about the work you're doing, and how you support Palestine, and I'm just wondering why it is that you don't support Israel."

"I do support Israel, I love Israel. As the article mentioned, we support both Israel and Palestine. I just don't think that supporting Israel means being uncritical. To me, supporting Israel means supporting peace. That's true support, that's thinking of Jewish lives now and of future—"

"Don't you see that your actions are effectively undermining Israel?" His voice is chilly.

"Actually, Mr. Cohen, I think that the actions of lobbying groups like the American Israel Political Action Committee are what undermine Israel, because they unquestioningly support an Occupation that is illegal, if one pays any attention at all to international law laid out by the Hague and Geneva Conventions." I feel my chest tightening, hear my voice growing shrill. "And the fact that AIPAC is allied, as you must know, with Christian fundamentalists who want to expand Israel to speed up the apocalypse—when, incidentally, all nonbelievers—that means you and me, Mr. Cohen—will be consumed in a gory—"

"Has. Anyone. Ever. Informed. You. That. You. Are. A. Self. Hating. Jew." He does not say this. He spews it.

I gently set my carry-on luggage down on the floor and slump against the wall. At the front of the line a woman with two children is arguing with a security guard about taking off their shoes. "Do you really think my six-year-old is a terrorist?" she demands, and he shakes his head and tells her, "Regulations, ma'am, since 9/11, regulations."

"I. Said. Has. Anyone. Ever. Informed. You. That. You. Are. A. Self. Hating. Jew."

From somewhere subterranean my voice locates itself, clambers to the surface, encounters oxygen. "Mr. Cohen, you yourself seem to be the one consumed by—"

"You're an apologist. You obviously hate yourself for being Jewish." He is roaring now. "But why make your fellow Jews suffer because you're so fucked up?"

The line is beginning to inch forward.

"How dare you?" I feel it. It's coming. "Honestly, how dare you?" People are turning now, looking at me. It's coming. It's coming. Water to blood. Boils. Locusts. The deluge. Reckoning. Reckoning. "Just who the hell are you to—"

"I'm the guy in the Warsaw Ghetto who fought back, Handler, that's who I am. You're the one who turned in her fucking neighbors. I'm the reason there's some of us left. I'm—"

"You're a total asshole!" I'm screaming now, riveted by fury, glued in place. A security guard approaches, nudges my elbow delicately. Everyone around me is staring steadily at the ceiling or the carpet, listening intently. No one cares if the line moves, I want to tell the guard. I'm more than entertainment enough. I take one step, two, three. "What is wrong with you people? Who are you without your hatred? You're a goddamn lunatic, and if you ever call me again, I'll report—"

I am at the security barrier when it occurs to me that I can hang up.

"This is what the Jews are doing to my people."

"Excuse me—"

"This man was killed at close range by an Israeli soldier. The soldier knew he was no militant, but he did not care."

"Moderator—" I wave my hand at the moderator, the blond student who just read her own paper deconstructing Zionist history. Fifteen minutes, ten pages of Times New Roman double-spaced, and the entire Zionist raison d'être trounced, just like that, in one fell swoop. "Hello, moderator—" But she too is staring at the giant photos Fareed holds up.

"And this boy. He is crippled for life, he will spend the rest of his days in a wheelchair. For what? For throwing stones at an Israeli tank—"

"Moderator!" I clear my throat into my microphone.

"Oh, yes. Miss Handler." Fareed pauses, lays down the photos with the kind of rigid resignation that says he knew it, knew the meddling

Jew wouldn't let him finish. He fixes me with a glacial stare. Four hundred heads turn my way.

"I just want to say... I just want to say that I believe it's vital to differentiate between 'the Jews' and the state of Israel. One is a people, the other a political entity. Of course we should critique the Israeli government for its wrong actions, as we should our own or any government. But blaming 'the Jews' is no different from blaming 'the blacks' or 'the Muslims.' It's anti-Semitism, pure and simple."

The crowd turns to Fareed. This is a serious accusation. They want him to put me in my place, I can tell. They want to keep the brutality of brutality simple. They want to know who is the victim, who the oppressor; who is good, who bad; what to sermonize, with untroubled conviction, when this topic arises at Thanksgiving dinner. They resent me for this complication, which is essentially academic, after all, in the face of so much maimed flesh. I search my brain for a good reason I accepted this engagement. I hadn't known that the pro-Israel campus group would cancel at the last minute. I had no clue I'd end up being the most conservative member of the panel—a position, incidentally, I find distinctly uncomfortable. Being the most conservative member of a panel addressing a U.C. Santa Cruz political science class is no walkover.

"Yet you insist on Israel remaining a Jewish state." Fareed is impassive, but I feel it. Colder than anger. Older. Loathing. "You call this upon your own heads. With no separation of church and state, there is bound to be confusion."

"That's no excuse for anti-Semitism. Saudi Arabia is an Islamic state, but I don't blame the Muslims for 9/11."

"Anti-Semitism, anti-Semitism. One word against Israel, and the Jews are up in arms crying anti-Semitism." Fareed is shaking his head with such vigor it looks like his kaffiyeh might pop off. "It's a pathetic excuse, a shield against addressing reality, a distraction. No one can suffer but the Jews."

The familiar rage, rising in my throat. I grit my teeth, willing my mind to clear, my voice to be strong.

"There are Jews who confuse criticism of Israel with anti-Semitism. And yes, this is counterproductive. It reduces substantive debate to meaningless rhetoric. But when you condemn all Jews instead of the

actions of the Israeli government, you play into their worst fears."
Look out, Fareed. Here it comes. "It's a dangerous move, and you do
your own cause a great disservice. There are many Jews who oppose
the Occupation. You lose allies. Like me."

Fareed stares at me, mask splintering, revulsion breaking over his
features. Finally, some authenticity. I actually feel relief. "You believe
my people should rot in refugee camps." An eyebrow tics above square
wire frames. "You are not my ally."

This has little to do with what I believe, I understand. This is
about who I am. What I was born. This man will never forgive me, no
matter what I say, what I embrace. I stare back.

"Then who is?"

The entire hall, as it turns out. The entire hall, stunned by bloody
photos of the Occupation's victims. The entire hall, spared the
equally gruesome photos of the bus bombings, the produce markets
sprayed with severed fingers and bits of skull. The entire hall being, of
course, a liberal class on a liberal campus in an uncompromisingly
liberal corner of an increasingly polarized nation.

It is early 2003. The Bush administration is pounding on the war-
drums again, ululating and strutting for oil in Iraq. I go to rallies and
marches against the impending war. I bring my friends and my homemade posters, and I look around me and see meticulously lettered
signs reading "Zionism Is Nazism." Signs reading "Death to Israel"
and "Sharon = Hitler." I see Israeli flags being burned, and it is like a
kick to the chest. Up to now, I have rarely experienced anti-Semitism,
but I am beginning to recognize it with regularity. It isn't obvious. No
one calls me names. I do not think, most of the time, it is even conscious. But it is present in the flavor of the fury directed against Israel.
I do not see such visceral hatred arising in discussions of other con-
flicts. No one gets nearly so enraged over the slaughter in the
Balkans or Rwanda. But when it comes to Israel/Palestine, white kids
who have no obvious affiliation to the region burn Israeli flags and
hurl invective at Israel, at Israelis, at the Zionist bastards. Occasionally, if you are listening carefully, at Jews.

Meanwhile we in the middle, insisting that a middle exists, hold our ground. The Tikkun Campus Network takes root and flourishes. Our first conference is a success. The Tikkun Community, for which I go on later speaking tours, also grows. As much as my job exhausts me, as much as I complain that I work all the time, I also love it: I love being at the hub, feeling I am making things move, feeling needed, relied upon. I am a leader, it dawns on me in the middle of facilitating a conference call. People are looking to me for guidance, for inspiration. How did I get here again? It strikes me as comical, in a number of ways, that I am working for peace. Most of the time my work for peace feels far from peaceful. Most of the time there is a lot of ego involved. How effective am I, then, I wonder. How helpful is my leadership, when I am so flawed? *Am I helping?* The anger that arises in my work: I thought of it as a side effect, but the more I look, the deeper it lies. When members of my extended family or friends from Israel send out emails lambasting the Palestinians and defending Israeli aggression, I discover myself whipping up impassioned diatribes and then hitting "reply all." *What are my motives here?* How much is anger determining my actions? Anger is natural, given the current state of our world, and anger is powerful. Certainly anger carries a formidable energy with which to wrestle injustice. But social-change work that is driven by anger will only push us further apart.

A local Jewish group organizes a demonstration supporting the U.S. and Israel in their "battle against terrorism." Three thousand supporters, mostly Jews, gather at San Francisco's Civic Center with placards and American and Israeli flags. I take it upon myself to organize a counter-rally, solely of Jews, calling for an end to both terrorism and the government-sanctioned terrorism of illegal war and occupation. There are about forty of us. We carry Israeli and Palestinian flags and signs reading "Jews for a Just Peace." As the larger rally marches down Market Street, the city's main thoroughfare, we move to the opposite curb. We stand in silence or sing peace songs in Hebrew and English.

Across the street many people ignore us, but some can't resist. They shout names at us, raise their fists and fingers and tell us we are betraying our own people. If this is indeed betrayal, then it is betrayal of a brittle and anemic dream. I see our activism as loyalty to a broader vision of our own potential. I have instructed everyone in our group on nonviolence, and we stand our ground—even my little brother, although he turns a worrying shade of purple at one point—and we keep singing. About halfway through, my co-worker's parents, who are Israeli and on the other side, catch sight of her in our line. They race across the street and try to drag her over to their side. "You are a disgrace," they tell her, and say they do not want to see her face. I am standing between my brother and my friend, our arms around each other. I am watching the expressions on the faces across the street, the disdain, the fury, the hatred, and I am recalling how I went to services recently, for the first time in ages. I held a prayer book and I sang the hymns and then I stood to say the *Shema,* the holiest prayer in Judaism. I held my right hand over my eyes and recited *Hear, O Israel, the Lord our God, the Lord is One,* as I have countless times since I first learned to speak. But this time the force of the Hebrew words ricocheted into me like a bullet, knocked me over and back into my chair, reduced me to a shuddering sodden mess as my sister bent over me asking, "What's wrong, Mims? Are you okay? What's going on?"

Unlike most prayers in Judaism, the *Shema* is not a prayer that speaks to God. It is a prayer that speaks directly to the Jewish people. *Hear, O Israel, the Lord our God, the Lord is One.* The *Shema* is an affirmation of the supreme unity of the divine. It is simultaneously a call to unity.

Hear, O Israel, the Lord our God, the Lord is One. All that we have suffered, all that we continue to suffer, flickering before my eyes in black-and-white eight-millimeter: the jumbled bones in yawning pits, the hills of gold fillings, the teenagers inside tanks, children sacrificed to soaring nails and chewing shrapnel, the habitual shattering of the mundane into the grotesque.

And you shall love the Lord your God with all your heart. All the suffering that we grapple with, that we feel and run from and feel and run from, that eats away at our vision so stealthily we do not realize we are peering through a tunnel.

With all your soul. And then all that we do not see, will not see. Do not feel, will not feel.

And with all your might. The other film: the other lives twisted by the quaking black-and-white farce of tragedy. The spine smashed for a pebble, the homes wrecked and rebuilt and wrecked and rebuilt and wrecked, the dust that will not settle, ash that the wind refuses to lift, the children claimed by holy and unholy wars.

And these words which I command you today shall be in your heart.

Is that the reason I am on this side of the street? These words, the vision of unity I have chosen? The insularity, the dissociation of our suffering?

You shall teach them diligently to your children. You shall speak of them when you sit in your home.

Is that the reason? I am deafened by the vitriol of my kin, hemorrhaging at the navel, and I can't remember now. Is that why I am here, standing opposite my own people, with four lanes of traffic and a freighter of rage between us?

You shall speak of them when you walk by the way.

When you lie down.

And when you rise up.

Seven:

San Francisco

"**Listen, I have to say** that I have pretty strong feelings on this one. There's no question in my mind: we really need the 'the' in there."

"I know you have strong feelings about this, Jumble, and I also feel strongly. The 'the' makes it way too specific. We aren't only about this war. We're about all war, right?"

"Jill. Just think for a minute, please. We are talking about war in Iraq here. We aren't talking about Vietnam or Afghanistan. People aren't going to get out in the streets over *some* war. They're going to mobilize around Iraq."

"Are you trying to build a movement destined to self-destruct? Is that what you're doing? Because then you're on the right path, my friend. I'm just thinking about the future. Holding the long-term vision here. 'Direct Action to Stop War.' It has a nice ring to it, don't you think? I mean, come on people, that says it all. We're against war, period. Right? Or am I at the wrong meeting?" Jill looks about for support. The other six people who are neither Jill nor Jumble gaze steadily at the table or the walls. We've been sitting here for two hours and the "the" debate is now hitting the twenty-minute mark. Initially there were a number of robust contenders, but now only Jumble and Jill remain in the ring.

We are meeting in the Art and Revolution space. The large, cluttered room reeks pleasantly of tempura paint. Directly opposite me stares a massive yellow molded cardboard face. It bears a wide grin, and a placard beneath its cleft chin reads "Direct Democracy." I slide down, down in my chair, till my chin is roughly at table level. I can see it now: tomorrow there will be competing direct actions at Sixteenth and Valencia. On the west side, we'll have the "Yes on The" coalition, with their signs, banners, and street theater. Giant colorful puppets will poke merciless fun at the harebrained pacifism and poor mass-mobilizing skills of the "No on The" folks, who will stand on the east side chanting passionately against those myopic fools, those reformist buffoons who believe that protesting one war will somehow amount to revolution. Eventually a few hardy souls from each group will sit down in respective intersections. "Hell no, we won't go" will be chanted in alternating choruses. The San Francisco cops will come in, cursing us for ruining their day off. They will duly handcuff and detain, and in jail amends will be made, solidarity will be conscientiously forged—

"Marisa?" It's Carwil, whispering loudly from two seats down. "Can you do something?" He has his 'fro mostly pulled back into a ponytail, but fugitive springy clumps bounce back and forth as he gestures. I met Carwil through "Alice in Oil-Land," and we've shared many a bullhorn and impassioned debate since. He invited me to come this evening.

"Oh, yes, sorry." I'm supposed to be facilitating this meeting. There was the usual dead silence when the topic of facilitation came up, and everybody prayed someone else would do it. Finally I volunteered, although I'm getting ample opportunity to repent now. "Look, I know this is important to both of you. We all respect that. But in the interest of time, can we wrap it up?"

"Sure, I don't mean to hold anybody up. We all want to get out of here." Jill is contrite. Jumble nods tentatively, reticent to fall in step with such a recent adversary. "But this matters, you guys." Jumble's nod quickens. "It may seem small now, but we're going to care what they're calling us, what the media is saying about us, when we have tens of thousands of people out in the streets and the city of San Francisco is paralyzed by our resistance."

Yeah right, I think. That's really going to happen. No one can accuse us of dreaming small, us radicals. Still, anything's possible.

"Listen, people." It's tiny Debbie in the corner, her usually soft voice now shrill. "I'm not sure we all get it." She bangs her hand on the table loudly. Pens clatter and heads start up. "There's a war that's going to happen, people." Her face is grim, lips tight and eyes wide. I do get it, suddenly. I remember why I am here. Bombs. Death. Mutilation. I remember why I am here and I'm cold, now, cold and crammed with dread.

"Do you get it?" Debbie looks around, meeting our eyes in turn. "We're talking lives on the line. Children's lives. Women's lives. Civilians. American soldiers." Debbie volunteers as a medic at actions. "We don't have time for this. We need to get moving."

There is silence as her words settle. Ruth, a member of the Gray Panthers, shakes her delicate white-haired head and wipes self-consciously at one cheek.

"Well, planning an action for the day *after* the war starts ain't exactly going to stop this war, folks." Pete shakes his head at the incomprehensible absurdity, at the burden of organizing with comrades who persistently assume they've already lost. "I've been saying this from the start, but nobody seems to want to listen. We're never going to win if we're convinced we're never going to win. What the hell's the point of an action the day *after* the war starts? For Chrissakes." Pete is a Vietnam vet. He's heavy and grizzled, long hair straggling out of a trucker hat. He's one of two seated around the table who is over thirty.

"Pete, we've already discussed this." It's Carwil, collected and focused as ever. "We don't want to do this action. We hope we don't have to. But we're thinking of it as a deterrent. If Bush insists on this illegal war, then what we can do is show the consequences. We can show that if this government isn't going to listen to its people, then we aren't going to allow for business as usual. And we all know that that's what Iraq is about anyway. It's business. The business of oil, the business of war." More head-shaking around the table, heads of people sufficiently infuriated by this administration's warmongering to determine to raise hell in response. People who care deeply what their country says and does. Patriots, in other words.

Speaking of raising hell. It's time to take the reins. "Listen," I say. "I know we're all tired, I know we're all frustrated, but let's try to keep hearing each other. No need to reinvent the wheel. We already know what we want to do. It's been discussed and decided. Now we need a name. How's about we take a vote."

Nods from around the table. Except for Jill, who looks ready to skewer me at a slow roast. Oh, Jill.

"I thought we worked by consensus process."

"We do work by consensus process, Jill, but it's pretty obvious that we're not going to reach consensus here. The past twenty-five minutes have been devoted to failed attempts to reach consensus."

"This is a crucial question. I'm not going to back down on this one." Watch out. Jill has An Issue. The woman is like a bulldog, working and working at the leash until it snaps. Which is precisely why she's also an asset to the movement.

"I hear you. I understand this means a lot to you, and yes, our name is important. Okay, how's about we take a vote on taking a vote." Groans from around the table. "Who wants to take a vote?"

Seven hands go up.

"Who doesn't want to vote?"

One hand.

"Listen, if everyone wants to abandon consensus process now, when we're just starting this movement, when it's in its vital formative phase, when it's like a defenseless newborn baby, fine—"

"Who exactly you calling defenseless?" Pete is miffed.

"Pete!" I glower at him. He hunkers down apologetically. Jill, meanwhile, has not paused.

"—but I'd like to register my opposition to that choice. As a matter of conscience. If we're trying to build a better world, a world that's directly democratic, then we need to be that world, folks. We need to embody people's democracy right here, right now."

And what if the people are royal pains in my ass? "Okay Jill, opposition registered. But as a reminder, the way consensus process works is that we try twice for consensus, and if we can't reach it, we move to a vote. So what you are now doing—inadvertently, I presume—is blocking consensus. Do you want to block?"

"No. I stand aside." Jill is somewhat mollified. Directly democratic principles have been upheld, if clumsily. There is a collective sigh of relief. A "stand aside" means that she doesn't support this, but will allow us to move ahead. She holds up a hand, drops and tilts her chin, lowers her lids. "For the sake of the children of Iraq, for the sake of harmony, I will not block." She is a martyr, a tireless martyr, and even we her comrades are a cross to be stalwartly borne. "I'm just glad we're not abandoning consensus when the rubber hits the road."

"Never, Jill, never. Okay, so it looks like we have consensus on a vote. Hallelujah!" Dry cheers. "Who wants to call it 'Direct Action to Stop War'?"

One hand.

"Who wants to call it 'Direct Action to Stop *the* War'?"

Seven hands.

And that's how Direct Action to Stop the War moves from the realm of idea to reality. From defenseless infancy, if you will, to squalling toddlerdom.

Since starting at Tikkun I have largely been on involuntary leave from direct-action organizing. Tikkun pretty much takes over my life and then some. After this first meeting at Art and Revolution, I am out of the loop on "Day After" planning for a couple of months. I spend most of this time on the road for Tikkun. But I get the announcements on the Direct Action to Stop the War (DASW) email list, which seems to grow every week. I finally manage to attend a spokescouncil in an office space in Oakland.

I arrive ten minutes early and settle down in a corner. There are only a few people here, and I don't recognize any of them. But they keep coming: Vets with canes and oversized glasses. Anarchists in black, their bags and hoodies safety-pinned with homemade anarchy patches. Bike activists with helmets and overstuffed shoulder bags. Palestine activists wearing kaffiyehs. Queer activists with rainbow buttons. And then there are the activists who aren't patently activists: their jeans and sweaters suspiciously resemble the Gap's latest crop, although no doubt they were purchased in good conscience at a thrift store. This is probably the category I am closest to, although—I glance down—I am wearing a shirt reading "Peace = Peace" in Hebrew and Arabic lettering. It was a gift from a Tikkun community member. Definitely a conscious choice. My activism, wretchedly, veers far from the species of noble selflessness that ignores wardrobe altogether. Probably this shirt was the wrong choice, I reflect. Probably I'm asking to get in trouble with the kaffiyeh-wearers. Probably I should have worn my "No Blood for Oil" shirt instead. I am interrupted in the midst of musings such as these by Carwil, who leaps on me in a bear hug.

"Hi sweetie!" He nuzzles me, rumples my hair. I give him a smacking kiss on the cheek, knocking his already-awry glasses further awry. "Where have you been?" he asks. "I was starting to wonder if you'd been body-snatched by little green men."

"Ah yes. To the parallel universe of a peaceful Middle East. Alack no, I've merely been organizing." I hold my hand to my forehead. Oh, the pain. "But I'm glad to be back. I've missed you guys."

More people are coming in, looking for space to sit in the lopsided circle. Then more people. And more. There's Jumble. And Debbie, who waves enthusiastically and heads over. By now there must be at least a hundred here. I'm impressed, I tell Carwil. He grins. "We've been drinking our milk and eating our brussels sprouts."

We both look to the front of the room as two young women start yelling for silence, and the din subsides to a muted roar. "Hello people, I'm Bernadette and this is Leslie, and we'll be co-facilitating this meeting. We have a ton on the agenda, so let's get started. First of all, thanks to everyone for coming. We are going to kick some Bush ass!"

Whoops and catcalls. The excitement in the room is palpable: sharp, nimble, vaulting. The fever of action finally sighted.

"Yeah folks, we are getting ready to build a resistance to be remembered." She looks to Leslie, who is busy scribbling last points on the butcher-paper agenda taped to the wall. "How about we begin with a go-around, then a quick review of consensus process, and then we'll go over the agenda and get moving. Sound good?" Hoots of approval. "Cool. So, the go-around. If you could just say your name and affinity group."

Affinity group. That's right. This is a spokescouncil, after all.

"Hi everyone, I'm Eric with Veterans Against the Iraq War, and we're real happy to be part of this."

"Yo. Bryan with the Bike Bloc."

"Callie with an affinity group that has yet to be named. We'll be part of the anti-capitalist cluster."

"Hey, I'm Kate with QUIT, Queers United against Israeli Terror."

"What's up y'all, I'm Rudy with Gay Shame."

I glance up as two more people enter the room. Dorrit and David, both of whom I know from organizing the May 7th action, ease their way into the circle. Dorrit catches my eye and waves.

"Hi folks. I'm Corey with Knitters for Peace."

"Jamie with the Brass Liberation Orchestra." A few whoops at this.

The BLO is a ragtag brass band that shows up at actions and toots, blows, and marches its way through the streets.

"Hi everyone, I'm Bernadette with Code Orange. And that's Code Orange for liberation!" Shooting her fist high. Scattered laughter. It has escaped no one here, the link between the government's color-coded "terrorist threat levels" — with orange signaling "high risk" — and its assaults on civil liberties.

"Hey y'all, I'm Justine with the yoga people. We don't have a name yet but we plan to do yoga in the streets." Applause.

"Hi, I'm Stacy with Global Intifada."

"Samuel. No affinity group yet. Hoping to find one that likes long walks on the beach and wine coolers."

"Pat with Guerrilla Gardening." He holds up a small spade and growls.

"Samantha with the Dot Commies."

"Raj from Freedom Uprising. We're an affinity group of people of color against the war."

"Hi, I'm Marisa and I don't actually have—" David is hissing my name from across the room. He gestures from me to him to Dorrit and back to me. I stare at him, puzzled.

"She's with us," says Dorrit.

"Yeah, you're with us." David smiles and nods, blonde curls bouncing. "With Code Orange."

I first heard of Code Orange roughly three point five minutes ago, but I feel gratified to be claimed by David and Dorrit. I've seen them in action, and I have a lot of respect for both of them. David Solnit in particular I am in mild awe of. He's been organizing grassroots action and street theater for nearly twenty years. He was a key organizer of the 1999 Seattle anti-WTO protests, and one of the founders of Art and Revolution. Soft-spoken and temperate, David exercises the sort of understated leadership that consistently provides wise guidance and strategic acuity to a movement that is relentlessly nonhierarchical and anti-authoritarian. I've already learned a lot, simply by watching him work.

"Oh. Got it. Hi again, I'm Marisa with Code Orange."

Thus the match is made, and I bumble happily into the arms of my affinity group. We are to have a vigorous and storied affair.

In the global justice movement, the affinity group is the basic unit of direct-action organizing. Groups are composed of five to twenty members; the prevailing idea is smallness and, by extension, trust and autonomy. When you're sitting in the middle of the street facing a line of riot police, you need to know that you can rely on the person next to you, and that the group as a whole is capable of fluidly responding to rapidly changing circumstances. Affinity groups are the legacy of anarchist organizing during the Spanish civil war; they were resurrected in the seventies and eighties by the antinuclear movement.

For larger actions, affinity groups gather in clusters. Decisions regarding specific actions or campaigns are made via consensus process at spokescouncil meetings, which are attended by representatives from affinity groups. While consensus process can be thorny and at times protracted, what consistently amazes me is how well it works. A proposal is offered, clarifying questions are asked, discussion is held, concerns are raised, amendments are made, concerns are resolved. Each person's needs and qualms are heard and incorporated into a process that arrives at decisions and moves forward. Facilitation of this process rotates. Every step of direct-action organizing strives at direct democracy, at locating the choices and decisions of a community squarely within the hands of that community. The concept of direct democracy appeals greatly to me because it places trust in the fundamental goodness of the individual, the fundamental wisdom of the community. But more importantly, these are models that work — and that, when judiciously enacted, tend to the needs of everyone present, without exception.

The decentralized mode of our organizing confounds the media, which cannot figure out what to make of the global justice movement. This is a movement that rejects traditional formulas for revolutionary change. Unlike many of our radical predecessors, we are nonviolent, and we aren't seeking power. We are, rather, seeking to return power to where it belongs: the individual, within the self-determining community. Believing in power-with instead of power-over, we endorse no hierarchy, and thus we have no pantheon of leaders. Countering the hugeness and homogeneity of corporate globalization with smallness and diversity, the global justice movement is not committed to any single overarching philosophical framework or ideology. Believing that the movement, like life, should self-organize, should straddle the shoreline between chaos and order, we often appear totally disorganized. Yet we nonetheless succeed where painstaking diplomatic efforts have failed. The wealthy nations of the WTO ignored objections on the part of poorer nations to the imbalance in negotiation power, but they couldn't ignore the massive street demonstrations that completely shut down the Seattle round.

In early 2003 the Bush administration plunges ahead with its isolationist agenda, dropping allies like flies, labeling dissent unpatriotic and even dangerous, manufacturing token evidence of weapons of mass destruction. Progressives are up in arms, and protests erupt with feverish frequency. On February 15 between eight and twelve million (according to official estimates; unofficial estimates run as high as twenty-four million) march for peace in thousands of cities across the globe. *The New York Times* calls us "the world's other superpower." In a matter of months, this new peace movement attains the kind of numbers that the Vietnam antiwar movement took years to accumulate. Yet there is no single charismatic leader inspiring resistance, no Gandhi or Mandela. Moreover, no single ideology unifies the protests. February 15th is the result of thousands of dedicated activists mobilizing locally while coordinating globally on the Internet—a consummately organized collective upswelling of conscience and empathy. See, I say to my friends, marshaling statistics and stories, look at this. Look at what we're capable of. Is the consciousness not shifting? Meanwhile, DASW is holding weekly spokescouncil meetings, and our numbers are snowballing. At these meetings, representatives from different affinity groups and organizations share details of their ongoing work against the war, and plans for the Day After ripen.

My work at Tikkun continues to consume me—my talks now address not only Israel/Palestine but also the impending war in Iraq —and I am often out of town. The next spokescouncil I make is in mid-February. I arrive half an hour late and press through the packed bodies to get to a spot where I can see. David is in the front of the room, tall spare body folded into a crouch.

"So we in the scenario committee took what was decided at the last spokes and met to develop a proposal for the Day After. First I'll do a quick review for any new folks." He gestures behind him, to several sheets of butcher paper filled with notes. "As many of you know, the plan is to target the financial district. The objective is to make clear the connection between U.S. militarist imperialism and the corporations that profit from war."

A low buzz of approval slinks its way around the room.

"As consensed on at the last spokes, we have three goals. First, if the government and corporations won't stop the war, we will shut down the warmakers. We'll impose real economic, social, and political costs. The point of declaring mass nonviolent action now, before the war starts, is to deter this and other wars."

A chorus of yeahs and right-ons.

"Second, to assert our power to transform our city from profits, oil, and war to resistance and life." David opens his arms wide, inviting us to consider the possibilities. "We will create an open and inspiring space that gives voice to the antiwar majority as an assertion of real democracy."

The buzz is high now, an agitated clamor of anticipation.

"And third, we aim to uproot the system behind the war, to help catalyze mass movements to challenge corporate and government power." David's blue eyes spark, his voice lifts. He is a preacher who knows his congregation is with him. "Our goal is to create socially just, directly democratic, ecological, and peaceful alternatives."

The room breaks into cheers. In this place, at this moment, we are all devout believers. A different world is possible, a gentler world, a world to which we would be proud to introduce our children. And with such an intoxicating brew of energy and commitment, how can we not make it real?

"So." David looks around him, voice back to its usual soft tenor. The room hushes instantly. We are eager to hear what's coming next, anxious to know how this fervor will be harnessed. "We took all of these ingredients, mixed them up, let them marinate awhile, and came up with the idea of a menu..."

The city is papered with flyers. Dedicated crews go on nightly wheat-pasting expeditions, plastering telephone poles, walls, cafés, bookstores. Cyberspace is duly clogged. The menu that is finally approved

Waiter!! There's a W A R in My Soup!

EMERGENCY "POTLUCK"
TO STOP THE WAR

7:00 AM
MORNING OF THE NEXT BUSINESS DAY
AFTER WAR BEGINS

Meet at: Justin Herman Plaza/Embarcadero BART, SF
Mass Nonviolent Direct Action

TRANSFORM OUR CITY
From Profit and War to Life and Resistance

Shut Down The Corporate Warmakers!

- Don't go to work or school
- Head downtown: Bring friends, music, art, performance, and food to share
- Join/create an ongoing transformation/occupation
- Form an affinity (action) group

is ambitious indeed. "A Moveable Feast" offers two full courses of major intersections and arteries to block — a buffet of over twenty delectable dishes native to the financial district. The "Traditional Sit-Down Dinner" presents government and corporate entrées such as the Federal Building, the Army Recruiting Center, Bechtel, Citicorp ("City Corpse"), and the Carlyle Group. For those with no time to dine, there is takeout. Bikes Not Bombs invites participants to support stationary actions through cycling, a "quiet statement against oil wars." The menu is accompanied by a map of downtown San Francisco, tagged with all the target locations. Finally, an "Open Letter to San Francisco" is wheatpasted to every available post, wall, and doorway.

The DASW media workgroup outdoes itself. It issues press releases, holds a well-attended press conference, and succeeds in getting our website and the action meeting spot printed on the front page of the newspaper and announced on every major television and radio station. All public statements are crafted to appeal to the widest possible audience. Instead of "activists" or "protestors," DASW uses terms like "residents" and "people from all walks of life" — language that underscores the broad-based nature of opposition to the war. As strategist and organizer (and fellow member of Code Orange) Patrick Reinsborough writes in a later essay, "Without sacrificing the opportunity to put out a systemic analysis, [DASW's] organizing appealed to mainstream values — democracy, security, justice, belief in international law, patriotism — and used them to leverage opposition.... [This] helped normalize resistance and expanded the appeal of the action."

On March 14 we hold a preemptive action at the Pacific Stock Exchange, billed by DASW media as a preview of the Day After. More than seventy people are arrested for nonviolent civil disobedience, including the former president of the Pacific Stock Exchange. Euphoric with success, we move to an intersection on Market Street, which a couple of hundred of us proceed to occupy. Someone hands me the bullhorn and I am prancing around in the middle of the street, comfortable with it now, comfortable enough to holler at people to dance, shake it, move. And then all around the intersection, jubilant protesters are dancing and singing. In the face of missiles amassing and artillery unshelved, we are defiant with life. For the sake of the living and their children and their children, we are snarling up traffic, we are causing

CEOs and stockbrokers to falter in their tracks, and a single block of Market Street is, for a couple of hours, transformed.

Five days later.

"My fellow citizens, at this hour American and coalition forces are in the early stages of military operations to disarm Iraq." I despise that voice. I am trying not to, but I can't help it, I despise it. I despise the twang, the arrogance, the complacency with which nameless thousands are condemned. I despise it with such a cold silvery knife-edge loathing that I am shaky and nauseous. I turn up the volume. "On my orders, coalition forces have begun striking selected targets of military importance to undermine Saddam Hussein's ability to wage war. These are the opening stages of what will be a broad and concerted campaign."

I am driving from Berkeley to San Francisco, and I have to concentrate very hard to stay in my lane. I have to pay very careful attention, minute attention to the lights in front of me, to the stripes on the asphalt, to accelerator, brake, accelerator. I am straining past my tears, I am doing everything I can not to slam on my brakes halfway across the Bay Bridge and bash my head over and over into the steering wheel.

Fourteen and a half years ago my family scraped together its resources and its nerve and pole-vaulted across the Atlantic to the United States of America. We came here from apartheid South Africa because this country, to us, represented everything South Africa was not: freedom, justice, democracy. Democracy. A novel and thrilling concept to me, and I fell recklessly in love with everything it boldly spelled out. Now I am left wondering: Can my country still be called a democracy when a miscounted vote in a single state makes for a president? Is it still a democracy when the government lies to its people? Which democratic ideals are we embodying in embarking on an illegal war in violation of the will of the global community? In Nepal, democracy may be a child. But in my country, democracy, by all indications, is growing senile.

"And I assure you, this will not be a campaign of half measures and we will accept no outcome but victory."

What does victory mean to you, Mr. Bush? Oil fields? Puppet leaders? What does victory amount to when the mightiest military in the world charges into a unilateral war? But Bush batters on, heedless of my ranting and that of millions of others, several solid tiers of Secret Service buffering him from meddling journalists and their troublesome queries.

"We will pass through this time of peril and carry on the work of peace. We will defend our freedom. We will bring freedom to others."

The freedom to work more hours than any other nation on the planet, grossly overconsume, and still feel we never have enough? Or the freedom for corporations to exploit workers and poison the earth?

"And we will prevail. May God bless our country and all who defend her."

What of the people of Iraq? Does their God listen when they pray? I blow my nose and pick up my cell phone.

"David?"

"Hi Marisa. You okay?"

"You heard?"

"Of course. Final spokes is at St. Boniface at seven. I'm heading over now."

When I arrive, the large hall of the church is overflowing with people. Person after person goes up to the microphone to introduce themselves as a representative of their affinity group. There must be hundreds of them. I find David and Dorrit. I sit with them and try to comprehend what is going on, which intersection is being held by whom, but I cannot take it in. I am numb, staggered at the thought of all that is to come, of the jets climbing toward Baghdad, their bellies heavy with the neatly stowed apparatus of carnage.

Thursday, March 20 dawns brilliant and lucid as a child's stare.

I clamber onto my bike at a quarter to six and start pedaling toward downtown. Even this early, to the knowing eye, Market Street is speckled with intimations of what is to come: small bands of the colorfully dressed gather on odd corners, ogling intersections and chattering animatedly, staking out the day's work. Minutes later I arrive at Justin Herman Plaza, a broad swath of red brick in San Francisco's northeastern corner. City-side, the plaza is surrounded by glittering blades of skyscraper. On the other side are the sturdy lines of the Ferry Building, leaning into the Bay, and then the swells of tide, hoary and ragged. I lock my bike to a parking meter and head in, scanning the scene. The DASW orientation team is at full throttle, checking their walkie-talkies and reviewing last-minute adjustments. Already people are beginning to arrive. They will be herded into groups, given an orientation, and dispatched to support actions throughout downtown.

First stop: the Mourning Mothers. This affinity group dresses up as the mothers of Iraq. They wear huge painted masks of grieving and carry cloth effigies of dead children in their arms. I have been asked to sing with them. I spy a giant cardboard face at the other end of the plaza and head over. Susie, one of the Mothers, welcomes me with a hug, and we chat as she puts the finishing touches on her black costume. "It's a hard day," she mutters through the pins in her mouth. "But resistance, at least, will be ours." Susie is one of those people who you don't expect to be a radical. She's middle-aged, incurably polite and placid, and works as upper-level management in a corporate job.

The plaza is rapidly filling up. Small knots of people arrive, locate their place, meld with the growing mass of bodies. I hum a few test notes into the microphone as the Mothers ready themselves. Then I close my eyes, imagine Baghdad, and begin to sing. The Mothers wait in a semicircle as a crowd gathers. One by one each proceeds solemnly to the front, holds up her child, and lays it down on a white sheet. I have not sung with the Mothers before, and I am amazed at the power of their performance, at how keenly it elicits the intimate horrors of war. Among the anger and confusion and fear, here is a space for grieving. At the close, a number of faces are wet, and some come up to place notes and flowers on the bloodied rag dolls.

My next stop will be Market and Sansome, where both City Corpse and the British Consulate are located. I thank and hug the Mothers, but reaching my bike proves no simple task: at this point, Justin Herman Plaza is sardine-stuffed with thousands of provoked patriots. I burrow my way through and am busy unlocking my bike before I think to look up at Market Street.

San Francisco's financial district is not a place I relish. Everyone is rushing: rushing to meetings, rushing to shop, rushing to lunch dates. Rushing because rushing is what you do when you're in the financial district. People are far too preoccupied to see each other. They are distracted by cell phones, by business papers or propositions or partners, by bodily urges that gallingly demand filling or emptying. It is a numbing place, a place both overstimulating and isolating, simultaneously busy and bleak. But today the financial district is on strike. Today the financial district is gone trekking on a vision quest, is lifting the veil to kiss its bride, thrusting out its first child. Today its streets are filled with human beings doing the kinds of things that render them human: conversing, dancing, shouting, laughing, sharing. *Feeling.* Today there is a clan of knitters occupying the sidewalk, churning out scarves and mittens as they chat. There are sweatpants-clad yogis doing downward dog in the Montgomery crosswalk. There are anarchists with bandannas over the lower halves of their faces reclining on plastic lounge chairs smack in the middle of Kearny. Police in riot gear stand watching. Helicopters drone overhead. The staccato lights that reliably regulate the rushing and the distraction are flashing yellow, red, green, yellow, red, green, but regulating nothing, a mute tribute to the orderly half-life of the world that yesterday was. I ride or walk my bike down Market Street, awed and giddy, whooping at the knitters and the yogis and the countless costumed and painted creative retorts to this war.

Market and Sansome: packed, jostling, panting, hectic. Alive.

"Dorrit!" She is talking strategy with someone from another affinity group, listening intently and then yelling into a walkie-talkie. She sees me, hugs me, pushes me toward the ad hoc stage. "Go sing!"

Our cluster decided to transform this intersection into a space for art and celebration, an enclave of music and poetry and performance grafted onto the concrete and steel. I am hefted up onto a crude platform and I sing the song I wrote days earlier.

> *I will fight against this war because I'm loyal.*
> *I am loyal to the rivers,*
> *loyal to the sky,*
> *loyal to this earth and the stars swinging by,*

loyal to what we share,
to the love that brings us here...

At first, it seems no one is listening. The sound system isn't loud enough to rise above the clamor of this howling body. But after an early stumble, I sing as if my life depends on it, because singing is something I can give right now. I cannot stop the war, but I can offer this—my anthem to my country, which is without borders. My paean to my people, who are without tribe. My voice grows strong and sure. It takes me over, wrings me out, leaves me emptied in its wake as it curls and dives and soars. At some point the rest of me falls away altogether, and I am pared down to voice, naked and true. I shut my eyes, move in closer, and when I finish, to my surprise, to my delight, there is a scattering of applause. Some were listening.

I open my eyes.

I have a bird's-eye view of the action, and there are people as far as I can see, up and down Market, up and down Sansome, people chanting and romping and snapping photos, people fierce with joy and anger, drunk with the elixir of our own power. Direct action is a salve on the lesion of our alienation. In times like this I am reminded of my own agency, and again I feel connected, enduringly fused with those beside me in the streets. Our society seems hell-bent on fragmenting us into ever-smaller isolated units, and confronting its institutions on terms entirely our own tastes to me like bread must to the starving. For a few hours, for a day, it is indisputable that change is possible, that we can make it so, that indeed we already are.

At 6 p.m. spontaneous waves of protest are still engorging Market Street. Thousands march somberly or stridently, moving with the implacable momentum of a force of nature. There are teenagers, businessmen, bus drivers, soccer moms, grandparents; the affinity group-spokescouncil structure allows for a widely diverse range of participants. At one point during the day my sister Gabi calls me on my cell phone to ask where I am. Market and First, I tell her. We have moved, as cops encircled the last intersection and ordered us to disperse. What's left of Code Orange—David was recognized by the police and immediately arrested, a few others are supporting different actions—is now roaming the streets fortified with a bullhorn and a devoted constellation of cohorts. "We're coming down," says Gabi, who has never before expressed interest in joining me at an action. She arrives with a couple of other attorneys from her corporate law firm, points me out to them with something like pride as I ramble hoarsely from behind the bullhorn, suddenly self-conscious.

A couple of months later I am in Columbus, Ohio, on another speaking tour for Tikkun. My host is an energetic young professor who teaches at the local college. We are driving through the city when the topic of the war comes up, and of the protests, and I mention the Day After.

"Were you there?" he asks. Yes, I tell him. Indeed I was. He chews on this for a minute. "You know, I'd like to thank you. You and everyone else who was a part of that. It's not easy living here with my politics. Every single one of my neighbors supported the war. I was close to despair when Bush gave that speech. But when I saw the footage of the shutdown in San Francisco—of all those people putting themselves on the line—it lifted me. It gave me back some hope."

On March 20, 2003, protests spontaneously erupt around the world: Greece, Costa Rica, Germany, the U.K., France, Syria, Jordan, Morocco, Egypt, Turkey. Thirteen U.S. embassies and consulates are closed due to security concerns. Meanwhile, in the belly of the beast, dozens of cities give way to resistance. In Chicago, thousands of demonstrators clog major arteries. In Philadelphia, over a hundred are arrested for blocking the federal courthouse. In New York, protesters stop traffic on Broadway for two hours. And in one legendary city on the western shore of the world's superpower, twenty thousand people step out of their jobs, homes, and lives. Twenty thousand nonviolently occupy the streets in protest of an unjust war. Over fifteen hundred of them are arrested.

Half a world away, bombs are dropping on Baghdad. But our vote is unmistakable.

Eight:

Miami

Run, Marisa, run. Go. Go. Go. Faster. *Keep running.*

There is no other line of thought in my brain. The panic stretches so wide it exiles all but the nonessential. Run. Run. I am clutching my sign, my backpack is jogging hard against me, and it will be simply a matter of luck if I don't slam into another runner. Sirens shriek. I am surrounded by choppy swells of black, a surging swarm of sprinters veering at manic angles. Cops at the jagged edges of the beast, prowling. Run. I'm not sure why, but I must keep running, can't be left behind. Go. Faster. Move. Can't see much in front: just bobbing heads. Behind: generous crescents of white around the eyes, pink Os of mouths.

Can't—get—quite—enough—oxygen.

"Run!" someone is screaming, as if we weren't already, as if hundreds of pairs of lungs weren't already aflame. "Run!" *Rape! Fire! Murder!* they may as well be howling. Panic stabs through the crowd, and the pace picks up. Somewhere in the conjoined brain of this terrorized animal the primal impulse to flee has been slumbering; once aroused it is overwhelming, irresistible, familiar. A cheer arises from my left. On a window glints the strident black of a fresh-scrawled anarchy sign. Running through the streets of Miami with the Black Bloc: not what I pictured when I contemplated going to Miami to protest the FTAA.

The Free Trade Area of the Americas: The more I learned about it, the more I felt compelled to come demonstrate. The FTAA proposes to expand the North American Free Trade Agreement (NAFTA) to the entire western hemisphere—with the exception of Cuba, of course. Yet NAFTA has already proven itself a lame donkey: as is invariably the case with free-trade policies, disabling a nation's capacity to protect and regulate its own economy has a nasty tendency to benefit the very wealthiest and punish the poor. I arrive in Miami in late November 2003. In the near decade since NAFTA was passed in 1994, an estimated 765,000 jobs have been lost in the U.S. Most of these jobs have turned up, unsurprisingly, in Mexico, where labor is far cheaper. Yet the number of Mexicans earning less than the Mexican minimum wage has increased by over a million since 1994. In the profit-driven race to the bottom that is corporate globalization, these jobs migrated to the underpaying border factories known as *maquiladoras*. Like NAFTA's infamous Chapter 11, the FTAA's rules on investment would moreover allow corporations to sue governments for future profits lost. Under Chapter 11, the American corporation Metalclad was awarded $16.7 million by the Mexican government after the toxic waste dump it planned to construct in Guadalcázar, San Luis Potosí, was banned. The message? Lower your standards, or pay up.

When I was new to this country, commercials were my best teachers, my earliest friends. They educated me effectively, smilingly, on the mores of my new culture. But over the past few years, my attitude toward the parade of friendly faced commodities has changed. In India, I glimpsed the underbelly of the consumer culture generated by massive transnational corporations that run roughshod over local cultures and environments, "improving" them, trampling them. Through my research and interviews, through my own observations, I came to recognize this glittery "monoculture" as the carrot. Invisible to the average consumer is the stick: a system of global economic policies that benefit the world's superpower—and its wealthy friends—while placing a stranglehold on the global south. Those who can afford it chase after the carrot. The rest are subjected to the stick. The International Monetary Fund, the World Bank, the World Trade Organization: during my travels, I saw the effects of the policies devised by these global financial and trade institutions. Created for the purpose of regulating the world economy, their antidemocratic governance now facilitates corporate colonialism. Their functionaries come from the halls and chambers of the global north, of the affluent. Most of them cut their teeth on trade or finance. Having been the beneficiaries of free-market capitalism, they share an ideology that worships the market as virtually infallible. And they wield the stick.

The FTAA is one more example of privileging the market over democracy, putting profits ahead of people. It covers services—everything from education to hospitals to water utilities. In competition with some of the mightiest transnational corporations in the world, Latin America's poorer nations wouldn't stand a chance. And a host of U.S. industries would be flattened by tariff-free Latin American imports. In short, the FTAA is a nightmare for the environment, human rights, and labor. Yet there is no process for public input—no hearings, no referendums, no plan to accommodate the voices of the communities the FTAA would affect and claims to represent. NGOs (nongovernmental organizations) are being offered what amounts to a suggestion box, while privileged advisory roles go to corporate representatives. Direct action is the last available tool in the box. Millions of those who will be most affected by the FTAA can't go to Miami to voice their dissent. But I can.

"Hey! Hey!" I turn my head. It's a young woman running next to me, one of the other few smudges of color amid the sea of black. Behind her the city flies by: right angles, concrete, flat pastels. She smiles, hair buoyant around her face. "I'm Jenny. What's your name?"

Hardly the time for chitchat. But then again I don't know anyone here, and am happy to make a friend. I manage to huff my name out.

"You with the Black Bloc?" She is lean and muscular, and looks like a born marathon runner. Maybe she'll carry me if I collapse.

"No, with Code Orange from California. In the FCAA." The Free Carnival Area of the Americas. An arts-and-celebration-themed cluster of nine affinity groups. I'd give my left pinkie finger to be among them now. "You?"

"Food Not Bombs." The good folk who reliably dish us up three steaming hot meals a day. Always vegetarian (if not vegan), frequently the product of diligent dumpster-diving.

"Cool. How'd you end up here?" I am matching my pace to hers.

"Wrong place at the wrong time, or something like that. I was supposed to be meeting a friend on the corner a few blocks back. You?"

"Also by mistake."

Today is November 20, the first day of the summit. I arrived at the Convergence Center at a pitch-black 5:45 a.m. with the rest of Code Orange. But when they set out with the FCAA, I stayed behind to do some media "wrangling." Just as the Bush administration had "embedded" journalists with army units in Iraq, we were assigning local reporters to various clusters. When I was done, I hopped a ride with some friendly North Carolinians. "That looks like the FCAA," offered one of them—a scoundrel I will not soon forgive—and I leapt out and skipped toward the three colorful signs at the rear guard of the Black Bloc. A loose affiliation of revolutionary anarchists that evolved out of the squatter protests in Germany in the eighties, the Black Bloc is infamous for its belligerent tactics and property destruction. Black Bloc protesters wear masks to symbolically elevate the community over the individual, and see smashing windows and burning dumpsters as an effective means of challenging the violence endemic to corporations—by garnering media attention and by demonstrating that these institutions are not impervious. They are the militants of the global justice movement.

Less than a minute after the North Carolinians dropped me off, the police started closing in and someone gave the order to run.

"Stop! Whoa, people, slow down, slow down!" Yells from the front end. Bless my stars, are we actually being asked to stop running?

"Stop!" A chorus, now. I brake rapidly, so rapidly that someone hurtles into me from behind and I career forward. Jenny catches and steadies me. I turn and scowl darkly at the perpetrator, who is panting out profuse apologies from behind her black bandanna.

"What's going on?" I drop my backpack and sign, lean over with my hands on my knees.

"No clue." People are milling about, lighting cigarettes, sipping from water bottles, sparking up casual conversations. As if the world wasn't about to cave in on us thirty seconds ago.

"Can you see anything?" Jenny is at least half a foot taller than me.

"No. Just a buttload of black. And beyond that some cops." Squinting. "Scratch that. Looks like the entire Miami-Dade police force showed up."

We settle on the sidewalk to catch our breath. I peer about, anxious for clues. "Hey, anyone know what's going on?"

"Unclear," says a guy standing next to us on the sidewalk. He's leaning on a hockey stick and pauses to drag heavily from a cigarette through the hole in his ski mask. "Word is we're surrounded by the pigs. There's a spokes going on in the middle."

"Yeah? I'm going to go listen in." I look at Jenny, ask her if she wants to come. She smiles and shakes her head. "I'm happier on the edges."

I pick up my backpack and sign and push my way through the thickening bodies toward what I imagine is the center. There, that must be it: definitely a circle, an urgent huddle half crouched, half standing. I walk up to the edge. "What's the situation?" I whisper to the person on my right.

"It sucks." The bandanna is pulled down to reveal a woman: very young, freckled, amply pierced. "Two circles of cops around us. It's dire, dude."

The voices from the circle are rising. "Listen, people, enough talk. We've got to make a decision. There's a fucking million pigs out there in full-on riot gear. And no doubt more are coming."

"If we start talking to the pigs, it's over."

"What choice do we have, Spar? We're surrounded. We're more than surrounded."

"I say fuck 'em. I say we make a run for it. What are they going to do if the entire fucking group starts running? What can they do?"

"What can they do? Have you seen how many pigs there are out there? They fucking hate us and now they've got us, dude. They're going to let loose their rubber bullets and their tear gas and close in. They're going to arrest every fucking last one of us. That's what they're going to do."

"Okay, right on, Nemo. Then you tell me how the fuck we're going to meet up with everyone else. There's no way they're going to let us get to Government Center." Government Center is downtown, about as close to the FTAA talks as the public can get. It's the convergence point for today's direct action.

"Excuse me"—a woman's voice, now—"I'd like to talk. From what I can tell, Spar, it seems like most of us want to negotiate with the cops. Can we try to consense on this?"

"Sure." Spar throws his hands up, dismissive. "If you all want to just roll over and lick their boots, go fucking right ahead."

"Who wants to talk with the cops?" A ripple of hands rising.

"Stand asides?" Two hands.

"Blocks?" Spar mutters an inventive string of obscenities but his hand stays down.

"All right. Who wants to police liaise? We need at least two."

"I'll do it." Nemo, moving from crouching to standing.

"Cool. Nemo, and we need one more."

No volunteers.

"Come on people, who's willing to liaise?"

Silence.

"I will." I step forward. I've liaised before. The circle of faces turns my way.

"Who are you?"

"Marisa. With Code Orange from San Francisco." Their suspicion is justified. No one here knows me, and infiltrators are common. Besides, I'm not in black—which would, on second thought, render me far too obvious to be an infiltrator.

"Code Orange, got it."

"Yeah, she's cool, I recognize her."

"I'm happy to do it if people feel comfortable," I say. "Keeping in mind that I don't belong to this bloc and don't represent any affinity groups here." A round of nods.

"Okay, Nemo and Marisa. Looks like we got our liaisons."

Nemo turns to me, juts his chin out. "Let's do it."

We walk out of the circle together. He offers his hand and smiles. "Nemo, as you may have heard." No more than twenty, delicate-limbed, with the kind of pristine good looks that would put your average adolescent girl in a mortal swoon. "Good to meet you." Pulling his black bandanna back up over his mouth.

An eager trail of press swarms around us out of nowhere as we walk. Pretty funny, come to think of it, because I'm press too. Well, press of a different sort: I'm writing a daily series, from an activist's perspective, for Salon.com. Not only listening and transmitting, this time, but speaking too—and amplified at that. I remind myself to start scribbling notes as soon as I get the chance.

"There they are." Nemo is looking ahead. I follow his gaze. I've never seen so many cops. Two solid lines of them. In front, the city cops on bicycles. Behind, the riot police. Heavily armed, slim swatches of skin shining wanly from under their marshmallow-suit body armor and helmets. They barely look human. We keep walking, Nemo slightly ahead. At the first line we pause. I look into the faces, into pair after pair of cold eyes. Behind the hostility: fear.

The Bush administration is not taking the FTAA protests lightly. Around $8.5 million of an $87 billion War on Terror package has gone toward "protecting" the city of Miami from us. Over forty law enforcement agencies are included in this effort. The money has also funded a host of new weapons—not just the same old tear gas and rubber bullets (yawn) but also fancy new gizmos like Taser stun guns, electric shields, and mobile water cannons. Miami police chief John Timoney—who has already earned himself a nasty reputation for his treatment of protesters at the Republican National Convention in 2000—calls us "knuckleheads," saying we have come here to "terrorize" Miami. He vows to "hunt [us] like a hawk picking mice off a field." In our honor, all of downtown Miami has been shut down, enclosed by a massive ten- to twelve-foot steel fence. By the time we reach the day of action, Miami police have already infringed liberally on both First and Fourth Amendment rights. Free trade, it appears, easily trounces freedom. This response indicates not only how much is at stake for Bush Inc. but also how much we scare them. A couple of thousand of us are exercising our First Amendment rights on the streets this morning. In response, 2,500 cops have been deployed. It seems a good three-quarters of them are looking at Nemo and me right now.

We stare back. Who knows what they have been told about us? As I study the closed faces, I struggle to remain open, to remember they are just doing what they believe they should, the best they can, same as me.

"We're here to negotiate," says Nemo finally. "Where's the captain?"

"Here." One of them pulls away from the line and approaches. He stands before us with his feet apart, hand massaging his baton. Middle-aged, red-faced, belly pressing at his buttons. I see him baking on the deck of a cruise ship while his wife pages through *People* magazine.

"Captain Serry. At your service." Cameras snap. I offer my hand. "Nice to meet you." Hi there, I'm the one-woman welcome committee of the Black Bloc. Care for some hors d'oeuvres? Perhaps a hockey stick or two?

"The pleasure's mine, young lady." He cracks a grin. There's a reason he's a captain. Maybe that reason has to do with his humanity. He holds out his hand to Nemo, and Nemo shakes it.

"We'd like to get to Government Center," Nemo says.

"Well now, young man, that may be so, but negotiation goes both ways, if you know what I mean."

"Uh-huh." Nemo is clipped, painfully conscious of his loyalties. "What do you want us to do?"

"Well, I see a whole slew of sticks and spray cans out there among your people. You get them put away, we'll see what we can do."

"You'll let us go to Government Center?"

"I said, 'You put them away, we'll see what we can do.'"

"Captain," I pipe up, "I thought you said negotiation is a two-way process. How about we commit to getting the sticks and cans put away if you commit to letting us move to Government Center?"

"We're not doing a single thing unless you let us get there," says Nemo. I look at him. What is this: good cop, bad cop?

Serry takes our measure. "We're not going to just let you people loose on the streets. Sorry, no deal. How about this: you put the sticks and cans away, we'll escort you there."

Nemo and I excuse ourselves for a brief consultation, waving the paparazzi away. I say we go with it. "You really think we can trust the pigs?" "I don't think we have much choice right now. Either we do this or we sit here all day." He nods. We turn back.

"Okay, Captain, you're on."

"I see a single stick or can out, and we go right in and arrest every one of you." Serry needs no foil. He's got the whole routine down to a one-man act.

"They'll be put away."

"All right. Go to it then."

We head back into the Bloc, split up, and distribute the message. I holler out our agreement in phrases, the group around me yelling back in repetitions. Sticks and cans are duly stowed in black backpacks.

We assure the cops that our part has been done, and the checkered group—Black Bloc, police, media, green-capped legal observers—slowly starts moving. Conscious of my role, I head to the front where Serry can see me.

"Fucking pigs."

"Pawns, man, pawns blindly defending the same fucked-up system that fucks them."

"Hey, look at that one. Isn't he the dude from the Village People?" Baying laughter. I look behind me. It's three teenagers, skinny and scored with acne.

"Funny, man, funny. What about that one—the scrawny one? Must be a bad bad cop. No donuts for him."

"You know the only reason cops are cops is because they couldn't follow the recipes at Burger King." More howls.

The police are well within earshot. None of them are responding, but I watch as the back of one neck steadily reddens. I turn around. It's not my role here, but I can't help myself.

"You guys, you're only pissing them off right now. If anything goes wrong and they decide to arrest us, you're going to be feeling it. And the more you heckle, the more they're going to want to arrest." They're just teenagers, I know, but I'd be hard-pressed to dream up a more counterproductive approach. The cops aren't the enemy. The cops are doing their job. A nasty job, granted, but are we so blinded by anger that we simply demonize the nearest target?

They stare at me, this colorfully clad upstart giving them a thorough dressing-down. One kicks at the ground, eyes me askance.

"Whatever, dude," he grunts. "They chose to be fucking tools of the system. They're gonna do what they're trained to do."

I'm well aware of the class issues here. Most cops are blue-collar. Most of the direct-action contingency comes from the kind of background that affords us the time and resources to travel to protests.

"No, dude, she has a point. I don't want to get beat up and sit in jail. I gotta finish up the semester."

"Me too, dude. Let the pigs alone, I say."

When we are a few blocks from Government Center, Serry halts the motley caravan. "There's been a confrontation," he tells us. "I can't let you move any further." Simultaneously, we learn via walkie-talkie that most groups have already left Government Center. For the next hour we sit in lengthy negotiations. "I see your people pissing in bottles," Serry says to me at one point. "Even one of those gets thrown at my men, and we go right in and arrest." I gape at him. These cops must have been subjected to some mighty persuasive propaganda about us deviant radicals. "Captain, we've been sitting in this intersection for an hour, and you're not letting anyone leave. Where else are they going to piss?"

Eventually Serry lets us disperse. Several members of the Black Bloc come up to thank me, pulling bandannas down and ski masks up as we talk. Before this morning, I haven't engaged much with the Black Bloc. Convinced as I am that enduringly peaceful ends require peaceful means, I don't agree with their tactics. But this has been a helpful reeducation. The Bloc is mostly young, and—contrary to my expectations—relatively gender-balanced. While I believe their militancy alienates others and generally does more harm than good, I understand, and share, their anger. And I am amazed and encouraged by the degree of conscience and empathy that inspires an eighteen-year-old to come here. I spot Nemo squatting on the sidewalk and head over. "Thanks for all the good times," he says, grinning, and we hug.

I cross the police line with all the elation of an escaped prisoner— Free! Free at last!—and head off in anxious search of Code Orange. The city is crammed with uneasy police. I am repeatedly prevented from crossing certain streets and frostily informed that I'll have to "go around"—seven blocks around—for "security purposes." One cop follows me from the Black Bloc and stands directly in front of me snapping photos as I try to reason with another captain. "For the FBI file, eh?" I pout for the camera. He is not amused.

Downtown Miami looks like it took a flying leap into the Twilight Zone. I walk rapidly, inundated with an amorphous, drenching fear. Where are the people? Swept up by extraterrestrials? Stores are closed, windows boarded up. The only vehicles in the streets are police vans. Helicopters whine above like gargantuan mutated mosquitoes. In this world, humans have been replaced by the robotic constructs of a dystopian future, and they march the streets in mechanized formation. I keep my head down, staying on the sidewalks and crossing only when the light is green. It's eleven in the morning and already the heat grips like a fever.

As the street numbers grow smaller, I spot people ahead: clumps of protesters surrounded by more riot cops, clubs at the ready. The air tastes brittle, curdled by tear gas. I walk up to the edges and scan the scattered crowd. There, there on my right—the huge sun-puppet—it's Code Orange! I break into a run, hollering their names, then leaping into the circle and bouncing between them, half-delirious with relief. The response is disappointing. My friends look exhausted, notably deflated from earlier this morning. They lean heavily on each other and the giant puppet sticks. "Where have you been?"

"Oh, you know, chilling with the Black Bloc, marathon training, that kind of thing. How was your morning?"

"Not pretty." David is flushed and grim, red-rimmed eyes set hard on the line of cops. "This city is under siege. We've been herded around like sheep. And Joshua got clubbed in the back of the head." I gasp. Joshua is also a writer, a poet. Brilliant, droll, and about as belligerent as a bunny rabbit. "He seems all right for now. He bled a lot, but the medics bandaged him up."

It's noon, time for the permitted AFL-CIO march. We pick up our puppets and flags and advance toward the gathering point. It is a relief to merge with the swell of bodies, to move through the streets without feeling like a hunted animal. There are twenty thousand marching. Later, we will learn that over a dozen buses were prevented from reaching the site of the march, that some people trying to join the march and rally were pepper-sprayed or thrown to the ground, weapons to their heads, without cause or explanation. But for now we are in the thick of it, riding the flow, buoyed by the movement and clamor. We fall in with a group of steelworkers. "Nice puppet," one says, pointing at the sun and giving me a thumbs-up. "Thanks. Nice slogan." Their T-shirts waste no words: "FTAA Sucks." The local union director bellows tirelessly through the bullhorn and we chant along, puppets bobbing. It's contagious, this energy, and soon I am high on it, racing about in a happy tizzy, greeting friends, snapping photos. A huge inflated globe, riding above the crowd, reading "Make Trade Fair." A Mexican contingency, marching with an oversized Mexican flag and signs reading "No al ALCA." United for Peace and Justice, the national antiwar coalition that organized the February 15th demonstrations, banner held high. A local environmental group, molded cardboard dolphins dipping and swooping through the throng. The Coalition of Immokalee workers, a local immigrant and workers' rights group that organized a three-day march leading up to today, calling for *uno centavo más*—one more cent per pound—for the tomatoes they pick.

Labor, environmentalists, immigrants, farmworkers, people of color, people of faith, the antiwar constituency: a very diverse group is making its presence felt today. The FTAA protests are proving to be a successful exercise in solidarity between movements. Yesterday, John Sweeney, president of the AFL-CIO, visited our Convergence Center. The AFL-CIO had initially requested that the direct-action contingency not organize for the first day of the talks, when the unions would have their permitted march. After months of discussion, an agreement was reached: we would schedule the direct action early in the morning, to avoid compromising their march. Sweeney stood in the center of the roasting warehouse, mopping his forehead. "We're delighted to be marching together tomorrow," he said, to riotous cheers. "I stand with you here in solidarity."

Despite our unity, both police and local journalists insist on constructing an artificial divide, repeatedly differentiating "good protesters" from "bad protesters." The labor movement, according to Timoney, is "credible"; we are of course the "suspect" ones, the "violent troublemakers with no message." And it is after the permitted march ends—cut short just as it reaches the point closest to the FTAA talks—that we "troublemakers" of conscience feel the brunt of Timoney's wrath.

"What's that?" Joshua pushes his glasses up on his nose, squints down the street. We are gathered outside the Arena, where the AFL-CIO rally has begun.

"Jesus. It's a tank."

"Oh. My. God."

The War on Terror has arrived home.

In the middle distance, blossoms of tear gas. Above, surveillance helicopters swarming. Ten yards away, a shriek as someone collapses. "Infiltrator! It's an infiltrator with a taser!" People are screaming and pointing. The infiltrator dashes away, wielding his stun gun in front of him. More screams as snatch squads move in, yanking people out of the crowd at random.

"Let's go." David is already moving.

"Where?" This from Tracy, recently doused with a faceful of tear gas. She holds a Maalox-and-water-soaked bandanna to her eyes, which are red and puffy and leaking.

"It doesn't matter. We need to move. Now."

I glance up at the tower of the Intercontinental Hotel, where the talks are being held. This mayhem must be visible to the delegates. What are they thinking? In September, the WTO talks in Cancún collapsed. Buttressed by activists and nongovernmental organizations, the nascent G22 — group of twenty-two developing nations — refused to negotiate until agricultural subsidies and protections for wealthy countries were substantively addressed. Led by Brazil, the G22 took an unprecedented stand against the U.S. and E.U. Stalemate resulted. What will happen today? What is being deliberated right now inside those rarefied rooms? Is any part of our message audible, or do the delegates hear only the thunderous static of the Bush administration, the mainstream media, the corporations?

We are running, now, running again through a city that has shrunk to a gray blur, a blur broken by shards of dialogue and color, oblique flashes against the concrete and keening sirens. We knew what was coming today, and we prepared. We reviewed street tactics with the FCAA outside the Convergence Center yesterday, practicing linking and locking our arms to hold intersections, rehearsing jumping and running together as a coordinated group. But nothing could have primed me for this. This is a police state, and those of us who are exercising our freedoms of speech and assembly are being treated like criminals. Someone calls my name and I turn to see Carwil jogging along with his affinity group. The lump just above his left eye is the size of a ping-pong ball. "Rubber bullet," he explains, as we hug and part. I race to catch up with Code Orange. We keep running, north toward the Convergence Center, pausing occasionally to catch our breath under cover of palm trees. There is a host of small groups tearing through the streets, some being followed by police, others getting ambushed.

"We've gotten word that the Convergence Center isn't safe," pants David. We are squatting on the sidewalk under trees, puppets propped against the side of a building. "What do we want to do?"

"Get rid of the puppets," says Nora. A Canadian here on a work visa, she's been especially vigilant about avoiding arrest, which would surely lead to her deportation. "They're slowing us down, and announcing that we're the bad protesters." She suggests dumping them. But others disagree: the puppets might get ruined, and our friends in the Coalition of Immokalee workers could use them again. We debate different options for a few minutes.

"Maybe we could leave them with someone who lives here," suggests Tracy, dabbing at her eyes. "Then we can pick them up tomorrow." We are in Overtown, not far from the Convergence Center. Overtown is African American and poor. Residents living near the Convergence Center have been friendly, despite having been warned about us by the police. We consense on this option, and decide to do our best to get back to our hotel. A small delegation sets out, knocking on the doors of the nearest homes. The second person we ask agrees—"Sure thing. They givin' y'all a hard time today, huh?"—and we push the puppets over the fence into his yard. Next, to the bus station. Calmer now, we slow our pace to a brisk walk.

"Look at this!" Joshua stops in his tracks outside a shop window.

"My lord." The television inside the shop is showing footage from the helicopters above. Journalists "embedded" with the police are filming us, and we watch wordless as protesters scuttle antlike through the urban grid. I stand stock-still. Television before me, playing the hunt in real time. Helicopters above me, simultaneously hunting and recording, constructing and filming the spectacle. And what of me—am I the hunted or the spectator? The subject or the audience? Am I creating or consuming this spectacle—and does it make any difference, really, as long as it keeps people glued to their sets? Survivor: The War on Terror Goes Domestic—the ultimate reality show. It is so riveting that for a minute I forget we need to move.

The level of cooperation between police and media in Miami is unprecedented. Media treatment of the global justice movement is invariably heavily biased. "If it bleeds, it leads" journalism unerringly homes in on the single smashed Starbucks window, ignoring the thousands of peaceful protesters—and, for that matter, the reasons they choose to protest. None of this is surprising, given corporate domination of the mainstream media: in the U.S, the five major broadcast networks control 75 percent of the prime-time viewing audience; worldwide, eight corporations control over 70 percent of the media. If we in the global justice movement were portrayed accurately, viewers might grow suspicious of the corporations, the institutions, the entire system. They might question their own level of consumption, or—worse still—the content of their consumption. With profits on the line, the mainstream media inevitably portray us as clueless, even dangerous, radicals. But Miami takes this one-sided narrative to a whole new level.

As Ilyse Hogue and Patrick Reinsborough of the smartMeme Project write in "Lessons from Miami: Information Warfare in the Age of Empire," the police operation in Miami is about far more than controlling the streets: it's military-style propaganda, pure and simple, aimed at controlling public perception of the talks and the protesters. Borrowing liberally from PR lessons learned in Iraq, TV correspondents in Miami are "embedded" with the police, and they appear on camera in flak jackets and helmets (to fend off us perilous protesters). Other than rare and brief "on the streets" snippets, interviews are limited to police spokespeople. Footage is eerily disjointed from voiceovers describing the circumstances, and the voiceovers themselves shift frequently and without clear identification between anchor, embedded reporter, and police spokesperson. "So far, we're winning!" crows an anchor from Fox affiliate Channel 7, to footage of squads of riot police pushing protesters from downtown with colossal force.

Timoney is repeatedly interviewed, and his descriptions of police tactics are simply untrue. He claims the police never use tear gas and arrest only "violent" protesters, and that peaceful demonstration is permitted. The protests are overwhelmingly nonviolent, but the anchors credit the "massive, well-prepared police force" instead of the explicitly nonviolent nature of the organizing. As for the print media, the Miami Herald Publishing Company not only runs editorials backing the FTAA, it actually donates $217,000 worth of advertising space in support of the FTAA and a full $62,500 in cash to subsidize the summit.

Half an hour later, we reach the bus station, which is brimming with agitated activists. We locate our bus and drop exhausted into the seats. Back to the nightclub fashions and art deco facades of Miami Beach. Back to devour what the Miami papers have to say about today. Back to discover that the FTAA talks adjourned this afternoon,

a day early, and that the delegates agreed to leave the harder decisions
— the real decisions — unresolved, indefinitely postponed. We go out
to dinner at a nearby restaurant and order pitchers of margaritas.

The "FTAA Lite," as the agreement comes to be known, allows
member nations to withdraw from any trade requirements they find
unsavory. Brazil, South America's economic heavyweight, objected to
the FTAA's rules on investment and intellectual property; the U.S. refused to relinquish domestic farm subsidies. The resulting compro-
mise carries about half a calorie, but the U.S. government has avoided
a humiliating repetition of Cancún. For us, it is a victory — of sorts. A
dubious one. What goes down in Miami sets a new standard in domestic repression. As the tallies later reveal, on this day — November
20 — over two hundred people are arrested. More than a hundred are
injured. Twelve are hospitalized. One prisoner, a Mexican man, is
beaten so badly during arrest that he is put in the ICU with a brain
hemorrhage.

Later that night, the streets are still filled with police. Cars are
halted at whim, guns aimed at drivers, passengers made to get out
with their hands up. The next day, at a peaceful jail support action,
fifty of two hundred demonstrators are arrested. The police open negotiations only to break their word, issue a three-minute dispersal
order, and close in, arresting everyone inadvertently caught in their
net. Six helicopters and 680 riot police are present for the occasion.

The militarized response to the FTAA protests will become
known as the "Miami Model." "This is the model by which the citizens of Miami, and of this country, get used to seeing tanks in the
street," says Global Exchange and Code Pink co-founder Medea Benjamin when I run into her the next day. "Viewers get used to a military state."

I am driving through downtown Miami with a friend that night,
our truckbed full of recovered giant puppets, when we are pulled over.
Police cars are still clustered on corners like feeding larvae. A Miami–
Dade County deputy sheriff leans into my window.

"License and registration."

"Yes, Officer." I'm starting to feel frightened when I see the police,
even though I've done nothing wrong.

He peers at the documents, then back at us. Unsmiling. Blank.

Trying, perhaps, to connect these two innocuous-looking young women with what he's been told about us. With the face-off in the streets.

"So, you having fun?"

"Not really." I am trying to see him as more than a cardboard cutout, more than a uniform with lethal toys. "How about you?"

"It's been an intense time." A flicker of human feeling plays over his pale face. Faint but there.

"No kidding." I am suddenly furious with him, livid at what he and his cohorts have put us through. Enraged that my friends have gotten hurt, that others are in the hospital, that we have been treated like reprobates for caring so much. And then sadness lunges, liquefies me, and I struggle not to dissolve into tears right there in front of him. I know nothing about this man. I don't know what he thinks, values, believes in. Or what his wife believes. Maybe they argue. Maybe she says, "Listen, honey, those protesters, they have a point." Who knows? Yet here we are on opposite shores, soaked to the bone with suspicion.

I watch him in silence. He examines the registration, nods and grunts, lets us go. They trail us for a while before losing interest.

I am in Miami for six days. Between organizing and writing, I probably get a total of about twenty-five hours sleep the entire time. Joshua and I are sharing a cab to the airport, both of us half-asleep, when the driver decides he's in the mood to chat.

"So, was it a good holiday?" He eyes us benevolently from the rearview mirror. He is black, somewhere in his forties, easy-featured. Speech tipsy with a swig of French. From Senegal, probably. Or maybe Niger.

I rouse myself with herculean effort from the sun-warmed leather comfort of the backseat. Outside the window, another immaculate day. Row upon row of squat cookie-cutter houses, paper-thin against a nondescript sky. "Not so great, actually. Sort of challenging." I am enervated and bleak. Did our efforts really make any difference? Was Miami simply a glimpse into this country's Orwellian future?

The cab driver smiles benignly back at us. "Too many lovers' squabbles?"

Joshua and I look at each other and cackle. Lovers. Squabbling. Both seem worlds away. Back on the planet where people go on honeymoons and fight over things like broken toasters. As a rule, I don't date other activists. Something happens to my sexuality while organizing direct action: overwhelmed by all the urgency, it curls up, hides in a dusty corner from my stentorian left brain. I'm not sure I could handle being in a relationship with someone equally impassioned and committed. I need calm, stability, grounding. I think of my boyfriend, Jonathan, who will be meeting us at the airport, who will take me home and feed me and run me a bath, and I feel a little better.

"No, nothing like that. Actually we were here to protest the Free Trade Area of the Americas. Did you hear about the demonstrations?"

"Ah, yes. Certainly." His face tightens into solemnity. "I have been following this with great interest."

"Really?"

"Yes. I am from Haiti." Haiti. Of course. We're in Florida. "I have been listening to the local Haitian reports on the radio."

I ask him what they are saying.

"They are saying what Haitians already know. What most of the world already knows. Haiti produces denim jeans and baseball equipment for this country, but Haitians themselves cannot afford to buy it." I am nodding, awake now. "The FTAA will make the rich richer and the poor poorer." He brakes at a light and turns to look at us. Stern, resolute. "This is not fair."

No. It's not fair. No, no, no. *No. We said no. Hell no. Not this time. Not next time, either.* There are multitudes out there suffocating under the pulverizing leviathan of free trade. People, yes, and beyond: we have not only toxic levels of flame retardant in breast milk but also whales with tumors, and radioactive soil contamination, and rainforests and polar icecaps and entire ecosystems staggering toward oblivion. We are officially in the midst of the fastest mass extinction in the planet's history. And still we are working ourselves to the bone for the consolation prizes, enduringly mesmerized by the siren jingles of a monstrous economy that is slowly but surely killing the vessel upon which we depend. That is robbing four-fifths of humanity, injuring our children, slaying our great-grandchildren before they even get a taste of fresh water, a breath of uncontaminated air. *DID YOU HEAR US? WE SAID NO.* This week I met people from Ecuador, Bolivia, Venezuela, Brazil, Peru. All around the world many are already resisting. Many more are forging alternatives through their own lives, work, and communities. There are millions who stand with us but could not join us. We are ourselves one small strand in an intricate and exquisite weave.

"Thank you." I look around the car to where his name is posted, just above his head. "Thank you, Marc. For saying that."

The light changes. Someone behind us honks and Marc turns back to the road. "Human life is important," he pronounces quietly, gently, as the car gradually picks up speed. He knits his brow at me in the rearview mirror. "It must be valued everywhere."

Nine:

Sarayacu, Ecuador

"Once, there were many *sabios* here. They were very pure. They were able to transform into snakes and tigers. They knew everything—sickness, healing, they understood it all." Atanacio Sabino Gualinga Cuji, a shaman himself, is giving me a crash course on three and a half centuries of Sarayacu history. His gaze is piercing, unbending from eyes blued by cataracts, eyebrows riotous as the jungle floor. "Then the Christians came to convert us. Then the companies came to drill for oil." He shakes his head. "In '35 Shell came and put a pipeline in. Before, there were lots of fish, turtles, alligators. After, nothing was left. Everything died from oil."

Atanacio is tiny, earnest, serene. His hair is oiled and neatly combed, his goatee white-filamented, his checkered shirt clean and pressed. We are sitting in his yard on two well-worn stump-stools, beneath the cool relief of palm-thatch. He looks beyond me to where Mario, my host here, sits with his wife, chatting in tempered tones, sipping homemade *chicha*. "I saw it. Everything died." He considers the sweat-polished wood of his walking stick, propped scepterlike beside him. "There is money. But here there are marvels. Here we have pure air. Here women can walk freely." He giggles, now a mischievous six-year-old dropping a punch line. "We only have to watch out for the snakes." Then he's abruptly somber again, with all the burden of his seventy-odd years. "The oil corporations—they want to kill everything here. They don't understand. They live apart from real knowledge. We wouldn't want that kind of knowledge." Atanacio pauses as a tame toucan—the family pet—dashes boldly at us, formidable beak parted in an ear-splitting screech. He tosses it a nut. "We want to maintain

our culture and identity. My role is to maintain the consciousness."
He looks past me, past the palm fronds, into the legendary *mar verde*
of Amazonia. Quietly, now: "The earth is our mother and father. We
can't sell our mother and father."

I see 2003 as a year of endless transition, always setting out, never
quite reaching my destination. In July, I quit my job at Tikkun, exhausted and emotionally drained. I take some time off, spending a
week backpacking solo in the Sierras, a week on a silent meditation
retreat at Spirit Rock, and a week working with one of my mentors,
Sharif Abdullah, on a project exploring issues of race and class in the
Portland Department of Transportation. We interview sewage workers, engineers, and upper management on topics ranging from homo-
phobia to gun control to abortion to the environment. I then take a
half-time job with a tiny local nonprofit running a *satyagraha* campaign.
Our target is Clear Channel communications, a corporate (and politically conservative) media behemoth. Our small staff begins exploring
models for bringing spiritually grounded principles of interconnection and nonviolence to bear upon our own organizing, and upon a
corporate target. The work is good and meaningful, but I still feel
somehow at sea.

Since my time in Phoolchatty, the question of meditation versus
action has wedged itself, burrlike, into my brain. I have maintained a
daily meditation practice, complemented by attending teachings and
retreats at Spirit Rock and self-retreating on solo backpacking trips.
And while it is my nature to hurl myself at life like a besotted puppy,
I can't shake the nagging feeling that my activism—not to mention
my psyche—would ultimately be most benefited by devoting myself
fully to inner work. I go to a day-long at Spirit Rock with renowned
Buddhist activist and teacher Joanna Macy. When we break for lunch
I approach her with this question. Later she addresses the entire group.
"So today I was asked the same question I hear over and over. 'Is my
time better spent working on the world or working on myself? On so-
cial change or practice?'" She scans the group, arms wide in petition.
"Isn't the answer clear?"

Well, to be honest, no. I've been chewing this over distractedly for a good year and a half. Pray enlighten me.

Macy looks expectantly around the silent room. "Both, of course!" People are smiling and nodding as if to say, Naturally, clear as day. "The world needs us too much right now to just work on ourselves. And we need the world too much to only work on it. Without practice, we lack the kind of awareness necessary to discern what is inspiring our actions, and whether they are truly constructive."

Both. Got it. Nice one.

In December, the nonprofit unexpectedly runs out of funding for our campaign. For the first time in two years, I find myself at a loss. What to do? The mere thought of taking on another full-time organizing position — another round of being overworked and underpaid — is exhausting. I cast about half-heartedly through the want ads. Nothing appeals. I have no idea, I tell people when they ask me what I'm doing next. But this isn't quite the truth, the whole truth, and nothing but the truth. I have an irksome feeling that I know exactly what to do next. That niggling suspicion is even more terrifying than not knowing.

Write. I want to write. Over the past couple of years I have continued freelancing whenever I've had the time and opportunity, largely focusing on issues related to globalization. But pay from most of the publications I've written for has been scant at best. Writing makes absolutely no sense. Unless I marry rich, which at this point strikes me as an idea worth considering. Since immigrating, my family has struggled financially; in college I relied entirely on scholarships and part-time work, and since then I've mostly earned what my grandmother called *bupkes*—"beans"—at my jobs. I'm already used to counting pennies, and shabby chic, I reason with myself. But perhaps even more daunting than assured poverty is the idea of investing myself in an endeavor with no established path or guidance and certainly no guaranteed success or even work. No, writing makes not a whit of sense.

On the other hand, since when have I chosen to do anything because it's sensible? If I'd been making choices based on prudence, I would've snapped up the job I was offered in management consulting fresh out of college. Instead I called them back to tell them I wanted to sing. I am still singing, still writing songs and experimenting with different collaborations—jazz, electronic, folk—but that's not going to earn me two nickels to rub together unless I sing covers at weddings and bar mitzvahs, which I can't find it within myself to do. No, I've been a stark-raving romantic for too long to stop now. Writing may not be a particularly practical choice, but I have seen through my journalism how powerful a tool it can be, how it can amplify issues and voices that too often go ignored. That, and I can't deny I thoroughly relish seeing my name in print.

Although my life feels like a rickety mess, I am starting to see where my work lies. My time at Tikkun showed me that I don't always have to pick a side, that speaking exactly what I believe is risky but ultimately strengthening. I also met many people who were listening, like I am, to hear the quietest of their own inner voices echoed, to be affirmed in their understanding that the way we change the world needs to reflect the world we wish to create. My time in the global justice movement has shown me the power that we have as individuals and communities, and has positioned me so I am directly facing the dragon's lair. I pick up my pen, and begin with a couple of essays examining the role of nonviolence within the context of corporate globalization. But without guarantee of publication—and the accompanying deadlines—I find it hard to locate the motivation and discipline to sit down and do the work I feel I need to do. Partly out of desperation, partly because the travel bug has been champing with increasing boldness, I decide it's time for another solo jaunt. The destination finds me.

I first hear of the Sarayacu from an acquaintance who works at Amazon Watch, an NGO with offices in San Francisco.

"They're amazing," says Leila. We are sitting at her desk, sipping maté. "What they've achieved so far is hard to believe. They've managed to resist some very powerful oil corporations backed by the government of Ecuador."

The Sarayacu, she tells me, are an indigenous community of Quichua in Ecuador's southern Amazon. She walks over to a large map of South America pinned on the wall and points to a bright green scrap. "They're being called the gateway to the south. Ecuador's northern Amazon has been devastated by decades of exploitation, but the south is pristine, untouched. The Sarayacu are on the front lines. And everyone is watching: other indigenous communities, the government, the oil companies." She pulls out articles and photos. I stare at the broad features, the squat bodies, the knotted backdrop of jungle. The faces are clear, resolute. Somewhere in the vicinity of my belly something tugs. And again. I ask Leila if she can put me in touch with them.

"Yeah. We've been working with them for the past couple of years. I can connect you with Mario Santi, their lead organizer."

"Great. I definitely want to write about this. I'm going to read up and start pitching today."

I tell my boyfriend Jonathan, whom I have been with for the past five months, that I'm going to South America, that I've found my next project. I tell him I'll be gone for four months, but I'm hoping he can visit for a couple of weeks. Jonathan is over a decade older than me, and pushing for more commitment, not less. He stares at me, hazel eyes wide, and I feel hideously guilty. "I can't believe you're going to do this."

"I'm sorry." I am a callous, evil woman. I must be, to hurt someone I love this much. "I just have to." It'll be a good few years before I'll consider putting the needs of a relationship before my own and those of my work. Today I have no regrets about this. I've been fortunate to have dated wonderful and devoted men, but none of them fit quite right, and somewhere inside me—although I push it away frantically at the time—I'm aware of this.

"Why? Why do you have to do this?" He offers to support me, which I consider for a delusional half-second before adamantly rejecting.

"I want to see South America," I say miserably. "You know how much I love traveling." I've always had the ability to adapt rapidly to new places. There's a sublimely lonely part of me that feels most at home traveling, that discovers itself and the world and the bridges between when the rest of me gets lost in a foreign place. I think of my great-grandfather Max. Perhaps it's as simple as a matter of believing in possibilities.

"Also I want to write this story."

Miami left me wondering: Where does the endemic violence of corporate globalization end? How do we defend what is precious to us? How do we protect our cultures and communities? How do we preserve what remains of this planet's biological richness and diversity—those places upon whose preservation our own health and survival ultimately depend? I had gone to talk to Leila because it occurred to me that those who live in close contact with the earth, with their own resources and culture and spirituality, must have a great deal to teach us. It is time, again, for me to listen.

I look at Jonathan, who appears far from convinced. "These are voices that need to be heard. I know you don't want me to go, but I've got to write about this. About how globalization is affecting indigenous communities in the Amazon." There. I said it. That's how I'll say it when I tell my parents, too. I pause, considering. "And about how they're affecting globalization."

Three weeks later, I leave for South America.

The children stare at me. Unblinking. Wary. Their faces laced with geometric designs, painted in traditional black *wituk* dye. Warriors already. Welcome to Sarayacu.

I arrive in Ecuador in early March 2004. I spend a week in Quito reviving my Spanish through an intensive, then take a bus to Puyo, the nearest city to Sarayacu. There, I meet with a couple of the community's leaders, to discuss the risks and convince them to let me visit. For good reason, the Sarayacu are very careful about letting outsiders in right now.

Mario, Leila's contact, is my traveling companion on the flight from Puyo to Sarayacu. When we climb out of the tiny plane, he is instantly surrounded, shaking hands, laughing uproariously. He vanishes into the small crowd. I stay put, somewhat shaken after our bumpy landing. I hang back from the children's gaze, looking elsewhere, embarrassed by my sunglasses and backpack, by my gringa-ness. Some of the younger boys play behind the plane, dancing in the tail winds as the engine ebbs. The makeshift runway lies in the middle of a large cleared grassy area, with a few low-lying buildings on the edges. "The high school," Mario pointed out as we descended. "And that, there, is the elementary school." Beyond, on all sides: the *mar verde* of the Amazon basin. Sprawling, dogged. Simmering, ticking, throbbing. Alive.

"*Venga,*" says Mario, emerging from the knot, reaching toward me. I take his hand and he leads me through the bodies. He is greeting friends and relatives, pulling bread, jam, and other urban goodies from his sack and handing them out. His face is lambent, transformed. He's a different person from the one I met three days ago in Puyo, where the Sarayacu office is located. The office, the nexus of their global campaign, is home to two desks, one desktop and one laptop computer, one printer, and one fax machine. Posters condemning oil exploitation are pinned to the walls. "Our land is our future," reads one. Mario wore jeans and a T-shirt, his long black hair pulled neatly back into a ponytail. "We are a warrior people," he told me, his face grim, composed. "If they try to come drill on our land, we will hold them off with our bodies. We'll form a wall with our lances."

That's precisely what they did the last time.

In 1996 Ecuador auctioned off a number of concessions for oil exploitation. Block 23, a 494,200-acre quadrangle of rainforest in the south-central province of Pastaza, was purchased by the Argentine-based corporation Compañía General de Combustibles (CGC). The CGC later sold a quarter of its shares to Texas-based Burlington Resources and another quarter to Paris-based Perenco. Roughly half of Block 23 is Sarayacu tribal land. But Ecuador's constitution retains the antiquated Spanish edict that regardless of ownership, the resources underground belong to the state. Faced with major political resistance, the CGC didn't enter Block 23 before 2000—which was when their legal right to conduct seismic exploration expired. Nonetheless, in late 2002 the CGC announced that it would be entering Sarayacu territory with the aid of the Ecuadorean military. In response, the Sarayacu declared a state of emergency. They chopped paths through the dense jungle, lugged out massive supply sacks, and built twenty-five Peace and Life camps along the boundaries of their territory. When the oil workers and soldiers arrived, the Sarayacu were ready. They interlocked their traditional *chonta* lances and bodily held them off. Every member of the tribe age ten and older participated. Most were at the borders for fifteen days at a time. Some stayed in Sarayacu Center organizing the resistance and communicating with local allies. Others, like Mario, worked from the Puyo office to mobilize an international campaign, coordinating with NGO partners in the U.S. and Europe and speaking with the media.

For three and a half months, this community of one thousand remained on their borders nonviolently defending their land and heritage. Eventually the CGC decided it was time to change tack. "Now things are normal," Mario said. "But when the oil workers come, everything will be paralyzed. We'll go into a state of emergency."

I am here writing a feature for *Orion Magazine* and a news piece for the *San Francisco Chronicle*. Over the course of my scheduled ten-day visit, I aim to conduct a broad range of interviews, to pull together a detailed anatomy of the Sarayacu's resistance. For the feature, I'll also need generous helpings of "vivid color, rich context, and telling details," as my editor put it. In other words, there's no time to waste.

"Take, take. *Por favor.*" A woman is thrusting a bowl, the shell from some species of gargantuan jungle fruit, toward me. I eye the murky contents charily.

"What is it?" I turn to Mario. She is a cousin of his — it seems everyone in Sarayacu is a cousin, or an uncle, or an uncle's cousin — and we are pausing en route to Mario's home, waiting for his wife Marcia to meet us.

"*Chicha.* Made from yucca. Boiled, pounded, chewed, then fermented. It's a bit like beer."

"Chewed?"

"Yes. The saliva helps it ferment." He smiles — accustomed, I am sure, to this gringo squeamishness. "The Sarayacu women work hard to make our *chicha.* It's delicious. Have some."

"No, thank you. I mean, thanks very much, but no thanks." I smile up at her feebly.

She smiles back, shifts the child on her hip, and moves to the next in the circle—her husband, who accepts it without relinquishing the reins of conversation. He takes a lengthy draft, smacks his lips, hands her the emptied bowl. She returns to an urn in one corner, dips from the larger into the smaller, runs a hand through to sieve the excess fibers, and tosses them in the dirt. The child jogs about uncomplaining on her hip. He stares at me until he tires of my strangeness, then resumes the consolation of her nipple.

The adults continue talking quietly in Quichua, laughing at intervals, our hostess periodically circling with the bowl. We sit on logs, under a roof of palm fronds. Chickens cluck through self-importantly. Several of the scrawny breed of mutt distinctive to Sarayacu snuffle and whine at the edges. Beyond the small circle a few children play, giggling and hopping about manically, still giddy with excitement over the bread and jam. And then there is the heat, heavy and wet as a tongue.

I am left out of their conversation, but I do not mind. I am overjoyed simply to be here—in the Amazon and among this community, which has occupied my imagination for over a month. I try to envision these tranquil people at their borders. But it's near impossible to picture them any other way than they are right now. This is how the Sarayacu lived two hundred years ago, and this is how I see them living two hundred years from now, molding to place and task like jungle mud to my feet. The land itself possesses a timelessness, a peace so self-assured that it is palpable. The peace of earth unviolated, of an essence inviolable. The languid coil of the Bobonaza River, the rhythmic ticking of insects, the shrills of birds and children: all a mantle over a much older silence. Like the silences that gird a long and fecund marriage. The people know the land and the land knows the people. Conversation eases into comfortable redundancies: bridges between stillnesses. I cannot understand what they are saying, but I can understand the gaps in between, the flow of words natural as rain. "It must be hard to leave, Mario," I'd said as we trudged through the sucking mud. "Yes, it is." He'd turned to me, exultant. "We're safe here." There is of course a constant metallic undercurrent of tension: the CGC could try to enter again at any point, with the government's declared support. But there is more to Mario's assertion than that:

the land actually somehow feels safe, as if in gentle collusion with its people.

"Marcia!" The conversation breaks off as Mario rises. His wife is emerging from the jungle path into the clearing, barefoot, arms filled with books. Marcia is in the teacher-training program at Sarayacu's university. They greet each other quietly, casually joyful. Mario has been living in Puyo working on the campaign, and it's been a full month since they last saw each other. He introduces me and she takes my hand.

"*Un gusto.*" A wide, gap-toothed smile. Marcia is tiny, self-possessed, very much at ease. She greets the circle briefly. "All right, let's go home. It's just about time for dinner. Fidel! Ligia!" Out of the jungle skip their two children: Fidel, already a sturdy model of his father at eight, and Ligia, a bewitchingly dreamy-eyed six-year-old. They hang behind their mother and titter over me at the other children. "*Bueno*, we're off."

I follow the family out into the jungle. They are all marvelously nimble in the stubborn mud. I scuffle along awkwardly behind, my gumboots sinking half a foot deep with each step. Next comes the rain. It is light at first, then more insistent, and then the sky unbolts and buckets down on us. By the time we reach home we are all drenched. Their *wasi* is a generous oval of around forty by twenty feet, sheltered with a dense weave of palm fronds and enclosed by a four-foot-high bamboo fence. The kitchen occupies one end. The other end comprises the sleeping quarters. The family sleeps on the ground and unrolls their bedding nightly; I, as their guest, am given the single raised wooden bed. I will spend the next nine nights on this bed, switching sides religiously every half hour on complaining hips.

We gather soap and towels and head down to a nearby tributary of the Bobonaza to bathe, Mario veering off to give Marcia and me some privacy. The water is cool, glassy, agile. Perfect. Marcia scrubs away industriously with a washcloth, while I recline languorously, limbs settling into the rocks' toothy embrace, velvet river-sand sifting between prune-puckered fingers. Greeting the odd fish jaunting by in a stutter of silver. Daydreaming, staring soft into a supple ceiling of green. Buoyantly, absurdly happy.

Dinner is fried yucca and bananas, with sugary decaf Nescafé and packaged cookies for dessert. The transmitter radio blares a constant stream of Quichua and Spanish, pop hits jangling against the bluster of news updates and the purr of community announcements. *Mi amor, how you make me suffer. Gutierrez alienating his indigenous allies. Rosa sends kisses to Eduardo in Puyo.* Fidel and Ligia long forgot to be shy, and they hang about me, sharing jokes and games, exploring the unfathomable contents of my bag, instructing me patiently in beginner Quichua. Mario and Marcia unroll their bedding. I hang my mosquito net.

"*Buenas noches,*" calls Mario from the other side of the *wasi.*

"*Buenas noches,*" shrieks Ligia, giggling.

"*Buenas noches, amigos.*" And then I am asleep, lulled by the pulse and swoon of jungle night, by the mellifluous rise and fall of conversation that is their reunion.

On the flight to Ecuador, I had plenty of time to think about the Sarayacu, to review my preparatory research and consider my fascination with them. Digging through newspapers and surfing the Internet in San Francisco, I had learned that partly owing to their geographic remoteness, and partly because the people have made a series of decisions not to barter their heritage for western accoutrements, the Sarayacu's indigenous culture remains largely intact. "Of all the Quichua communities, the Sarayacu are the most traditional, and rooted in their territory," Kevin Koenig, who has worked with the Sarayacu for two years as the Amazon Oil Campaign Coordinator at Amazon Watch, told me in San Francisco. "They present their own vision of the future, and pick and choose what of the world out there they want to incorporate." The Sarayacu live, as they have for centuries, off what the land provides: they fish in the Bobonaza, and hunt wild game in their territory. They farm yucca and banana in small fields, and collect fruits and nuts from the jungle. The community still relies primarily on age-old shamanic wisdom for medicine; the *sabios* cultivate gardens of traditional healing plants, including the famous *ayahuasca*, a potent hallucinogenic used for entering spiritual trances.

The Sarayacu move slowly. They laugh a lot. They do the work they need to do, and then they sit back and relax. The CGC could enter at any time, and they'd be ready, but you'd never guess it by watching them. I think of my life back home: constantly rushing to meetings and appointments, constantly feeling pulled between activism and music and social obligations and every other essential thing on my endless list. I have to pencil in "nothing" when I want an evening off. Every activist I know is similarly overburdened and stressed, staggering around like Atlas beneath a world only we can save. It can't be helping our work.

In Quito, I conducted a series of interviews with outsiders who have worked with the Sarayacu. When I asked them what sets the Sarayacu apart, how they have succeeded where so many others have been overcome, I heard the same answer again and again. They are rooted in their culture, land, and, most importantly, their spirituality. "The Sarayacu are a center of spirituality for the Amazon," said Mario Melo, a legal advisor to the Sarayacu from the Quito-based Center for Economic and Social Rights. "They are very powerful. They have no money to confront the corporations, but they do have their spirituality and a very long tradition of battling."

On the bus ride to Puyo, watching the Andes unfurl into the Amazon, I thought about how the Sarayacu found the courage to defend themselves. In 1989 they used civil disobedience to prevent ARCO from completing drilling in Block 10, a chunk of which falls in their territory. Their opposition led to the Sarayacu Accord, which pledged to the tribes communal title to all indigenous land in Pastaza, and halted oil operations until environmental measures could be put in place. A year later the government renounced the accord. In 1990, along with tens of thousands of others, the Sarayacu demonstrated in the first of several massive nonviolent indigenous uprisings. In 1992, following a mass march to Quito, President Rodrigo Borja acquiesced, granting title deeds to Quichua, Achuar, Shuar, Shiwiar, and Zapara tribes for three million acres of land—about 70 percent of the province of Pastaza. Excellent, except for that tricky old clause under which the government retained rights to subterranean resources. But as the CGC discovered, a clause does not a conquest make. By the time I get to Sarayacu, the CGC has hauled out virtually every tried-and-true tactic in the oil industry's bag: threats and intimidation, bribing other indigenous communities in Block 23, attempting to bribe individuals within Sarayacu, and finally—when that fails—

offering the whole community $60,000. "That's a lot of money being offered to very poor people," says Esperanza Martínez, founder of the Ecuadorean NGO Acción Ecológica. *No,* said the Sarayacu.

For the crowning oily feather in their cap, the CGC neglected to file an environmental impact report on the seismic testing it tried to conduct in 2002. "That's required by the constitution," says Mario. "They broke the law." Nonetheless, in March 2003, following the CGC's abortive attempts to enter Sarayacu territory, the Ecuadorean government extended their contract. In February 2004, just weeks before I arrive in Sarayacu, Minister of Energy Carlos Arboleda states that the government "is prepared to provide all security guarantees to the CGC so that it can continue operations in Block 23."

I spend my first full day in Sarayacu interviewing, interviewing, and interviewing some more. I start with Atanacio in Sarayacu Pista, then Mario leads me across the river to Sarayacu Center to speak with Romel Cisneros, one of the youth directors.

"We went in groups to the borders, ten to fifteen of us, aged fifteen to eighteen," Cisneros says. "We tried to resolve the conflict with our words." He is twenty-two and looks younger. He sits opposite me bare-chested, cross-legged, nervous. "We just want to protect our land. Our grandparents tell us that the trees have a spiritual life, and the land too. Before, we knew this." A toothy grin. "Now we are getting back to it." I recall Atanacio's words an hour earlier. "Once," said the *sabio,* "we talked to the moon, the stars, the sun. We can return to the way of the wise."

The Sarayacu are making a concerted effort to recoup the aspects of their indigenous spirituality and culture that have been displaced by the icons of Christ and capital. Attendance at the local church — built decades earlier by missionaries — is steadily dwindling, according to Mario (and to the consternation of the devout Christian elders in the tribe). The *sabios* are training a select few in the art of shamanic horticulture and practice. Many of the young men are again wearing their hair long, as is traditional. Later in the day I interview Johnny Dahua, a twenty-three-year-old who worked out of the Puyo office during the resistance. "What's important is that we don't forget our culture," he says. "Our elders tell us to preserve the land because it's our life, because we are interrelated with the jungle. It fortifies us, this idea." I nod. My heart is with him, but I have to admit I'm losing steam, and my pen is dragging on the page. Dahua is approximately my fourteenth interview so far. It must be at least 105 degrees, and I'm drenched in a layer of sweat that stubbornly refuses to evaporate, plastered with mosquito bites, and dog-tired from trailing my indefatigable host through the vile, odious, godawful jungle mud.

I'm trying to be inspired by his words but having a little difficulty. Is this really what I want to do with my life?

"Money comes and goes," Dahua continues, finger wagging. Schoolmarmish despite the bare chest, galoshes, and loose, waist-length hair. "But if you guard the jungle, it will be here a thousand years."

"Uh-huh. Lungs of the earth and all that." I glance over to Mario, who is schmoozing with Dahua's mother and young wife. Lunchtime, anyone?

But Johnny remains on target. He keeps talking, and I automatically keep scribbling. At some point his daughter, a winsome two-year-old in a frilly dress, toddles over. He picks her up and deposits her on his lap, where she engages in the hands-down favorite pastime of Sarayacu's below-seven constituency: staring at the gringa. I smile and give a few feeble coos. I ask Johnny if he thinks it's possible his children will want different things—money, material goods.

"No. We're not going to lose our traditions and our way of life for things, for material things. I'm totally sure that the next generation will be aware."

It occurs to me that culture, spirituality, and nature are inseparable here. In the west, we divide them into three categories, and I struggle conscientiously to make time to engage with each.

I thank Dahua and close my notebook. Despite my exhaustion, I feel somehow lighter than I have in months—since Miami, probably. Every interview I've conducted so far has moved me, given me hope. Dahua calls over to his mother to bring the *chicha,* and politely inquires whether I'd like some. Mario looks up at my face and snorts. "Virginia's *chicha* is delicious," he sings. "Don't miss out."

This must be the twentieth time I've been offered *chicha* in under twenty-four hours. *"Bueno.* Hand it over." Virginia comes, smiling as she proffers the bowl. I grimace and take a sip. Okay. Okay. Not bad, really. Sake with sass.

Later in the week, I will help Marcia as she makes the family *chicha.* I will take large handfuls of boiled, mashed yucca and fill my mouth, chewing and chewing and then simply sitting with engorged cheeks —as instructed—trying my best not to gag. And Marcia will laugh and laugh at the squirrel-cheeked gringa, laugh until I can't take it anymore and yucca is coming out my mouth, out my nose, yucca all over their floor, half-choking, the two of us rolling around in hysterics.

"What do you think?" asks Mario. "Do you like it?"

"Claro. Es muy rica." I reach for the bowl.

The next morning Mario is taciturn, brooding. "Are you okay?" I ask, as we sit down to breakfast. The *wasi* is unusually quiet: Marcia has gone off to classes, Fidel and Ligia to school.

"I had a bad dream." Terse. He spears a few slices of the fried plantain Marcia has left on the table. Spoons coffee into hot water. And then sugar. One, two, three.

"I'm sorry. Do you want to talk about it?" I help myself to some plantain. Outside, the Bobonaza ambles at a steady gait. The sun has shouldered its way through the clouds, and everything dazzles, every last leaf is cluttered with the costume jewelry of daybreak. It's the kind of morning that makes me want to belt out an aria.

Mario takes a swig of coffee and clears his throat. "I was working in a factory." His voice is low. "A huge factory, with people in long lines. All the other workers were wearing ear protectors. But not me." He considers the plantain, lays down his fork, scowls. "My ears were deafened by the noise. I walked outside and came to a river." Shaking his head. "But not a clean river, like the Bobonaza. It was a river of chemicals, red and black. I walked through it and it burned my feet." Now he looks at me, fierce, so fierce that I am struggling to hold his gaze. Mario is a man of great dignity and composure. That was evident within two minutes of meeting him. He's the kind of person who leads by nature. I'm learning just by watching. But this morning Mario is like I have not yet seen him: hard, smoldering. He turns away now, to the jungle, to the river. "My heroes are Gandhi and Mandela." Resolute. "We will not sink to violence."

A gargantuan butterfly flits into the *wasi*, drifts casually across to the other side and then, with a single languid beat of stained-glass wings, out into the sunlight.

Mario's hands are clenched around his mug. "If they come with weapons, they'll have to kill us to get in here." Quietly: "Then the world will see that there has been a massacre, and there will be an outcry."

The massacre in Ecuador's northern Amazon has been slow and skulking, shape-shifting into all kinds of macabre perversities: neurological disorders, spontaneous abortions, extraordinarily high rates of cancer; vanishing game and ruined soil. And the banshees of cultural genocide: displacement, alcoholism, prostitution.

In 1971 Texaco entered Block 1. In 1991, carpetbags dripping dollars, they departed, and Ecuador's state oil company took over the operations. "People in Block 1 are sick," says Luis Yanza, who works at the Ecuadorean NGO Frente de Defensa de la Amazonia, which is coordinating a historic $1.5 billion class-action lawsuit against Chevron-Texaco. I met with him in Quito before coming to Sarayacu. "They are still drinking contaminated water. Their animals are dying. They can't cultivate the land."

The more I learn, the more horrified I am. Three decades of drilling have produced 18,000 miles of seismic trails (set with explosives every hundred yards to sound for oil), 339 wells, 300 miles of roads, and 600 toxic waste pits. Yet thanks to the work of some very dedicated activists, this disaster has also become a powerful educational tool. Acción Ecológica and the Center for Economic and Social Rights have organized visits between indigenous communities in the north and south. Leaders from the north discuss the many impacts of oil exploitation, and speak about how the oil companies have deceived them regarding these impacts. Those from the south witness for themselves the fallout from the worst oil disaster in the western hemisphere.

Every indigenous person I talk with in Ecuador knows about

the disaster in its northern Amazon. The Sarayacu's resistance has everything to do with Block 1. And when it comes to the future of Ecuador's southern Amazon, all eyes are on Sarayacu.

Day Five.

The army helicopter hovers like a holdover from the Mesozoic era, massive, small-brained, coolly surveying its prey. It lowers and settles into the runway clearing, the long grasses flattening in frenetic undulations as the blades ease into visibility, the engine drones toward silence. It seems as if all of Sarayacu is gathered here. What is going on? Why are they coming? I ask around me, pad and pen at the ready, but no one knows.

The belly snaps open. The community hangs back, anxiety skittering about like something feral and trapped. My heart gallops at a manic pace. Will they come out shooting? I move forward shakily, conscious of my status as a gringa and a journalist.

First emerge civilians, waving and shouting in greeting. Then come the soldiers, uniformed but unarmed. A few of Sarayacu's leaders walk toward them, Mario included, and I follow.

"Colonel Marco Rentería," says one of them, giving a gap-toothed grin, shaking hands. Mario and the others introduce themselves, wary, waiting to hear what this is about. Mario gestures toward me. "A journalist from the United States."

"Mucho gusto, mucho gusto." He pumps my hand vigorously. "I very much look forward to visiting your country myself one day." Rentería is thickset, red-faced beneath the brim of his cap. He puts his arm around me and addresses everyone else as I squirm. "This is a federally funded medical visit," he declares. "We are here in response to your invitation."

The doctors, as it turns out, were indeed invited, although months earlier. The military, of course, were not. One of the soldiers is strolling around filming everything. When asked to put the camera away, he protests, then complies when Rentería orders him to.

The visitors are escorted across the river to a palm-roofed gathering spot atop the bluff adjoining Sarayacu Center. A circle of chairs is arranged: Rentería and the soldiers on one side, Sarayacu representatives on the other. The Sarayacu officially welcome the visitors. Then: "It's uncomfortable for us that you are in uniform," says David Malaver Santi, a Sarayacu leader. "As a community, our experience with uniforms has been frightening."

Rentería listens, nodding, the radio at his belt sputtering intermittently with unintelligible directives. When it is his turn, he stares at the ground for a while, apparently lost in weighty contemplation. Letting the apprehension blossom. "I have worked IN THE AMAZON for twenty-three years," he finally begins, voice booming. It isn't an oratorical affectation, I realize after a minute; it's just the way he speaks. He looks at the faces around him, arms flailing emphatically. "We have NO INTENTION of dividing this territory. You are OUR BROTHERS. We are FILLED WITH HAPPINESS to bring and distribute WHAT YOU NEED."

I do not trust him. I turn to look at Mario. He is standing with his arms crossed, sturdy body tense. Mouth compressed. Eyes vacant, looking nowhere and beyond nowhere.

I think of the burning red-black river, and of the butterfly.

"Why was the soldier filming?"

"We film LIKE TOURISTS DO. It's routine, just a graphic reference."

By this point I've had a good deal more practice asking difficult questions. And it's definitely easier when I don't like the person I'm interviewing. "Will the video be used to assist the army in escorting the CGC?"

Rentería's flushed face flushes deeper. "No, OF COURSE NOT." He's angry, now, at the gringa journalist with her spotless principles, her holier-than-thou politics. It's easy to be virtuous when you live in gringo-land. "We are here to HELP THEM DEVELOP. Nothing more. NOTHING MORE. Look around. Don't you think there can be MORE PROGRESS here?"

We are sitting on two stools outside Sarayacu's dilapidated clinic. The line of mothers stretches well out the door. Mothers with babies in their arms, children hanging on their thighs. They are coughing and whimpering, or pale and quiet with exhaustion, these children. Blank-eyed and bloated, with the species of stolid endurance largely unknown to children of the industrialized world. Inside, I watched for over an hour as the pediatrician handed out drugs for parasites. "They still drink the river water," she told me, shaking her head.

Rentería leans forward until his face is inches away, small black eyes beating into mine. He's liking me less and less. "There are TWO TYPES of invasions," he rasps coldly. The back of his shirt is dark with sweat. "VIOLENT and peaceful. This is a PEACEFUL invasion. NOT like the U.S. in Iraq. Now that was terrible. Your government DID NOT CARE AT ALL what the people of the world thought."

If he's trying to piss me off, this is definitely the wrong tack. In fact I'm starting to develop a moderate affinity for the Colonel.

"Look, Maritza"—leaning back now, hands off—"government is government. It changes." And forward again, eyes rapt. "But THE ARMY IS PERMANENT. Our role is in the constitution. What we do is serve our country. Nothing more. NOTHING MORE." His arms are outstretched and thrashing. This man has missed his calling. He belongs in the pulpit, not the barracks. *Give yourself to Christ. Nothing more. NOTHING MORE.* All that fire and brimstone, wasted. "And so"—the denouement, now, with a rapid flourish of palms—"we JEALOUSLY GUARD OUR BORDERS to keep our own people safe."

I wait. I have a feeling he's not done yet. With most people I interview, I need to actually pose questions. Others, however, multitask.

Rentería inhales sharply, lifts an index finger. "You see, Ecuador is a DEVELOPING country. Our MAIN PROBLEM is our POVERTY. But you know what the REAL PROBLEM is?"

"Tell me, Colonel."

Rentería smiles, visibly more relaxed. He's liking me again, now that I'm not picking fights. Maybe the gringa isn't quite as naive as he'd thought. "The MOST serious problem, OF COURSE, is GLOBALIZATION." He is gesticulating again, arms waving in an interpretive dance. Taking in more than this country, more even than this continent. "You see, *señorita,* we are LOSING the concept of BOUNDARIES." Those arms are taking in the whole world now, all seven of the Continents Formerly Known as Pangaea, the whole GOING-TO-HELL-IN-A-HANDBASKET planet with its EVERY-COLOR-IN-THE-RAINBOW races, its grab bag of religions and cargo of cultures, so intricately and fabulously diverse that EVEN the MOST INVENTIVE human brain would FAIL ABYSMALLY to grasp its proportions.

He's got me there. I lay down my pen and smile broadly at the colonel. And Rentería — soldier, preacher, citizen of the world — steps down from his pulpit and smiles back.

The Colonel has a point. Ecuador owes $14 billion to international creditors, who refuse to forgive the debt, citing the nation's oil reserves as assets to be liquidated. The International Monetary Fund is pressing Ecuador to pry open its southern Amazon, in order to continue making interest payments and receiving loans. "Oil," says Martínez of Acción Ecológica, "is at the heart of all the social and environmental crises here." Oil accounts for close to half of Ecuador's national income (its chief customer is the U.S.). But 70 to 80 percent of the nation's oil revenues go directly to servicing the interest on its debt. In thirty-five years of drilling, Ecuador's debt has only increased. So, for that matter, has its poverty rate: from 47 percent of the population in 1967 to 70 percent in 2000.

"Globalization," said Rentería, and when globalization meets oil, it's no holds barred. If Ecuador isn't proof enough, we need only look to a more contentious corner of the globe. Less than a week after invading Iraq, the Bush administration began handing out contracts for the "reconstruction." Dick Cheney's former employer Halliburton won the largest initial prize: overseeing repair work to Iraq's oil infrastructure. In late May 2003, Bush signed Executive Order 13303, granting complete legal immunity to any U.S. company that produces, ships, or distributes Iraqi oil. Spills, explosions, labor debacles, impacts upon communities and the environment: all were exempted from any form of accountability. Chevron-Texaco began transporting oil out of Iraq as early as June. ("Iraq possesses huge reserves of oil and gas," said Ken Derr, CEO of Chevron-Texaco, in 1998, "reserves I would love Chevron to have access to.") British Petroleum followed in July 2003, and eight other oil giants hastily queued up to claim their spoils.

Despite all evidence to the contrary, the Ecuadorean government continues to promise that oil exploitation will bring development. "Development?" scoffs Mario. "The word *development* is a lie. It only means poverty for the indigenous. The 'developers' have wreaked five hundred years of barbarism in our world." I ask him about the line at the clinic. Yes, he concedes, there is value in some western medicine. "Development itself is not the problem. We have our own alternative development; the difference is that it is sustainable."

As I learn over the course of enough interviews that my hand starts cramping up, Sarayacu is home to a number of groundbreaking programs. In collaboration with a German university, the community has developed a sophisticated plan for natural resources management. The community has also created an indigenous education system, extending from preschool to university. And the women of Sarayacu run a microlending bank, the Caja Ahorro y Crédito, which began with fifteen members and currently offers assistance to seventy-two. Marcia is the elected director of the Caja—a task she juggles along with mothering, studying, and the numerous household demands of a Sarayacu wife. Traditionally, Sarayacu's women have been conscribed to the domestic sphere. But the active role women played in the resistance offered the community a memorable lesson in feminism, and conceptions of gender roles have adjusted accordingly. As Marcia puts it, when I interview her in the Caja office: "During the resistance, the men saw that the women were stronger and more courageous. Not only were the women confronting the workers, they were also making the food and *chicha* for the camps."

"How did you confront the workers?" I certainly wouldn't want to get on the wrong side of this woman. I'd place bets on her over Rentería any day.

"We would challenge them, shouting that this is our territory, and we wouldn't let them pass."

These women could have taught us a thing or two back in

Womyn Aloud. I ask Marcia if she was afraid, and she pins me with the same look she gives her children when they say something particularly obtuse. "No, of course not." Impatient with my questions now, ready to get on with the work at hand. "The company officials and workers are people, just like us. Why would we be afraid?"

Mario steers the canoe expertly downriver, standing straight-backed at the rear. I squat low in the middle and cling to the sides. I have not an iota of balance in this vessel, and get nervous even rising to clamber onto the banks—a source of high merriment for Fidel and Ligia, who relish rocking it and hearing me screech. We are headed to Sarayacu Pista, where the runway lies. My visit to Sarayacu is drawing to a close, but my leave-taking depends on the next plane to arrive from Puyo, and we're not sure whether it's coming today or tomorrow. I sit with Atanacio in amiable silence, chewing on the leathery jungle peanuts, while Mario goes to check.

"No plane today," he announces, upon return. I try to hide my disappointment. The more I've seen of Sarayacu, the more of its people I've met, the more I am in awe of this incredible community. My time here has been revelatory, and so I'm rather ashamed to discover how much I'm itching to return to showers and mattresses. But then I'm also eager to get back to write my stories. By now, I've collected enough material for a dissertation.

Mario watches me. "Want to go to a party?"

"A party?" I conjure up visions of icy cocktails with miniature hot-pink umbrellas and stuffed olives. Women in slithery satin dresses and stiletto heels, floating above the mud. Dapper-clad men lining up to buy me drinks. I smooth the bedraggled nest atop my head self-consciously. By this point I must have at least two respectable dreadlocks.

"Why yes, I'd love to. What kind of a party?"

"A graduation party for one of the high school seniors."

"I see. Is that what the racket is all about?" Strains of pop music are drifting tinny from somewhere across the river.

"*Sí. Vámonos.*"

The party is in a palm-covered yard adjoining a *wasi,* and our arrival is greeted with shouts of welcome — barely audible, however, over the bleating of the giant speakers. *Mi corazón, I would give everything I own to kiss your sweet lips.* As with other social gatherings I've attended here, the women are sitting in one corner, murmuring quietly together over babies and the *chicha* urn. I, as usual, follow Mario into the ring of men. The women are friendly, but I seldom have anything to contribute to their conversation. It takes me all of about three minutes to run out of interesting things to say about babies or *chicha.*

"Marisa, Ramiro." Mario leads me to a young man in a button-down shirt. His hair has been coaxed into a towering wave with a good half-bottle of pomade. "Ramiro is the graduate."

Ramiro is also thoroughly smashed. *"Mucho gusto."* He smiles, revealing two rows of oversized and blindingly perfect teeth. He sways, steadies himself, and bows gallantly. "Care to dance?"

"No thanks. I'll just sit over here." I scurry over to an available spot on a bench. Ramiro follows. Mario, curse him, sees a friend and deserts me.

"You are the journalist from California, right?"

"That's me."

"Welcome to Sarayacu." Again, that smile. I squint back at him. "Thanks."

"Would you like to dance?" The hostess arrives just then, bowl of *chicha* at the ready. I accept it and drain half the contents. The stuff is growing on me. Ramiro asks again, scooting toward me a couple of inches. I scoot away a few more. "No, thank you."

"Please."

"I really don't feel like it."

"Please, please, please." The boy is begging.

"No. Maybe later." I invoke the unyielding tone of voice used for dog training. "Not now."

"But why not?" Guileless as a five-year-old.

Hmm. Let's see. Because I already said no twice, obviously am not remotely interested, and feel sufficiently self-conscious without prancing about gawkily in the middle of the circle. Because the men on the other side of you who are prattling away in Quichua keep looking over here and hooting. Because if your hair comes within inches of my face, I'm going to break out. Because your teeth scare me. "I—I'm just not in the mood."

"But dancing feels so good." Ramiro gets up and proceeds to energetically shake what his mama gave him. Which isn't, at least from this vantage point, a whole lot, although he scores extra credit for enthusiasm. The men in the circle cheer boisterously. "Dance with him! Come on, dance!" I shake my head, unmoved. A new contender materializes in my peripheral vision. Gray and paunchy, but no less tenacious. Ah, men. It makes not a whit of difference where you are on the planet.

"*Corazón,* let's dance." He's missing a few teeth, but that giant rhinestone belt buckle just about compensates. Gracious me, here comes the hostess again, thank the lord, with the *chicha*. I suck it down like water. "I do declare, this *chicha* is no less than exquisite." Handing back the bowl. "The crème de la crème of *chichas*. You simply must give me the recipe. What's your secret?" She stares down at me, smiles, heads back to the urn. Gramps leans in, breath ripe. "Come on, just a little salsa."

"Not now. I've got a headache. Maybe tomorrow." I leap up, scuttle across the circle to where Mario is sitting, and plop down awkwardly next to him.

"Why won't you dance?" Mario is chuckling.

"I don't feel like it. Why don't they ask any of the other women?"

"They know they have no chance."

Mario is sitting next to Franco, another leader type in his early thirties. I met Franco a few days ago and liked him instantly; he is candid, thoughtful, needle-sharp. The local philosopher. With a splendid mullet in the bargain.

"We were just talking about another recent graduate, who left and went to Quito."

"We think he may be a... a... " Franco is reluctant. "I think there's a good chance he is a... homosexual." Grave.

"Uh-huh. And?"

"Well, that's rather serious. To be a homosexual is... it's wrong."

"*Wrong?*" I can feel my hackles rising, pricking to attention like well-regimented foot soldiers. Mario is silent, listening. "I'm the wrong person to have this conversation with, Franco. I'm from the Gay

Fiefdom." Blank faces. "San Francisco. You know, heaps upon heaps of happy queens and glowering dykes."

"*Perdón?*"

"I come from a place where there are a lot of homosexuals. I don't think it's wrong." Where's the *chicha*? I spy the hostess, playing hooky in the womenfolk corner. "*Amiga, por favor, más chicha!*" She laughs at me.

"Well, it's definitely not natural." Franco is distressed. "God didn't make us this way for no reason."

"Did God make women to be warriors?"

"God made women to be mothers, to raise children." This is a line so hackneyed it's threadbare. He knows it, and he knows what's coming next.

"That's not what you were saying during the resistance." I glance over at the women in the corner, hoping faintly that one will leap up with a mutinous howl. And then bring over the *chicha*.

"True." His head is lowered, his palms face upward. "We men learned a good lesson. But that was different. That was protecting the community. This is dangerous to the community." A few nods from the men around us, who have quieted to listen in on the debate. "What if he forced his homosexuality on others?" Franco is getting riled, gesturing sharply. "What if he turned normal people into homosexuals? That would be a menace to Sarayacu." Franco's left hand is missing two fingers. He sits back, now, delicately unruffling his feathers. Taking his left hand into his right, he massages the stubs of knuckle.

I ask him if he is attracted to men, which elicits yelps of mirth from those around us.

"Of course not!" He is incensed again.

"If a man came on to you, would that change?" He regards me silently. Waiting. I'm not telling him anything he hasn't figured out. But I'm going to say it anyway, partly because I still haven't learned to keep my mouth shut, but mostly because Sarayacu has been an amazement to me, and I know it is capable of this too. I tell him that if homosexuality was accepted here, it may turn out that there are a few more homosexuals than he'd thought, but that would be because they were already there. And they would no longer feel the need to leave. The men around us shake their heads and mutter, but Franco has his elbows on his knees and his face in his hands, examining the ground. Quiet.

The hostess rolls up with the *chicha*. Franco takes a swallow, passes it to me. I sip daintily. I'm detecting the inauspicious beginnings of a fearsome headache.

Then he looks up, cocks his head coyly. He's rather attractive, once you get past the mullet. "Care to dance, *amiga?*"

"I'd like nothing better."

And then we are up and whirling around the dance floor, *ay mi amor, how you tease me,* Franco firmly in the lead, very serious as I giggle helplessly, surrendering without grace to my assigned role as the muddy, stinking, flea-bitten belle of the ball.

I have only a few hours left in Sarayacu and I have come here, to the banks of the Bobonaza. I lay out my poncho and settle down on it, journal and a book of poetry beside me. Then I sit, meditating on the sound of the river, its many conversations, the sweep and song and scour of it. I open my eyes to circus tents of green far across the wide brown scrawl, and closer, to the bobbing dugout, the spongy red earth before me. To the leaves dead and dying, the reeds sprouting resilient from the chaotic necropolis. And closer still, to a flock of tiny fungi, polished snowy lollipops atop stems so slender it's unfathomable they do not collapse. Then insight coasts, bursts, splashes soft in the back of my eyes.

Marcia's fearlessness. Atanacio's "real knowledge."

They have it, the Sarayacu.

They are it.

When the CGC announced it would enter Sarayacu in 2002, the matter went to the *Consejo Gobierno,* the democratic council that handles the logistics of running Sarayacu. But before any decisions were made, the question of organizing the Peace and Life camps was debated by the entire community at a lengthy people's assembly. Every major decision the Sarayacu have made has been through a thorough and open process of consensus.

They took their battle to the Organization of American States, and they won. The Inter-American Court of Human Rights found in favor of the Sarayacu over the state of Ecuador, commanding the government to "comply strictly and immediately... in order to effectively protect the life, personal integrity and free movement of all members of the indigenous people of Sarayacu." But the Sarayacu didn't stop there. "This is a battle of all the peoples of Amazonia," Mario told me minutes after I met him. The community played a key role in organizing a two-day summit with representatives from all five indigenous groups in Ecuador's southern Amazon; out of the summit emerged an alliance of 100,000 people and an unprecedented mutual-defense pact against oil exploitation. "This isn't happening anywhere else in the Amazon," says Koenig of Amazon Watch. "These are historic adversaries. But there is a common threat now, with the Sarayacu thrust to the forefront."

There is no doubt in my mind that the Sarayacu will win this battle, no matter how much the government blusters or the corporations cudgel. They have it. They are it. Gandhi's *satyagraha,* his way of truth and love. Martin Luther King's love that does justice. This is what a spiritually grounded campaign guided by life-centered principles looks like. This is the community rendered powerful through the empowered individual. This is where life encounters the struggle, laughing, and the struggle encounters life, and it is all simply the work at hand. This is direct democracy, feet firmly planted in the same soil on which we all stand.

"We are 'saved' through our own spirituality," said Mario, in conversation with Rentería. "Through our original knowledge that we are one, indivisible from the earth. Our ancestors, our knowledge, our programs: therein lies our salvation."

Amen.

I sit dazed, barely able to comprehend the magnitude of what I've been given. Much less hold it, or the gratitude that comes next, blazing like a flash flood, exploding clean and brilliant as lightning out of the dense jungle sky.

Ten:

Urubamba, Peru

"Adiós amigos! Take care!"

Pablo and Campbell stand waving on the riverbank, growing smaller and smaller against the long, skinny curve of bridge and the stocky cement houses. Ivochote: the last town in Peru's southeastern Amazon reachable by road, where last night we sat eating *sopa de gallo* as Arnold Schwarzenegger gunned down terrorists on a forty-inch TV and half the tiny town watched blank-eyed, squatting in front of the screen or hunched over the wall or reclining luxuriantly at tables over their pricey desserts. Across the street blared the competition: here the other half of the town sat, squatted, or hunched as Sylvester Stallone stalked his prey. "What do you think they did before TV?" asked Campbell. "Talked?"

Ivochote, being the jumping-off point into the remote lower Urubamba region, has made a modest mint since the Camisea Gas Project began. Or at least its two inns have.

Pablo and Campbell are still waving and hollering their good-byes. I will miss them. It astonishes me, traveling alone, how quickly strangers become family. Even after a few days shared, I miss new friends abjectly when we part. I wave until they are the size of my fingernail, then turn around, leaning into the wind, and settle onto my bench. I watch with satisfaction as the blade of our motorboat slices neat through the obliging glide of the Río Urubamba.

"Warm enough?" Rufo eyes me. It's early enough in the morning, and high enough in the Andean foothills, for the Amazon to be cool.

"*Sí, claro.* You?"

"I could use a warm body, but I'm not complaining." His eyes are amused, as usual, above the wide cheekbones, burly nose, plum lips.

I chortle. Rufo is a strategic planning consultant for a couple of Peru's indigenous organizations. I've known him going on four days now. But it's been a full four days.

"Too bad you left your girlfriend in Lima. You're just going to have to suffer, *pajero.*" We both laugh uproariously. The other passengers on the boat inspect us dubiously from behind their bundles and packages.

Pablo took it upon himself to enlighten Campbell and me in regard to a certain key Peruvian colloquialism. *Pajero:* from the paja leaves gathered on the high Andean plains, an epithet meaning both "redneck" and "masturbator." The four of us devoted at least a half-hour of hysterics to that one on our lengthy road trip to Ivochote. Things tend to loosen up right quick when you're bumping down an atrociously rutted, pothole-crammed, single-lane dirt road at forty miles an hour. "A little slower, perhaps?" I offered helpfully from the back, smiling solicitously in the rearview mirror at our just-kicked-puberty driver. "I like fast cars and loud music," he retorted, grinning behind mirror sunglasses, gunning the engine. "This," said Campbell, delicately dislocating himself from my chest, where he landed after one particularly enlivening jolt, "is when you truly feel the prayers of those who love you."

It was just past dawn when we loaded our bags into the boat, the sun still tucked drowsing under the horizon. First light was slow, reaching pale across the listening distance. Then quickening like it remembered what it came to do, remembered with a jerk of panic all those seeds waiting to crack, flowers dreaming of fruit, all the children creaking sleep-faced from under scratchy blankets, the mothers with their tasks lined up patient as sheep. Now the sun is officially out. I raise my face and it beats red through my eyelids, pours into my throat, prickles down my spine.

Rufo bellows something incomprehensible from a couple of benches up. I open my eyes reluctantly. "Yes?"

"We're getting close. Start paying attention."

The land is rising around us now, swelling until it is broad-shouldered and brash. The river narrows, the current grows urgent. I hold fast to the sides of the boat, watching the green above us, green everywhere it can get a foothold, trees clinging to cliffs or, to hell with it, bungee jumping straight over, vines leapfrogging without a second glance, leaves the size of my thigh hurdling one over the other to come to rest coquettish inches above the current.

"There it is," says Rufo, making his way toward me, hanging on to the sides as the boat gets tossed around like cardboard. He settles next to me to watch my reaction, but I am looking behind us at the boy steering the boat, at his tight frightened face and his companion barking out commands. I am wondering whether I should be terrified or merely worried. Then Rufo is tugging at my shoulder and I turn and we are in it, of it, the Pongo de Mainique, the Gran Pongo, the grandest Pongo of them all — or so the Machiguenga thought when they named it, and I fully concur; as magnificent a sight as I've ever seen or will ever see; water everywhere, water bursting from the rock face, water trickling and spurting and cascading from skyscraper cliffs, heaving through cracks and crannies and over whole walls, torrents jostling on all sides. Rainbows a dime a dozen. Waterfalls by the fistful. Machiguenga legend holds that a river demon lurks here, but what I see are endless blooming blossoms of white taffeta, a line of brides perpetually awaiting their prince. I can barely breathe. I am inside the veil now.

I arrived in Lima, Peru, on March 29, after a thirty-five-hour bus ride from Quito, Ecuador. I discovered, too late, that there was a major soccer game taking place in the city at the same time as the Inter-American Development Bank (IDB) summit. By the time I looked into flights, they were all booked. But I had to get to Lima for the summit, because that's where I was scheduled to meet up with Pablo —the president of the Federation of Indigenous Machiguenga and my contact for my second story on globalization and indigenous communities in the Amazon. Also, I'd been reading up on the IDB, and I knew that there would be activists from all over the continent demonstrating against it. I filed my articles on the Sarayacu, packed my bag, and got on the bus.

Two hours after reaching Lima, I arrived at the Museo de la Nación, where the summit was taking place. The area surrounding the museum in central Lima had been cordoned off for three blocks, and 2,500 armed militia were patrolling the blockades. It took me a while to locate the protesters. They were rallying in the permitted area, well beyond earshot of those attending the conference. *"No al BID!"* chanted indigenous leaders in feathered headdresses. Activists milled about, greeting friends, grumbling over the heat. Some crouched on the sidewalk, sharing soft drinks and talking shop. I roamed through the scattered crowd, exhausted but happy, spiked on adrenaline. There were representatives from Peru's indigenous groups and from NGOs, and labor and environmental activists from across the hemisphere. All sorts of people with lengthy catalogs of grievances to present to the Bank.

The IDB is financing the controversial Camisea Gas Project, and that's what I came to write about. Deemed by Amazon Watch to be "the most damaging project in the Amazon basin," the Camisea project is located smack in the middle of one of the most biologically diverse regions in the world: the Urubamba. Home to the Machiguenga, Nanti, Nahua, and Yine indigenous communities, the Urubamba also contains vast pools of natural gas. Up to 75 percent of gas extractions are to be operated within a state reserve set aside for indigenous communities living in voluntary isolation. A contractor for Pluspetrol, lead operator of extractions in the lower Urubamba, recently violated internationally recognized indigenous rights by contacting members of the Nahua tribe living in this reserve. In the 1980s, when Shell was conducting drilling in the area, up to half of the Nahua population was annihilated by diseases introduced by the workers. In addition to the gas extractions, the $1.6 billion project has a second consortium managing transport: the Transportadora de Gas del Perú, or TGP, is constructing two pipelines leading all the way to the Peruvian coast. A processing plant is being built within the buffer zone of a marine reserve.

The Camisea project proposal was so flawed that the Overseas Private Investment Corporation, the United States Export-Import Bank, and Citigroup all rejected requests for financing. But in September 2003, the IDB, notorious for its bare-bones environmental policy, approved a $75 million direct loan and a $60 million syndicated loan. The Camisea project is not the Bank's only controversial investment: it is funding a laundry list of projects that have environmental and social justice activists up in arms across Latin America.

The World Bank has such a high profile that it has been the target of extensive scrutiny. In contrast, the IDB has succeeded in remaining quietly beyond the spotlight of your average western activist. I'd never heard of it before researching this story. "Public pressure has modified the policies of the World Bank," Juan Houghton, an organizer with the Indigenous Organization of Colombia, tells me. He is demonstrating outside the Museo. "So now the IDB does its dirty work. It makes loans in order to facilitate privatization and corporate investments." Indeed, the IDB evinces a rather unsettling tendency to issue loans directly in line with structural adjustments imposed by the International Monetary Fund—such as, say, opening up energy resources to maintain debt payments. "The IDB is a tool of the IMF," Houghton says. The IMF dictates the policies, and the IDB provides the financing—at a price, of course. Despite the "Inter-American" in its name, the IDB's "nonregional members" include roughly a dozen European countries, Japan, Israel, and South Korea. And while the Bank is owned by its forty-seven member governments, voting power is proportional to capital contributions—and the U.S. holds 30 percent of the votes.

According to a study by the Sustainable Energy and Economy Network, the IDB invested $6.27 billion in financing forty-nine fossil fuel pipeline, power, and sectoral reform projects between 1992 and 2004. These projects together will generate over double the emissions produced by all of Latin America in 2000. Of the top fifteen corporate beneficiaries, half are based in the U.S., and only one in Latin America. The TGP—the Camisea gas transport consortium—is but part of a vast transportation network in the making, an ambitious integration of infrastructure to steer the movement of energy and other resources northward.

Back in Camisea, a full half of the gas being extracted is destined for shipment to the west coast of the U.S. But as it happens, Peru has other things to worry about besides oversensitive ecosystems or the quality of life for a few thousand natives. The country is in debt to the tune of $30 billion, with the IMF hovering like Don Corleone at the door. Peru's principal creditor is the IDB. If I were Peru, I'd keep my mouth shut, too.

I locate Pablo inside the NGO room of the summit. He is loud, jovial, with bulldog jowls and an immense belly. He introduces me to Campbell, a biologist collecting data for Amazon Watch. Campbell is affable and bespectacled, a master of the grammatically flawless, twangily American variety of gringo Spanish. Along the way we pick up Rufo, and the next morning the four of us fly east to Cuzco. From Cuzco we take an eight-hour bus to Quillabamba. Then we hire a car and driver, drive six hours, and we're in the Upper Urubamba region. The four of us will spend a couple of days meeting with Machiguenga, and then Rufo and I will continue on by boat into the far-flung wilds of the Lower Urubamba. I do not have a commitment from a publication for this story yet, but I feel it's an important one, so I plan to write it anyway and then shop it around to some of the progressive magazines. After I'm back in the U.S., *Earth Island Journal* picks it up.

I've read Mario Vargas Llosa's *The Storyteller,* and I am intensely curious about these people, the Machiguenga, who have been persecuted since the time of the Incas. They were enslaved during the rubber boom, decimated by malaria and smallpox, and wooed by a colonial God through the exploits of Jesuit, Franciscan, and Protestant missionaries. Many of the Machiguenga fled to the depths of the jungle, living in voluntary and complete isolation. In the 1940s evangelical missionaries entered the Urubamba with the goals of translating the New Testament into native languages, spreading Christianity, and generally "Peruvianizing" the indigenous peoples. These missionaries trained schoolteachers and health workers, started community stores, and introduced the Machiguenga to cash crops and commerce. While they ultimately succeeded in tethering the Machiguenga to the outside world, it took decades of devoted toil on the part of the missionaries to win some of these people over. How, I wonder, are the Machiguenga handling this new breed of zealots? Have the prizes of hydrocarbon exploitation proven as compelling as eternal salvation?

The first place we visit in the Upper Urubamba is Shimaa, a community of six hundred that lies directly in the path of the TGP pipelines. We are seated across from a semicircle of village representatives, who proceed to detail their grievances, one of them translating from Machiguenga into Spanish.

"There was a water tank that burst because of their construction," says Laura, young and heart-faced, her voice cracking. "From the landslides. Now, whenever the river rises or it rains, we drink dirty water. And also my field of coffee and medicinal plants was ruined when they laid their lines."

"The TGP offered us their support," says Angel, thirty-something and resentful. "So we signed the paper. But they haven't followed through. The clinic has not a single pill. There is no teacher for the primary school. They made promises, but we have nothing to show for it."

And then there was the gas spill in September 2003, offers another. There used to be a lot of animals and fish, but now there are none. And the diseases, adds a fourth. Malaria, dengue, diarrhea. Yes, and the house they built in compensation for one destroyed by a landslide: terribly constructed. And the noise from the machines. The bridge they promised.

I grow depressed listening to them. Fierce with empathy, but the brand of empathy that climbs walls in a windowless room. They believe they are defeated, these people. I remember Mario and Marcia in Sarayacu, and I look at the bleak faces before me, the hands leaden in their laps; I listen to the voices, barren as dry riverbeds, and I think, they are defeated already.

When they are done, Pablo lectures them. "Don't sign anything until it's properly arranged," he scolds, and they hang their heads like penitent children. "You should know this already. Nothing good comes from these companies." I look away, cringing, trying to make sense of my emotions. Pablo is right, yet his paternalism riles me. I feel pity and embarrassment for the villagers, but also disappointment at their submissiveness, at their aura of defeat. Then I am angry with myself: who am I to pity them, to be disappointed?

After the meeting, Damian Torres Esteban, the president of Shimaa, takes us to see the project. A 20- to 25-meter-wide path has been razed through the forest for the pipelines. The builders did not bother to cover the pipes with earth. They snake down the hill, across the river, and continue west in zigzagging lines until they fade into the horizon. They have been constructed along the ridgetop: the shortest, cheapest, and most environmentally destructive option. Consequent erosion has led to the heavy landslides that Laura mentioned.

The top of the hill is shaved clean. A generator buzzes insistently; behind barbed wire squats the shiny yellow jungle gym of a pump.

"There's one every eight to ten kilometers," a guard tells me. He is young, sullen, reluctant to talk. "There are two of us stationed here at all times, to guard the pump." I ask him if he has friends in Shimaa. "No," he says. "We are prohibited from talking with the community." I feel a wash of sympathy for these pariahs. "It's the law," he continues, eyes on the skyline above my shoulder. "We don't bother them."

The final phase of the Camisea Gas Project is the construction of a plant to liquefy gas for export to the U.S. This will cost another $1 billion to $2 billion. The lead corporation is Texas-based Hunt Oil, which splits majority shareholder status in the Camisea consortia with Pluspetrol. Ray L. Hunt, the chief executive officer of Hunt Oil, is close to the Bush family: George W. appointed Hunt finance chairman of the Republican National Committee's Victory 2000 committee, and Hunt secured the status of a Bush "Pioneer" by raising over $100,000 for his buddy. Hunt also sits on the board of Halliburton, Dick Cheney's former clubhouse, and Kellogg Brown & Root, a subsidiary of Halliburton, is in line to build the plant. The site is a scant five miles from the 830,000-acre Paracas National Park, Peru's sole marine sanctuary for endangered birds and sea lions.

It's simple geometry to connect the dots between the Bush administration's approval of this project and the generosity showered upon him by the oil and gas industry in 2000. According to the Center for Responsive Politics, Bush's campaign received $1.7 million from the oil and gas sectors, over three times the amount given to the industry's next most-favored candidate.

After parting from Pablo and Campbell and crossing the Gran Pongo, our first stop in the Lower Urubamba is the community of Nuevo Mundo. Rufo and I gather our bags and clamber off the boat and up the riverbank. Before us lies a wide clearing lined with small tin-roofed wooden houses, loosely constructed, separated by patches of palm and hibiscus. Teenagers are playing volleyball. Peruvian pop blasts from somewhere. Rufo asks a passerby if he can direct us to the president of the community, telling him Pablo sent us.

The man eyeballs me, then squints up at Rufo in a not especially friendly way. "It's Sunday. He's drinking beer with his friends. I'll let him know you're here." He walks off.

Rufo turns to me. "Well then. What do you say we get something cold to drink?"

We are now officially in the Amazon basin, deep in the lowlands, and it feels like being sautéed. What's more, my belly's been acting rather odd lately. I generally take great pride in my cast-iron stomach: I only got sick once in India, and by month four I was drinking the tap water. But lately this mutinous organ has been sending me lurching off on frantic dashes to the bathroom at least five times a day. I'm definitely off-kilter, and I resolve to begin taking my antimalarials. At least I can try to fend off that evil.

We locate the closest thing to the village café — a family that cooks food and sells soft drinks — and collapse at the table. Three hours later, Ismael, the president of Nuevo Mundo, shows up, a mite toasted but with a lot on his mind.

"The problem here," he begins pointedly, "is that we don't have coordination between communities." As it turns out, there are three Machiguenga organizations, constituted roughly along religious lines. The Federation of Indigenous Machiguenga is the Dominican branch. Nuevo Mundo belongs to the Organization of Indigenous Machiguenga of the Lower Urubamba, an Evangelical association.

Rufo and I are taken aback. Pablo had led us to believe that he was the elected president of the whole shebang. "Pablo didn't tell you that we were coming?"

"Not a word."

Once we get past that, pleasantries proceed, and the interview begins. I ask Ismael how the project has affected Nuevo Mundo.

"Well, we've seen a lot of change. As soon as money enters, there's change. Now, for example, we have beer. Actually" — defensive, sucking in his gut — "I like beer. But now we also have alcoholism. That's new." Speaking more slowly. "And the workers, they came in and talked with our youth. Now the young are more interested in leaving."

I ask him about the wildlife.

"The animals are gone." Sober now, his eyes on the dirt line where the bank veers down to the river. "There are no fish left in the Urubamba." Ismael considers the empty beer can on the table between us. He lifts it, tilts it, and sends it spinning down the table, where it drops onto the ground. No one moves to pick it up.

"We wanted development. We wanted tin for our roofs." He's waxing maudlin, the pleats on his round face creasing deeper with the sinking dusk. "But we were mistaken." He lifts his shoulders and straightens his spine, pulling himself together. "We have a different definition of development now: sustainable development, and it depends on us."

Rufo asks him if the community has a vision of the future, of how to proceed.

"No. Not really." He's downcast again, his Sunday beer-glow completely evaporated. "I guess what we want is to improve our community with running water and electricity. Also, and this is very important, we don't want to lose our biodiversity or our culture."

I feel the same despondency I felt in Shimaa. Are these just platitudes, or is he taking refuge in denial? He wants it all, but surely he understands what has already been lost.

"Do you have any kind of plan? A scenario of some sort?" Rufo is hopeful.

"No." Ismael's face is barely visible now. His eyes gleam dully in the dark, reflecting the electric lights snapping on a few houses away. His voice is flat, weary. "The company hasn't fulfilled their promises. I'm not sure exactly where things went wrong." A hand in the air, fending off invisible accusers. "Maybe we negotiated badly. I don't know."

Ismael tells us there is no place for us to sleep at Nuevo Mundo, and waves us on to our second destination, Kirigueti, a community ten minutes upriver.

Our first sight in Kirigueti is a huge television, sitting on a raised platform in the middle of a clearing in the jungle. Behind it, what looks like a home. Commercial jingles prod and jostle at top volume. No one is watching. We walk past, into the village. The homes are spread out evenly among the palms and tropical plants: new, tin-roofed, some of them two stories. Gas bulbs are strung about like Christmas lights.

No one here has been informed of our arrival, either. "Of course you can sleep here," says the vice president of the village, to our relief. He directs us to a platform on the outskirts. It is a raised bamboo structure with a palm-thatched roof and no walls.

We lay out what bedding we can concoct from the contents of our bags.

"Hungry?" Rufo is glum.

"Starved. What do we have, *amigo*?"

"Let's see. Ten pounds of rice. Ten pounds of sugar. Flour. Pasta. Gallons of vegetable oil. Tuna. Matches. Cookies."

Pablo instructed us to buy supplies to offer as gifts to the villagers, who, he'd assured, would house and feed us. We didn't bring any food to prepare for ourselves. Or pots and pans, for that matter.

"Sounds like the main course is tuna. And cookies for dessert."

We eat the oily chunks with our fingers.

"Not bad." Rufo's buoyancy is returning. "Could be worse."

"Could be raw pasta."

"Or vegetable oil with matches."

"Oh my—Rufo—what is that?" Something is moving at the edge of one of the bamboo slats we're sitting on. Scuttling. Glinting. And then I see them: antennae.

Shark fins knifing my way.

White-eyed zombies closing in.

"Cucarachas!" Rufo is laughing. "They're hungry too."

"Kill it, Rufo! Go get it! Please. Go!" But Rufo is rolling around on the floor in fits. "Please! If my friendship means anything to you! I'm begging!"

I can put up with a lot. Namibian giant jumping spiders? Sure. Baby scorpions? No problem. Tarantulas? They're kind of cute. Rattle-snakes? Okay, from a safe distance, fine. Even bedbugs in Singapore I dealt with. But not cockroaches. It's the antennae. The way they wriggle is satanic.

"Rufo! Rufo, please! Rufo... I think I'm going to... uh... vomit."

My belly is gurgling ominously. Months later, back in San Francisco,

I will find out I have giardia. For now, my belly has become a take-no-prisoners battleground, the Gettysburg of parasites. I crawl to the edge of the platform and retch. Rufo collects himself.

"Are you all right?"

I wipe my mouth and hoist myself back into a sitting position. My head is spinning, and I'm concentrating hard on not crying. Who do I think I am, for the love of god? Jane of the jungle? I just want to go home. I want my own bed, my own room, my own chunky granola and yogurt for breakfast when I wake up in my own civilized metropolis. Where smart cockroaches fear to tread. Where the TV is permanently off.

I avoid Rufo's eyes. "I'm fine. No thanks to you, *pajero*."

"I'm sorry."

"Yeah, I know. You should be."

We clean up the tuna cans and arrange ourselves in our improvised beds. Rufo reaches over and taps my elbow.

"Do you forgive me?"

"I suppose I can find it within myself to do so. But you have to swear to keep them away."

"Not a problem. Those fiends shrivel in terror when they get a load of Rufo the cockroach-slayer." His face is lit up, suddenly, in a fearsome scowl.

Lightning. Followed by the bone-crack of thunder.

We spend the rest of the night curling pathetically away from the chilly needles gusting through the open walls.

In the morning Rufo pays a local family to cook us breakfast. We gobble down our fried eggs and bananas, sitting on a mat in the yard with the family and their dogs and roosters and pet guinea pig.

"*Masato?*" The father offers me a plastic cup filled with something that vaguely resembles Pepto-Bismol. Or could it be...?

"Is that *chicha*?" My spirits are lifting already.

"What?"

"You know, *chicha*, from yucca. Boiled and pounded and chewed." They all look at me and laugh.

"We call it *masato* here," Rufo corrects gently.

"But we don't chew it," the father says, wiping his eyes. "We haven't done that in years. We have a hand-grinder." His wife retrieves it from a shelf, exhibits it with pride. No doubt that little gem of technology makes her life a whole lot easier.

But the flavor is bland, circumspect. The Miller Lite of *chichas*.

Rufo and I visit Kirigueti's clinic. Built by optimistic Catholic missionaries, it has a laboratory and pharmacy, as well as rooms for examinations, surgery, dentistry, gynecology, and pediatrics. But the clinic has no medical staff. The building is run down, the equipment obsolete. I walk slowly through the empty rooms, examining the dusty surfaces, running a hand over quaintly outmoded instruments. The despondency returns.

One hundred and fifty new cases of syphilis were recently reported in this community of two thousand. These cases can't be directly traced to the Camisea project, but the introduction of foreign workers has historically proven dangerous—or, as in the case of the Nahua, lethal—to indigenous populations. "Last year," Marcelino Turco, vice president of Kirigueti, tells me, "a full half of our community was sick with different diseases."

Pluspetrol paid the community $266,000 for the right to conduct a two-year project on their territorial land. But the payments have been divided among the families, rather than being invested in significant development programs—like staffing the clinics or schools. In some communities, the companies of the Camisea Consortia have tried to illegally extend their initial offers to cover the full forty-year estimated duration of the project. I think of the vast sums corporations in the U.S. invest in public relations. Here, they're not even bothering to pretend they're trying.

"Oh, yes, there have been many impacts, both positive and negative," says Father David, a missionary from the Basque region of Spain. We are sitting on his blessedly cool patio, next to a lovingly cultivated garden, sipping iced tea. For a minute I forget entirely where I am.

"On the positive end," he continues, "their living conditions have improved. For example, now they have tin for their roofs."

Father David has lived in Kirigueti for the past two years, after having ministered for several years to another community downriver. He is young, ivory-pale, with a narrow face and aquiline nose. He positively hums with energy: his fingers drumming on the table, his foot coaxing rhythms out of the concrete.

"But then there are the helicopters. I've never seen helicopters like here, twenty to twenty-five a day. Of course that affects the animals, the hunting." Father David speaks at breakneck speed, his Spanish thickly accented. His words blur pleasantly in my ears, a mellifluous and passionate sonata. And then, he continues, some of the young men go to work for the companies. That changes family and social dynamics. "Most tragically, one little girl drowned in the high waves from a cargo boat. They paid her family eighty thousand soles, but how can you compensate for that?"

You can't, I think, suddenly angry. You can't compensate for any of what is being destroyed right now. "Money comes and goes," said Dahua in Sarayacu. But here it's still coming, and I wonder if that's not for the worse.

Father David leans back, taps an elongated finger against his chin. What is needed, he tells us, is not development for the Lower Urubamba region, but rather development for the indigenous people of the Lower Urubamba. He sighs, fiddles with a crease in his robes. "Still, this is just the beginning. There will be unimaginable changes here. But you know what the worst impact of all of this is?"

Rufo and I shake our heads, both of us mesmerized by this intent, fast-talking believer.

"The worst of it is that they are forgetting how to do things for themselves. And this is the fault of the NGOs as much as the companies. The Machiguenga have come to believe that they have the right to all kinds of stuff, and that they deserve to have it handed to them on a platter."

For some reason what comes to me now is the Gran Pongo: the water cascading from the cliffs in stunning abundance, the white blossoms of taffeta.

The brides waiting for their prince.

On our way back upriver, we pay a visit to Camisea, the community nearest to the gas extractions. There is a large new building in the center of the village, and a second one is under construction. Piles of lumber lie about the central clearing. Electric saws drone. A huge bonfire is burning waste, and the smoke saturates the area, searing my nostrils, graying my vision.

We ask if we can speak to the village's leadership. By now we don't bother mentioning Pablo. "Certainly," says the first person we approach.

We are escorted to a low-ceilinged classroom, where we settle down into two of the desks. The walls are decorated with shiny Pluspetrol posters extolling the project's virtues. One lists its production capacities. Another details how modern and high-tech the operations are. A third catalogs its benefits to mankind. We wait.

"So sorry to keep you. I'm Bernave, vice president of the community of Camisea. And this is Camilo, the secretary." Bernave is young, unusually decorous in a button-down shirt. We all shake hands. He tells us that Miguel, the president, will be coming soon.

We sit, and I ask him how the project has affected Camisea.

"Very positively," says Bernave. "When the company came, we met and made agreements. They've fulfilled all the promises they made. They've helped us with the construction of new buildings and with electricity. They've also given us televisions, radio communication, and all the tin we need."

Rufo asks how the extractions have affected their natural resources.

"Oh, everything's fine with them."

"Do you still have the same numbers of wildlife?"

"Well, there aren't as many animals. The helicopter noise scared them away, so now we have to walk a day to find them. As for the fish—"

"There are hardly any fish left. I'm Miguel, glad to meet you." The president paces across the room, shakes our hands, and sits down next to the secretary, who is busily recording the interview. I ask him the same question I asked his vice president. His jaw tightens.

"It's affected us negatively in many ways. The animals and fish are gone. We have all kinds of new diseases: diarrhea, parasites, malaria, rabies." Miguel is middle-aged, grave, cautious. He weighs each word, gauging its heft and merit before putting it out for consumption. "They've only hired a few indigenous to work on the project." He

looks across the secretary, now, at Bernave. Suspicious. "As indigenous, we've always respected our cultural identity and customs. Now
we don't even wear our *cushmas,* our traditional dress, anymore."

Miguel watches Bernave, who is quietly examining his fingernails.
The secretary keeps scribbling furiously, although I'm not sure what
he is recording. I am astonished by the tension between these two
men. How do they work together? How do they lead Camisea?

"None of this is going to benefit us in the long run," Miguel continues, his face heavy, his voice low. "It's only going to benefit the
companies."

I am certain that he would rather not be here, rather not speak any
of this. He would rather not have this role, rather not be living in
these churning times. I feel an intense sympathy for him.

"Bernave," I hazard, when the silence is verging on unbearable.
"What do you think this community will look like in ten years?"

Bernave looks up, face instantly bright. "Oh, it will be totally different. We'll have electricity everywhere. And running water. Televisions
in all the homes, with a lot of different channels. Even the Internet."
He is eager. "We'll be very developed."

"Miguel?"

Miguel waits, bringing the ends of his fingers together and flexing
them gently. "It will be very different, Bernave, you are right."

He does not look at his vice president. Instead he watches my pen
as I take notes. He speaks as if dictating a shopping list: "Many more
colonists will come in. We will lose our animals. We will lose our natural resources."

The president of Camisea seems to be aging before my eyes, shrinking, a tired old man curling toward the anesthetic of a second infancy.
A Cassandra vanquished by his own prophecy, by the ears riveted to
the rumble of construction, the jangle of televisions. "Our children
will forget their traditions. We will lose our language." Speaking very
slowly now, each word a struggle, a step closer to the abyss. "Our way
of life will change completely. Yes, Bernave. For the Machiguenga,
things are going to be very different."

We are back in the boat, throbbing our steady way out of the Lower Urubamba. The flatlands gathering gradually into goose bumps, hinting at voluptuous curves. Rufo sits in the back chatting with the driver. I am on the very front bench, wind slamming at me, spray tickling. Pretending I am flying over the water. Skimming low, very low, close as muscle to bone. A sheer lining between river and sky and nothing more, just a layer spread thin, straddled by all the other layers. One striation of clay in shale. That's who I am right now. Lacking the organ to think. Or feel.

But it's not working. I lean into the wind, letting it lick the tears from the corners of my eyes, daub them cool across my cheeks.

The Camisea Gas Project will ruin the Machiguenga. It will trample their land, livelihood, and culture. And it is obliterating a heritage that belongs to all of humanity, for the Lower Urubamba is a region of global ecological import. The rainforest plays a crucial—and immeasurable—role in maintaining the delicate and mysterious balance of the earth's systems. The Amazon basin is the most biodiverse region on the planet, home to the world's largest expanse of tropical forest and one third to one half of all species. The basin is being destroyed at the rate of eight football fields a minute. Over the past century of exploitation approximately ninety Amazonian tribes have disappeared, vanished into oblivion when their homelands were destroyed.

In 2000 a Pluspetrol oil spill damaged one of the largest protected regions in Peru, the Pacaya-Samiria Reserve; it contaminated the food and water supplies of the Cocamas-Cocamillas community, wreaking havoc on their health. But unlike Ecuador, there has not been a Block 1 here. Yet. Is that what it takes? The people of the Urubamba are neither unified nor organized in defense of their land. They lack the political education to understand the future that awaits them: they can have either televisions or their traditions—either the money or the environment. But not both.

And many of them want the money, the stuff. Why not? Their lives are so arduous, so tenuous, so impoverished. Who am I to say what they should think or want? I'm a gringa with the resources to flit about the globe, with access to every sliver of technology I want, with the prerogative to turn up my nose at television. I'm no better than a two-bit bleeding heart sitting in a mobile ivory tower, mourning the demise of my idyllic fantasies of the natives. I am furious with myself, now, furious at my lofty ideals and my privilege, at my own guilt and at how I back up like a nervous colt in the face of it. Furious at the limits of journalism and furious also at them, the Machiguenga, for letting me down. I laugh, and the laughter rattles out soundless, invisible fists against the punchball of the wind.

How will I write this story? I came here to report on how corporate globalization is laying waste to communities and cultures and the environment. The Inter-American Development Bank, the IMF, and Bush Inc. all fit neatly into the framework of my own radical critique. And most of the Machiguenga I spoke with lament the effects the Camisea project has had on their culture and environment. Yet they are simultaneously riveted by the power and prizes of technology. They want these, and they want their culture and an uncontaminated environment to boot. They want it all, and they are being paralyzed by wanting it all. Father David faulted the NGOs for encouraging the people to believe that they deserve it all. But why shouldn't they have it all? Why can't they, when some of us do?

I came here to listen — or so I thought. I came to listen, but what do I do when the voices contradict my own? As a community, the Machiguenga are ambivalent, and their ambivalence, I predict, will likely destroy them. Can I be both radical and objective? What is objectivity, anyway, when the world is stark raving mad, when war is presented as just another foreign policy option, and pillaging an economic solution?

All journalists choose their quotes, I tell myself. Every writer has an angle, conscious or no. So do the progressive magazines for which I am writing, and their audiences know it. And so we should: there's no firm footing on the middle ground in a lopsided world. That's why I wanted to write these kinds of stories — so I could go beyond a glib synopsis that begins on an "objective" note and ends with the party line. Those of us who actually have some kind of feeble grip on the bigger picture — and have the freedom to explore and present that, as I do as a freelance writer — are obliged to, right?

But I wonder about the voices I will be leaving out. And whether, ten years from now, those whose stories I do tell will be grateful or angry. Will their grandchildren call them right or wrong? Traitors or visionaries? Will history call this tribe assimilated or broken?

I wonder if history will call them anything at all.

Maybe there will be a national holiday to commemorate the vanquished indigenous peoples of Peru. Families will dish up great steaming bowls of fried yucca and banana, drink chilled *masato* out of cans, and give thanks for all that their ancestors did or did not do. For all that they have. And remind each other not to forget the sacrifices or the history or, most importantly, who they are.

I know what I need to write. I have been listening, and one of the voices I am obliged to render is my own. I watch the hills rising as the boat moves up the river, against the current. Mostly what remains now is empathy for these people and how trapped they feel. For Miguel, watching his world collapse around him. For Ismael, wondering where things went wrong. I will try to tell their story, but it is not my place to judge them.

The land is high around us now, ripe thighs and ample bellies, and ahead lies the Pongo de Mainique. Grandest Pongo of them all, the Machiguenga said, where the river demon lurks. The water is growing choppy, rushing at us in flaring squalls, but now I remember that fear is only fear, my old companion, and that it can be held, like a baby. So I rock it gentle against my chest and stay right where I am. Up ahead the brides are waiting, waiting for their prince. I can see them now with their veils in place and bouquets fresh, riveted by the annihilation and the glory, by the roaring silence.

Eleven:

New York

It is Thursday, September 2, 2004, the final day of the Republican National Convention. George W. Bush is about to accept his renomination. He will thank the delegates for their support and speak of the American soldiers who have charged through sandstorms and liberated millions.

Hundreds of demonstrators have gathered in Union Square tonight, huddled over candles flickering in jars and paper cups, keeping vigil, silent or praying or sharing stories. A single saxophone moans in sluggish sobs. Meanwhile we in Code Orange are staging some guerrilla theater of our own.

We move slowly through the crowd in a single-file line, timing our steps with the person in front. Left, pause. Right, pause. Our hands behind our heads or joined behind our backs. Gags over our mouths reading RNC and CORPORATE MEDIA. Signs on our chests spelling out PEACE and DEMOCRACY, HEALTH CARE and EDUCATION. People stare at us and whisper. We snake through the plaza for a while before pausing at the front, where we spread out in a line at the top of the stairs and stand immobile. We are silent, our eyes fixed ahead. Passersby point and snap photos.

"Get out of there!"

After five days of watching the First Amendment repeatedly trampled, I'd thought I'd seen it all. But no. A police captain is running toward us, baton raised. He bellows like a bull fresh out of the pen, his face purple. "I've had enough of you people! Get down from there immediately or we'll arrest every one of you assholes."

"Whatever happened to freedom of speech?"

"This is a peaceful—"

"I don't want to hear about it," he roars. "Unless you want to rot in jail for the next month, you get your asses down from those stairs right now. And take those fucking gags off this instant or I'll—"

I come home from South America in the middle of June 2004, right in time for the fanfare and hullabaloo as the parties primp and prime their candidates. I'm more than a little jaundiced, having just returned from a part of the world being systematically plundered by the policies touted by this administration. I am itching to demonstrate, more motivated than ever to get Bush Inc. out of office.

The Republicans decide to hold their convention to renominate Bush in New York City. As if the city hasn't been through enough over the past four years. The site of the World Trade Center is still a massive hole in the earth, fences bedecked with memorabilia and dedications of grief. But here was where the president had so publicly and brazenly embraced aggression and isolation. Here was where he told us there's no other way. So, there you have it, onward and eastward for the Grand Old Party! The machine is firing up now, gears clanking into motion. We'll speechify and proselytize till our heads swell to the size of Coney Island. We'll have ourselves a grand old time. Let's not discuss the ongoing siege in Najaf, with U.S. forces bombing the holy city to bits, making mincemeat of Muqtada al Sadr's army and assorted hapless civilians—but failing to kill the man himself, or the thousands more lining up to fight. Let's not mention the number of Iraqi civilians killed, estimated by Iraq Body Count to now be thirteen thousand. Certainly we'll avoid referring to the nearly one thousand American soldiers who have died, and the thousands more wounded. And as for all that nasty tumult around civil liberties, the environment, welfare, and reproductive rights... Well, let's just concentrate on pleasant things, shall we? Like the fact that Paul Bremer got out safe and sound, having successfully implemented his one hundred corporate-contrived orders to render the Iraqi economy naked and defenseless. Like the billions in reconstruction contracts jingling in the pockets of our GOP donor buddies at Bechtel and Halliburton.

And so the Republican National Convention rumbles and bombasts its way into New York City.

As the 4,800 delegates head east at the end of August, so do tens of thousands of protesters. About fifteen of us from Code Orange scoured the Internet for cheap flights and begged our East Coast friends for couch space. New Yorkers have been bracing for the onslaught for weeks. Local activists have been mobilizing for months. "There's a real New York energy to the organizing," says Carwil, who arrived in early August, when I call to interview him for a story I'm writing on the buildup. He's working with the A31 Action Coalition, which is planning a series of direct actions for August 31, the second day of the convention. When we in Code Orange get to New York, that's where we'll be plugging in. "Here's a political party coming to New York," he says, "that rejects so much of what the city is—immigrants, people of color, artists, queers, renters. It's generating all kinds of local organizing."

In response, Bush Inc. resort to their usual tactics: lock the city down, up, and sideways. The Department of Homeland Security designates the RNC a "National Special Security Event," which puts all security for the city—including the New York Police Department—at the behest of the Secret Service. Seventy-five government agencies are enlisted in the siege. Madison Square Garden, the site of the convention, is walled in by both a fence and movable barricades, its checkpoints reinforced by heavy weapons. And then there are the helicopters, armed federal agents, undercover cops, fighter jets from a nearby National Guard unit and—the coup de grâce—huge "frozen zones" that are closed to the public.

Miami's Timoney would have been proud.

After arriving in New York, I head uptown to the United for Peace and Justice office. UFPJ was the national antiwar coalition responsible for the marches on February 15, 2003, and it is coordinating a massive demonstration for August 29, the day before the Republican Convention begins.

Today is August 25, and the office is frantic with activity. I put myself to use stapling posters — "The World Says NO to Bush" — to be used as signs in the march. The people around the table are from all over the country, and we chat hopefully about the chances of beating Bush, and about the organizing in our hometowns.

"Who wants to come to the press conference?" A woman in the center of the room spins around as she bellows. "We need volunteers to hold signs when the verdict comes in."

It is estimated that 250,000 people will participate in the march and rally on the 29th. Although it will be the largest of the planned demonstrations, the city has refused to grant a permit for the rally to be staged in Central Park. The city's Republican mayor, Michael Bloomberg, argued that a crowd of 250,000 would cause irreparable damage to the grass on the Great Lawn. Lawn care, of course, is not the real issue. Bloomberg is a billionaire and a major supporter of the GOP: he donated $7 million of his own money and raised millions more to support the host committee of the RNC. UFPJ challenged the denial of the permit, and a judge is set to rule today.

"I'll go." I stand up.

"Great. You, you, you, and you." She points around the room. "Grab all the signs you can and let's move."

We pile into cabs and head downtown to the courthouse. Outside a million reporters are barking into cell phones or scrawling on notepads as crews set up half a million TV cameras. I spy Medea Benjamin, another Bay Area resident, and head over to say hi.

"What do you think?" We stare at the pillared, porticoed wedding cake of a courthouse. The ruling was due at 4 p.m., ten minutes ago.

"No. That judge isn't going to do it." She shakes her head and smiles brightly. "But let's keep our fingers crossed."

I ask her what she makes of the "National Special Security Event" designation.

"I think a response like this begins erasing the margins between terror and dissent," she says. I nod, recalling how Bush framed the "war on terror." *You're either with us or against us,* he said. Not much room for nuance or subtlety there.

A murmur rises from the crowd. Camera crews leap to attention. The UFPJ team is descending the courthouse steps, and I dash into position behind them with my sign. Reporters jam their headphones onto their heads, cameras start rolling, and I try not to wilt too visibly when they announce that the appeal has been denied.

The next day I return to the UFPJ office, this time to paint giant pink doves on behalf of Code Pink. Then I head over to Columbus Circle. A hundred activists have spent the past three and a half weeks marching here from the Democratic National Convention in Boston, a 258-mile trek. At the DNC all demonstrators were consigned to barbed-wire and razor-wire "protest pens." As if criticizing Kerry will doom the left, as if pulling ranks and tight-lipped timidity haven't helped land us in this reactionary nightmare. Still, that's small potatoes compared to the siege of New York. "The Democrats," Medea said, "are mildly afraid of the people. The Republicans are intensely afraid."

The DNC to RNC march is due to reach Columbus Circle this afternoon. They arrive before I do. I feel the familiar rush of excitement as I slip into the grungy crowd of radicals. These are my people, or at least some of them. There's David, holding up giant yellow bird puppets stenciled with "Yes: Direct Democracy. No: Bush, War, and Empire." There's Carwil in his Zapatista T-shirt, and there's Debbie, and there are Nora and Tracy and Sarah from Code Orange.

"Can I have a bird?"

"Sure. Hold it high." David hands me one, and then we are all marching down Broadway toward Union Square. We are marching and we are chanting and whooping, taking over a lane of traffic, police grim beside us on their motorbikes. *Move, Bush, get out the way. Get out the way, Bush, get out the way.* New Yorkers are stepping out of stores and homes to see what the fuss is all about. Some are just staring, others cheering us on. "Thank you!" yells one man in a turban. "New York loves you!" And for a minute I am silent amid the gust and tumble of it, a pebble in the stream, feeling what it is to be lifted and carried by the current. To let go with the full faith that I will be held, that the river moves with or without me. This is what I love. This is when I know we cannot lose, because this—the striving toward dignity, meaning, and connection—is what makes us human. *El pueblo unido jamás será vencido. The people united will never be defeated.*

We reach Times Square, and I am chanting again, captivated by flashing lights and soaring jingles, by the vast advertisements, the colossal teeth and eyes and breasts, the gargantuan print goading us to buy, buy, buy. *Drop Bush not bombs. Drop Bush not bombs.* Don't even dream of getting this lipstick unless you're ready to look like I do, a platinum blond simpers. Across the way a redhead dares me to off-road Manhattan in her glossy monstrosity of an SUV. I am immune to none of this. Whenever I come to New York, I get the irrepressible urge to shop. Everyone looks so painfully hip that I can't help but feel hopelessly dowdy. I religiously scour the sales racks in the Soho boutiques, figuring I may as well savor what I can of capitalism before advancing its collapse. As for SUVs, I drove one briefly during a speaking tour in Colorado. At the counter I protested, but it was all the rental company had left. Once I got used to it, I loved it. I felt protected and, dare I say it, powerful.

"You okay?" David is next to me, and his blue eyes show concern. "You look a little out of it."

"Yeah, fine." But I'm not fine. I am mesmerized. My lips move with the chants, but I am barely whispering. I am amazed at our audacity, that we do not balk and run from the brawn of this spectacle. Capitalism's hall of mirrors. According to the perpetrators, this is why thousands died and why the World Trade Center is now a hole in the ground. Because we are a godless society in thrall to greed. Of course, it's not quite the moment to discuss the merits of a god that smiles on terror versus the merits of no god at all. Certainly Abdul Bakr's Allah would not look kindly upon the wholesale slaughter of innocents. But I have to concede that they have a point, these plotting lunatics. We are a society of unparalleled abundance, and still we grab madly. I saw it when I returned from India and again when I returned from South America, and it is becoming clearer every day: this consuming need to fill, this inability to recognize what we already have, is rooted in a collective void, a spiritual void. And our culture, which keeps us constantly distracted, incessantly scrambling for material stopgaps, both generates and magnifies this void. To continue wanting in the face of so much abundance: this is a supreme dearth of faith—faith in ourselves, each other, the universe.

Drop Bush not bombs.

There are chain-mail links between the lipstick and the Camisea Gas Project, between SUVs and the war in Iraq. Things. We are a godless society in worship of things. And I can't say I blame us, because I look at the two-hundred-dollar jeans and the skinny thighs and I want them too.

I can hear the mayhem at St. Mark's Episcopal Church all the way from Thirteenth Street. I walk down Second Avenue through the East Village, smiling. The melodious chaos drowns out even the drone of helicopters. At Tenth Street the scene splits open like a ripe fig: the wide cobbled plaza seething with people, milling about beneath trees set against a cloudless sky.

The Rude Mechanical Orchestra is plucking and blowing away vigorously at something jaunty and familiar-sounding. Flutes quiver and pirouette. The trombone pumps like a windup toy. A woman in a green hat and umpire-striped shirt tosses a baton, catching it with flourishes and bows. Passersby pause to bang enthusiastically on upended twenty-gallon cans. "Hey hey," calls out a girl from the side, "These streets belong to us. Hey hey..." and the call is picked up by one voice, two, chanted by several, then drifts back down to three voices, two, hers alone. Until she gives a final hoot and returns to her sandwich.

Cops line the sidewalk, eyeing the revelries impassively. Green-capped observers from the National Lawyers Guild eye them back. Across the plaza, people cluster to eat lunch. It is Tuesday, and Tuesday is the farmers market—rain, shine, or revolution—and so the farmers peddle their wares: lustrous peppers, fat fists of garlic, eggplants purple as a fresh bruise. I ask one vendor how he's doing. "It's tense." He frowns. "You don't know what's going to happen."

St. Mark's had been billed as the Wellness Center, a place for fatigued or injured protesters to rest and get medical attention. But it has morphed into an ad hoc convergence center for the direct-action contingency. Inside the churchyard, a group called Seeds of Peace doles out hearty veggie fare: stir-fry, brown rice, salad. More people sit and eat. "Ho ho ho," calls out a man in a top hat and vest. "Let them eat cake!" Behind him shuffles a chain gang of American soldiers, eyes fixed ahead. Guerrilla theater. A former Deadhead squatting beside a blanket of bumper stickers grins at me, points to one that reads LICK BUSH AND DICK. I smile, shake my head no. "Drop Bush not bombs, right on!" he howls fiercely out of nowhere, and everyone around him leaps.

"Yo, people! Jail solidarity training at the back of the yard in five minutes!"

I head over to listen in.

A small circle gathers around the bespectacled, black-clad facilitator. "There are already five people doing jail solidarity," he says. "They're a little ahead of you, but I assured them you'd catch up." Laughter. "Who here can explain why we do jail solidarity?"

One woman raises her hand. "To protect undocumented people and also those who are typically targeted: people of color, queers, transsexuals, et cetera."

"Precisely. The idea is that everyone who commits the same act should be treated equally and fairly in jail as well as sentencing." He speaks rapidly, urgently. "When we practice jail solidarity we choose to act collectively, refusing to identify ourselves and then refusing citations or fines or bail or what have you, depending on what we all decide. Then we can negotiate on our terms instead of submitting to divide-and-conquer tactics." Heads nod with the ardor of the converted.

I've never been arrested. I'm always writing about the actions, and my deadlines make for an effective preventative. I can't risk arrest this time, either: I have an article on the protests due in to the *Chronicle*. But I'm starting to feel rather like a thirty-year-old virgin. A little shamefaced, a little scared, waiting for the right opportunity to break out. Or in, as it happens. I leave when he asks who plans to risk arrest, and head off in search of a church official for an interview.

"We haven't taken a position on any of the issues," says Jerry Long, a member of St. Mark's board. "But we sympathize with the struggle to improve the lot of all peoples, especially the poor and oppressed." Long is middle-aged, clean-cut, ruddy with the heat. He has to yell to be heard, but he doesn't look the slightest bit flustered by the racket. "For two hundred years this church has offered a place for people to exercise their right to free expression." I ask him what he thinks of the protesters. "We are very impressed by the cooperation and gratitude of every one of our visitors." He looks about us, taking in the various antics: the musicians, baton twirlers, guerrilla theatrics; the assortment of quaintly dressed rabble-rousers munching, chatting, napping, or otherwise generally lolling about. "I think they appreciate the fact that a church has opened its doors to so many of America's young. To God's children."

Sunday, August 29, 9 a.m., Union Square.

"Many times when we have sat down, we think immediately that we're arrested. But there's often space for negotiation." Starhawk and David are co-facilitating a training on nonviolent civil disobedience. Twenty people stand in a circle listening intently. The paparazzi do their thing, clicking and scribbling. So do I, for that matter—but as usual I am on double duty, jotting down notes while I participate. A few New Yorkers en route to work poke their heads in to listen. "Sitting down is a really good tactic," continues Starhawk in her usual placid sotto voce, somehow audible above the Rude Mechanical Orchestra fifteen feet away. "It's extremely rare that cops will charge a sitting group of people. When we sit down, the police feel safer too."

They run through the basics: picking a buddy, de-escalation tactics for cops or irate New Yorkers, protecting at-risk people, legal issues, jail solidarity. And finally, the scenario, courtesy of the direct-action constituency: Today, following the march, we head to Central Park, in defiance of the city's ruling. Tuesday, A31, we meet at 6 p.m. on the steps of the public library. We give a rousing cheer and then begin dispersing. "Did everyone get an NLG tattoo?" hollers David. "Make sure you have the phone number written somewhere on your body. There's a whole legal team waiting to support you."

10:30 a.m., Eighteenth Street and Seventh Avenue.

We wait for the march to begin. The streets are packed full, crammed to the brim. Protesters are everywhere you look, blooming in all directions, common and lovely as cornfields in Iowa. Protesters impatient and holding their signs erect, protesters sitting on the sidewalks, protesters grumbling over the heat and Bush. I move through the crowd, handing out flyers for our call to Central Park this afternoon and our action Tuesday night.

"Oh my gosh, there are so many people here," an elderly lady gushes at me, accepting my leaflet. "There are people from everywhere, and we are getting the message out loud and clear. Isn't that so, honey?"

"Absolutely." Bush Inc. have succeeded in riling people from all walks of life: there is a wide cross-section of ages, races, and cultures represented here. In front of me strut the Code Pink ladies, in their lacy pink slips, carrying signs reading BUSH, CHENEY, YOU'RE FIRED. To my left stand the Christians for Peace, with cut-out cardboard doves upright. To my right, in the "no justice, no peace" corner, a flock of immigrants rights activists chant in time with several drummers. Thousands of others carry homemade signs, UFPJ signs, or—a highly popular item today—printouts of Bush looking especially dim-witted, with the caption DARN GOOD LIAR.

A cascade of cheers behind me greets an approaching fire engine. The crowd parts for these indisputable heroes of 9/11. Most smile and wave like beauty queens. A couple stonily ignore us.

Then, without warning, we are moving. Jerking into motion as the waves ahead roll back and collide with us. I run over to Code Orange.

"We're off!" Grabbing our signs and giant painted hand puppets: "Healthcare and Education NOT Warfare and Occupation," "Clean Air and Water NOT Bush, War and Empire." Pulling my brother Marc and my friend Nancy, both of whom have come to demonstrate, up off the sidewalk. And then pressing into it, caught up by it, chanting and laughing and smiling at the strangers around me, who smile right back and ask how I'm doing, tell me how they're doing, comment on my sign. The entire rollicking sea of us sparking electric. Images and sounds filtering through my senses in disjointed, adrenaline-kindled flashes.

America, know your enemy: Diebold, Halliburton, Bechtel.
Redefeat Bush.

A spontaneous cheer rising somewhere and swelling into a vast symphony of whooping-whistling-catcalling release. Wild, unrestrained.

Ban the nonconsensual testing of weapons on humans.

Here Lies Bush. Over a big red map of the U.S.

Axis of Eve. On the T-shirts of three women walking with arms linked.

I am marching for my grandma and she's pissed.

"Oh my God, there are so many good signs. Where are you from?"

"Boise, Idaho. You?"

"Right here, the Bronx. Welcome to the Big Apple, baby!"

"Thanks. Nice sign."

Protest etiquette.

No Bush No Dick. In glitter and pink, wielded by a flaming couple wearing tiny shorts and flip-flops and nothing else.

got democracy? Beneath the photo of the hooded, wired prisoner from Abu Ghraib.

A marching band, swaggering down the middle of the street to riotous applause. *There's a terrorist in the White House.* A procession of coffins covered with flags. *George W. Bush: Over 2,000,000 layoffs served. People's Rule, Not Market Rule.*

I am watching and I am listening; I am walking and I am thinking. When I came home from India it struck me how afraid we all are, how we struggle to avoid each other. In such a fragmented society, it takes a leap of faith to connect with a stranger. We must summon faith in the other, in their humanity, in our own need and ability to connect. I thought our fear was of rejection. But I see now that we're just as terrified of actually connecting. Or I am, at least. What happens then? What will the other expect of me? What if I'm incapable? Inadequate? When material things clutter the spaces between us, when wanting and having and achieving colonize the space within us, we don't have much authentic left besides our fear. But when we let fear dictate how we live our lives, we are defeated. We slide further away from each other, away from a real sense of ourselves. We believe fear, practice fear, vote for fear. And we buy fear. Fear sells like nothing else.

This simple action—showing up, marching, chanting—is one of the greatest risks we can take. We are hazarding expression over apathy, togetherness over the sham security of isolation. Hope over fear. And that's precisely why it's so liberating. Why we're all delirious with joy right now. In a society that defines us by what we have, that gauges our worth by how much we are capable of having, and that reduces our options to which furniture and which car and which box to check every four years, this is a gargantuan leap of faith. A ritualized rediscovery of who we are. A return to the power of our own hands and minds and hearts. Poetry slams, green festivals, bike workshops, yoga, Billionaires for Bush, a Fox News Shut-up-a-thon, a massive pro-choice rally: you name the issue and the medium of expression, it's happening this week.

You say war, we say no. George Bush has got to go. You say war, we say no. George Bush has got to go.

We are approaching Madison Square Garden now, and the mood is beginning to shift. A giant television screen high above the street broadcasts Fox News, the script streaming at the bottom of the screen. *Terror Alert,* it reads. Boos issue from the crowd. A Barbie-beautiful newscaster declaims soundlessly, staring out earnestly from beneath her flawless blonde helmet and triple layer of mascara. *What to do in case of an attack.* She is grave now, teacherly, as the people around me hiss.

"Fearmongering!"

"Change the channel!"

The chant is picked up: *Change the channel, change the channel, change the channel.* The crowd pushing up against me now, keen, urgent, and it feels different. Jagged. Volatile.

"There it is," David says, and I look. We have reached Madison Square Garden, and everyone around me starts going mad, releasing four years of pent-up fury. David is shaking his fist and yelling, Nora and Tracy are screaming, my brother is roaring, and I am too, but somewhere inside something lifts, shifts, snaps into place. The words wilt in my throat. Directly in front of us are the lines of police, tight-jawed and white-knuckled. Faces behind their dark glasses hard as granite; antagonism shot through with fear. Far behind the fence: more police, journalists, a few janitors and service people. Any actual delegates? Maybe a couple. Who can tell?

Our rage storms down upon the undeserving, and they hate us right back.

The blond is looking out with blank eyes and eyebrows high, wondering now: *The Republican Convention: will there be any surprises?*

A puff of tear gas before us, scattered screams, and people are running, the Black Bloc pushing the police lines back. We in Code Orange grab each other's hands and snake through the bodies toward the refuge of a subway station.

Tuesday, A31, 5:45 p.m., Thirty-fourth Street and Broadway.

"David. It's Marisa. You're on tactics, right?"

"Uh-huh."

"Well, I'm at Thirty-fourth, and it's crawling with cops. They've set up netting around the intersections, and they're controlling foot traffic."

"Got it." David is with the rest of Code Orange, back at the apartment where we held our final pre-action meeting. At 7 p.m., those choosing to risk arrest will be sitting down in Herald Square with the "True Security" cluster, sharing songs, stories, and ideas about how to end the war and create a world of genuine safety. A second cluster, focusing on environmental issues, is gathering at 6 p.m. at the public library on Forty-second Street. That's where I'm headed now.

I walk rapidly, scenes from Sunday's march replaying in my head. It was an indisputable success. Estimates of marchers ranged from 250,000 to 400,000, and even with the Black Bloc's antics, it was overwhelmingly peaceful. Afterward, thousands of demonstrators ignored the ruling and moseyed over to Central Park, where we schmoozed, picnicked, tossed Frisbees, and met to finalize plans for tonight.

Despite my brisk pace, it takes me a long time to reach the library. The vast frozen zones have turned the city into a convoluted maze of dead ends, and every time I round a corner there are huge barricades and cops redirecting me. Cops everywhere: on rooftops, on sidewalks, in the streets, checking bags. Cops lining Madison Square Garden when I finally pass it. Beyond the cops: an array of expensive suits standing about exchanging pleasantries. A woman in pancake make-up intoning solemnly to a camera.

I am moving at a slow jog now, wondering how the evening will unfold. The aim of the 6 p.m. gathering at the library is to direct demonstrators to civil disobedience sites. It's been widely publicized, so I'm sure it'll be swarming with police. The Herald Square location has been kept under wraps — or at any rate that was the idea. But I'd be amazed if at least one tentacle of the "National Special Security" behemoth hasn't extended into our spokescouncils.

6:15 p.m., New York Public Library.

"Whose library?"

"Our library!"

"Whose city?"

"Our city!"

Jumble is behind the bullhorn, standing stalwart in front of an American flag with the stars replaced by a peace sign. The police line begins moving in, shields over their faces, batons at the ready. But Jumble continues, undaunted. "This is an exercise of our First Amendment right, on public property —" A cop grabs the bullhorn and shoves Jumble down onto the sidewalk. The crowd boos and hollers. There are at least a couple of thousand people here, jostling and angry as the police push them back off the steps and begin arresting. I veer back, scribbling and snapping pictures.

"Excuse me, ma'am, are you a journalist?"

"Uh-huh."

"Do you know who organized this protest?"

I look up. Gray suit, mirror sunglasses, buzz-cut, and clean-shaven. On the card dangling over his abdomen: SECRET SERVICE. Is this guy for real?

"I'd rather not talk with you."

"Were you involved with organizing this protest, ma'am?" He is grinning relentlessly, eerily. A jack-o'-lantern triangle in a face that just might be plastic. His hands in his pockets.

"I'm under no legal obligation to answer your questions." My voice is hard.

"What's your name, ma'am?"

I start walking away.

"Ma'am, do you live in New York? How did you know about this protest?"

He keeps barking questions at me as I scamper back into the mayhem, as if my objections were meaningless, as if I'm going to telepathically transmit answers to him once I've vanished.

7 p.m., Thirty-seventh Street and Broadway.

There's no way we're going to reach Herald Square in time.

"Can you see anything?" I ran into Joshua near the library. He's also writing about the demonstrations, and we resolved to join forces. But for the past five minutes we've barely moved. The streets are packed solid.

"Just an endless sea of writhing bodies. Oh, and a couple of Republicans."

I crane my neck. Two delegates are moving through the crowd, clutching Starbucks coffee cups in front of them like talismans.

"Fascists go home!" a demonstrator screams.

"Yeah, that's what we are!" one of the delegates yells back. "We're fascists, right. Glad you're so liberal-minded."

A smiling woman in a white skirt prances in front of the delegates like a flower girl, flinging rose petals in their faces.

7:45 p.m., Thirty-second Street and Broadway.

Jackpot. I've finally caught up with what's left of Code Orange, and we appear to have stumbled upon the mother lode: a convoy of SUVs and limousines carting delegates toward the convention.

Bush lies, thousands die. Are your kids fighting? Are your kids dying?

None of us can risk arrest, so we wait until the light is green, then cross the street back and forth in front of them. We hold our signs high, chanting at top volume, pointing into the vehicles. Most of the windows are darkened. But some aren't. The well-groomed occupants and their chauffeurs stare straight ahead.

Six members of Code Orange were arrested minutes after sitting down. The police weren't gentle with them, either. Despite not resisting arrest, one woman was flung down on her chest, another dragged by the arm. By the end of the night, nearly a thousand demonstrators will have been arrested. Many will be kept in filthy "holding pens"; many will be held far beyond the twenty-four-hour limit for arraignment. A judge will find the NYPD in contempt of court and fine the department one thousand dollars for every person held in custody over twenty-four hours.

Bush lies, thousands die. Are your kids fighting? Are your kids dying?

Every now and then a small cluster of delegates walks past at a rapid clip. Almost all of them ignore us. One woman, in a flawlessly cut suit and heavy jewelry, looks straight at us. "But this is so silly, just so silly!" she says, arms raised in perplexity. I feel the anger rising lightning-quick, flooding me.

Silly? Now honestly ma'am, would you choose that adjective if your child had been killed in Najaf, or Basra, or Baghdad? I glare at her, loathing her for all she has, for the ease with which she will spend her entire life floating above the trenches. *Are your kids fighting? Are your kids dying?* I'm shouting at her, now, for her blinders and her diamonds and her privilege. For the snapshots of bleeding Iraqi children whirling through my head like a lurid carousel.

But there it is again: lifting, shifting, resettling with a jarring tremor in my belly. Again my voice dies in my throat, and I am abruptly nauseous, squirming away from myself. The visions of Iraqi children colliding with an image of this woman sitting with her own child, helping him with his homework. My rage crashing up against this and slopping back and forth, reeking shame. I am soiled with self-righteousness. Where can I aim this anger? Who can I blame? We have a president living so far "apart from real knowledge," as Atanacio put it, that he values the approval of his wealthy friends over the well-being of his people and the planet. Our soldiers are returning without legs or arms, waking in the middle of the night shrieking at the horrors that visit them. And this woman, the one walking the gauntlet and calling it silly, one of the many supporting Bush Inc., she is summoning the courage and fighting with her husband, shouting at him to come home by 8 p.m. just one goddamn night a month please to be a fucking father to his only child please. Her husband is pacing in a vast office, shaking his head at rising oil prices, barking orders, slaving and slaving and running and running and thoroughly lost to himself. And she sits alone in some massive dark house while her son sleeps, drinking her fifth scotch and thinking how can I, there's no way, I just can't, I have to.

I sit down on the sidewalk. Lay my sign beside me and my anger with it. What remains is grief. They keep walking and driving past, these people looking anywhere but at us, and every one of them is human. All of them with parents and spouses and children who love them. Or loathe them. Every one with a personal story to share or not share, depending on what each has been taught about how to win, ensnare, or embezzle love. Every one hard as nails right now.

We all suffer.

I watch my friends walking and chanting. They are good people, so good that they care about men and women and children they do not know and will never know. They are the conscience of this nation; they will not let these delegates forget what this administration is perpetrating. But this, what we are doing right now — is it helping? Or is it pushing us further apart? We didn't come here to convince the delegates to change their minds, or to win their esteem. But I can see what they are thinking. Faced with hatred, they hate us right back. That's what we've all learned to do. What would we risk if we tried something different?

Bush lies, thousands die. Are your kids fighting? Are your kids dying?

Is anger possible without hatred? What is nonviolence? Everything we have done this week has technically been nonviolent. No one has been physically hurt by our actions. "Tactical nonviolence," we call it. But is that enough? "Nonviolence," Gandhi said, "is not a garment to be put on and off at will. Its seat is in the heart, and it must be an inseparable part of our very being."

Is it possible to effect change without dehumanizing others? Without someone to hate? Can we connect with each other as we have this week — can we build a movement — without a common enemy?

Twelve:
Fort Benning, Georgia

Have you ever stuck around after they've all gone home? After the march has passed through, the rally run its course? There isn't a whole lot left. Papers littering the ground announcing upcoming events, pleading for a wealth of good causes. Posters pimpled with the imprint of street and sole, leaflets tattered and grimy. Trash cans towering, cathedral-like, amid variegated landscapes of aluminum and plastic, a topography molded from the drained and consumed. Wind shuffling these crumbs about, or stillness amplifying their silence. These intersections are the loneliest of poems, the ghostliest of towns. Everyone gone back to their bunkers to wrestle with the same doubts and the same people they wrestled with the night before. The echo of songs and speeches, of outrage and hope and entreaty, bouncing against the concrete and glass like rubber balls in a lockbox.

Later the city's forces will emerge—those forces that tidy and groom the apparatus being protested—to clean it all up. Laborers who can't afford to live in the city they clean will sweep away what remains, and the next day the apparatus will trundle on, humans in tow like ducklings. One day closer to demise. Nothing lasts forever, and that which consumes its own flesh falls a good deal short of forever.

I return from New York feeling ambivalent. I am inspired by the protests, by their range and creativity. But I am also decidedly pessimistic about my own place in this movement, and dubious about what our organizing is achieving. I have no doubts about the power of civil disobedience and direct action. But I am clear that both are most effective within the framework of a broad strategic resistance. Direct-action organizing, in contrast, seems to operate in emergency mode: a war arises, a multilateral trade talk is scheduled, and we rush to react. Within that urgency, we summon the energy to achieve amazing things through inclusive processes. But it's not enough. Our activism is rushed and lacks the grounding and alliances that grow from proactive, consistent, and patient organizing. Moreover, it lacks sustainability. If we are constantly stressed and harried doing the work of change, then we aren't living the world we say we want. And if we can't live it, how can we build it?

I'm starting to think our vision must be broader, our goals larger. The models are out there: India, Ecuador, Brazil, South Africa, Venezuela — movements in villages and cities are pressing and hammering this world into a new mold. We need to build our connections with these movements, learn from them. We need to continue to develop our vision of what we want and our analysis of how to get there. And indeed this is happening: the World Social Forum — an annual meeting of global justice advocates from all over the world to coordinate campaigns and share and hone strategies — is about to enter its fifth year. This is a young and vibrant movement, and thankfully, given its openness, there is ample room to grow, and in a variety of directions. But I'm not sure of my place within it.

I am increasingly convinced that tactical nonviolence is not enough. Gandhi and King maintained that civil disobedience must be more than symbolic and strategic. To be effective, it must also be principled. In 1930, after marching to the seaside to protest the British salt tax, hundreds of *satyagrahis* were beaten savagely as they approached the Dharsana salt deposits. Yet they kept coming, columns of them, without fear or fight. Gandhi's Salt March is generally recognized as the turning point in the Indian resistance to British rule. In 1965, in Selma, Alabama, when police turned tear gas and billy clubs on the nonviolent civil rights marchers, they knelt in prayer. This event too is now recognized as a turning point: the nation clamored in protest, and two marches and five months later, President Johnson signed the Voting Rights Act into law. The Sarayacu are winning because their forms of resistance align with their deepest-held values.

The strategy shaping their campaign is grounded in their spirituality, wisdom, and culture. Stemming from a nonviolent vision of interconnection with the earth and humanity, their means are congruent with their ends.

I do not feel like our means are congruent with our ends.

I go to direct-action organizing meetings and return disheartened. My fellow organizers have so much compassion for the oppressed, but they often completely demonize the police, the government, the people who work in corporations. *Why should we have compassion for them?* a friend asks, laughing in disbelief. *They perpetuate and profit from a system dependent on slave labor, highway robbery, environmental devastation.* Why? Because they suffer too. Because they're so busy pushing away their own suffering that they can harden themselves to the suffering of others. Because hating them certainly won't open their hearts. Not to mention that we're also a part of the same system. *So you're going to love them into starting a revolution?* Think of it as tough love. Like Gandhi said: "I can combine the greatest love with the greatest opposition to wrong." Compassion doesn't turn a blind eye to consequences. But when compassion exiles any human being, it lacks wisdom. *Okay, Marisa, whatever. Like anything's going to change that way.*

Then Bush wins. Fox, CNN, and *The New York Times* all attribute his victory to the "moral values" votes of the religious right. I am stunned, dismayed. All that energy and commitment in New York, all the grassroots organizing to get out the vote, all the young people newly politicized by his first term, and still we lost. Republicans now control both houses of Congress. We have a president, vice president, and secretary of state who are all former executives at energy corporations. Two of the three have more years of experience in energy companies than in government. The nation's left rants, tears out its hair, grieves, and collapses in a stupor of exhaustion and befuddlement.

Back home, Code Orange slowly falls apart. There are questions we have delayed addressing that now, if we are to continue organizing, demand our attention: Do we want to be an affinity group or, as we've sometimes functioned at major demonstrations, an organizing collective — planning actions for others beyond ourselves? Do we want to commit to one or two ongoing campaigns or mobilize on an action-by-action basis? We try to answer these questions but repeatedly become mired in process. Interpersonal issues arise, along with communication glitches. It seems we lack the energy to address it all. We limp along for a while but eventually stop meeting altogether.

How dare you look at me like that?

You, yes you, with the tie-dyed shirt and tie-dyed skirt. I saw that sidelong look. Who dressed you, anyway? Haven't you ever heard of solid fabrics? Very much in demand these days. One tie-dye at a time, how's that for starters. Or perhaps let's take a stab at limiting ourselves to ten colors in combination, shall we?

As for you, I saw that. I saw you cut in line. Think you're better than all the rest of us, don't you? I know your type. Weekly pedicure followed by a satisfying whine at the injustice of the world over hundred-dollar lunches with your face-lifted pals in Sausalito. Just because everyone else is too spineless to do anything doesn't mean I didn't notice. If I could only talk, you'd be up to your ears in it right now. Speaking of which, I'd seriously consider getting those mothers pinned a few inches closer to your head. You've obviously got the resources.

For now, I'll content myself with a malevolent glare.

And you behind me — yes you, I know who you are, the one with the face only a mother could love — if you step on my shoe one more goddamn time I swear to Jesus I'm going to turn around and throttle you. Can you imagine it? All these timid do-gooders. "Now, dear, let's cast our minds back to right action..." What if I picked up a kitchen knife and started yapping like a dog? Would they break silence? Maybe bray faintly? I'm about ready to do it. Where's the knife? Someone hand it to me so I can save us all from ourselves.

I've had it with these retreats. Why am I here? Why choose to torture myself like this? Surround myself with people thinking all manner of foul things about me? (I know they're thinking about me, they must be, I'm far too compelling for them not to be.) What the hell was I thinking?

Wait, what the hell *am* I thinking? Where is my mind?

I'm evil. I'm a bad person surrounded by good people who are thinking nothing but virtuous thoughts. I am utterly vile. I honestly cannot stand myself. How can anyone stand me? I've fooled them, evidently. On top of it all I'm ugly as sin. My hair is more like a hairball, my hips elephantine, and I look like I haven't slept in the entire Cenozoic era because we have to get up at the freaking crack of dawn to meditate. What's so urgent about sitting on your ass watching your breath that you have to get up at 5:30? I should just go back to my tent right now. I don't deserve to be here. I don't deserve to eat lunch, and I'm harboring strong suspicions I don't deserve to exist. Surely they can tell. They can all tell how despicable I am. And did I mention self-obsessed, neurotic, and paranoid?

I have come to recognize my aversion phase. It happens early on at most retreats. I dislike everyone and logically presume everyone dislikes me. But this retreat is different. By this time I've been practicing daily for over three years. But I'm still astounded by what hits me. Every retreat I sit with what comes up, both unpleasant and pleasant. This time, I'm bowled over by it.

It is a women's retreat taking place in a county park. We sit in a circle, outside, beneath madrone and redwoods. Grief pins me, anger rages like a forest fire, and hatred throws fists, knives, Molotov cocktails at all of it. What is this torment? Who knew it was in me? For days I sit with my own fury and hatred, watching them storm, wondering if I'm strong enough to overcome them. Yes, I think, I can beat this.

It hits me with such impact that my eyes startle open.

Madrone trees arching red. Dead leaves skittering across the tarp.

It dawns on me that I am fighting the grief and the anger with hatred. And it is fueling the cycle. This resistance is simply a different kind of clinging. It depends upon what it reacts to for its own survival. I begin to practice *metta*, giving all of it love. And the war starts to subside.

What I have been stymied by my whole life is the *why* of it. Why is there so much unnecessary suffering? Why do we keep engaging in actions that are obviously destructive? In wars, occupations, economic policies that rob from the poor to ornament the rich? Why, when people, I am convinced, are fundamentally good?

Because we do not see our own goodness.

Every action I take is a reflection of my own heart. It's not simply that in harming others I hurt myself. The harm I inflict on others reflects where I am myself broken, or barren. How much love I can give others is an indication of how much love I allow myself. The woman in New York I hated for her privilege—how could I not see that what I loathed in her is what I loathe in myself? Guilt is just anger turned inward. The violence I despise in the world is the same violence I push away within. We aren't separate, and neither is our suffering. There is no enemy, or at least none that doesn't exist within our own hearts. It is in me, all of it—the terrorist and the president, the homeless man and the CEO—and it's just a question of how much I'll let myself look at. How much compassion I can allow. How much faith I can have in myself, in others, in the universe. In a sense, it's really about saying yes. Until I can look at and hold—with patience, if not love—the ways that I have been hurt, that I am still hurting, I will not understand how they govern me. I will be unconsciously reacting instead of consciously acting. I will be unable, moreover, as Joanna Macy pointed out, to clearheadedly discern whether my actions are actually helping or harming. "For what is evil but good tortured by its own hunger and thirst?" Kahlil Gibran asked. "Verily when good is hungry it seeks food even in dark caves, and when it thirsts it drinks even of dead waters." We cannot see our own goodness because we are terrified of letting ourselves come to know all the ways it is blocked. We are invariably well-intentioned. But our own unacknowledged pain, our ignorance of our own hearts and motives, defeat us.

The revolution is happening. Right now as I study the faces around me, each is astonishingly lovely, really, in its own way. One biting her lip, lost somewhere far from here. Another nodding, giving in to sleep. A third with tears skidding down her cheeks. It's happening quietly, one by one. Within, and then without.

How much of my activism has simply been a vehicle to justify my own anger and hatred?

I pull back from organizing direct action. It just feels wrong. I don't like who I become at the planning meetings I attend. I find myself defensive, harshly critical of my harshly critical friends. I realize that the work and growth I need to do require some space to germinate.

I returned from South America determined to write, and knowing what I wanted to write about. There is a relationship between our own consciousness and a globalized economy playing demolition derby with the planet. Just as the Sarayacu's processes and councils are manifestations of their shared consciousness, so our systems and institutions are manifestations of our collective consciousness. Corporate globalization is a highly convoluted form of escapism, a marathon race away from ourselves and each other. We are letting fear dictate. We are buying and selling and voting for fear. But until we stop running, until we pause and look at the violence within us, we will continue creating violence in the world. What we are facing is not simply a political or economic predicament. It is a spiritual crisis. As such, it requires a spiritual accounting. I begin reading voraciously in the areas of economics, spirituality, philosophy, ecology, and psychology. I take a part-time position as a nanny and spend the rest of my time reading, organizing my ideas, and writing.

I recognize that I am ready to leave this phase of organizing—for now, at least—in order to do the work I feel I need to. But this realization also saddens me and leaves me feeling estranged and frustrated. Inner work is crucial, but so is wise action. Our situation is too dire to do otherwise. Where can I put my activist energy now? What will feel right?

"There is a great spiritual pain that progressive movements have not addressed," says law professor Peter Gabel. The audience roars its approval. "The right has addressed this, within a narrow moral discourse. But it is time now." He holds his hands aloft in petition. "It is time for us progressives to build a spiritual politics that speaks to the universal human need for meaning." He gets a standing ovation.

It is the first morning of the first ever Spiritual Activism conference, organized by Tikkun at U.C. Berkeley in July 2005. It feels more like a revival. The goals of the conference are to challenge the misuse of God and religion by the religious right, and to build a space for people of faith within the culture of the left. I am invited to speak on a panel addressing a values-oriented economy, and also to sing.

Far more people come than can be registered. The huge plenary hall is packed to the gills for the entirety of the four-day program. At every workshop I attend, people are exulting and effusing over walking into a community of the like-minded. According to the most conservative estimates, 78 percent of Americans believe in God. Bush won on "faith" votes. It is patently obvious to me—and the others here—that we on the left are overlooking something fundamental and profound. The conference is a massive celebration, a giddy and jubilant stampede out of the secular closet. "It is in the convergence of spiritual people becoming active and activists becoming spiritual," says Van Jones, director of the Ella Baker Center for Human Rights, "that the hope of the world rests."

Amen and hallelujah.

I leave feeling affirmed and elated. I'm eager too, like I'm five years old and just met my new best friend: I can't wait to have her over for a tea party and play with my favorite toys. For the first time in months —to my immense relief—my old comrade, hope, returns for an extended visit. She has a few gray hairs and crow's-feet, but she's still lugging her backpack crammed with maps and tackle, still flaunting sequin-green satin with her workboots. Still keen as mustard.

"So, what kind of Buddhist are you?" Sheilan asks.

"Well, I'm not really a Buddhist. I'm a Jew."

"Oh. So why—"

"What I mean is, I was raised Jewish and I love the culture and have no desire to stop being a Jew. But my main practice is *vipassana*, insight meditation, and it's been no less than transformative. I guess—I suppose—well, if I had to label myself I'd say I'm a Buddhist practitioner."

In November 2005 I move into the San Francisco Buddhist Alliance for Social Engagement (BASE) house. The vision of the house is for us to support each other in both our inner work and our work in the world. I see it as an opportunity to try to live what I preach. Community, as the Sarayacu showed me, is where we need to put our ideals into practice. If I want to change the world, I need to figure out how to start at home — with what I have before me, with friends who are also committed to this path, and with all that comes up as we negotiate it together. As I discover, living in an intentional community has its challenges, but the shared commitment to developing our awareness and compassion establishes a crucial groundwork of trust. We implement a number of processes to facilitate our practice and strengthen our community, among them communal weekly dinners. One week, the Buddhist ethic of "right action" — acting with wisdom and compassion — comes up within the context of social change work. Spring, one of my housemates, asks the table what the point of right action is when the system operates by no such ethos, and activism so often feels like a losing battle. We all have a lot to say in response, but Diane puts it best.

"You have to remember interdependence," she says, "if you want your work to be sustainable. We need to recognize that our actions are only a small part of a huge web. It's a challenge because we get so attached to having certain results. But interdependence also means that every action we take does matter, that any action that comes from a place of wisdom and compassion will bear fruit, whether or not we can see its effects. The key is going ahead and acting anyway, but with an understanding of our own place in the scheme of things, and without being attached to the results."

"Is it possible to act without being attached to results?" Scott asks.

"Yes. Gandhi did it."

"Oh sure, Gandhi. A walk in the park."

We begin opening our home up to the greater community. We start a weekly meditation group for activists, and a monthly speaker series on Spiritual Activism, drawing from recognized leaders and thinkers in the fields of nonviolence and social change. Every two months we plan an engaged retreat, where we spend one day practicing together and a second day volunteering on a project in our neighborhood. One afternoon Spring asks me if I would talk to the house about globalization and direct action. Sure, I say, and attempt a brief synopsis for my housemates. They are an attentive and curious circle of listeners. They share my view of the correlation between our systems and our consciousness, and their responses add significantly to my own thinking. I am midsentence when it occurs to me that perhaps the next locus of my activism has located me.

Hey hey hey, justice will have her say.

Maybe. No, not quite right. Makes justice sound mouthy and ineffectual. Definitely wrong. *Justice is A-OK?* Lord, where have my creative juices run off to? Wait, wait, I've got it: *Justice will make you pay.* Right. Maybe coming from the German-accented cop-gone-cracked in a B flick. Then there's the blue version: *Justice could use a good lay.* Now that'll get the people to rise up. Until they sprout a few grays, that is, and start taking long walks on the beach with their Volvo station wagons and 401(k)s. Okay, enough now. Concentrate. I'm feeling it. It's coming.

Justice is on her way.

Could work. Simple but rousing. I try it, humming low, bouncing around in my seat as I experiment with rhythm and pitch. *Hey hey hey, justice is on her way, close the gates on the SOA, close the gates—*

"Ma'am?" A sternly courteous gaze is leveled my way.

"Yes?"

"I was just asking what beverage you'd like with your snack pack."

"I'll take a glass of peace, no ice, and the veggie justice meal, please."

"Excuse me?"

"Tea. I'll have a tea."

Yesterday I spoke with David, who was already at Fort Benning. "Write songs," he instructed. "Bring music. We're in the Southgate Apartments, building 21. There's no power and the plumbing isn't working. But we are right outside the gates."

I've been hearing about the annual School of the Americas protest for years. Multiple VW-busloads of global justice activists went directly from Miami to Fort Benning in 2003. David was over to dinner a few months ago when he mentioned he was going. "I'll be with the Puppetistas," he said. "Making giant puppets and art." He encouraged me to consider coming, telling me that it was a faith-based movement started by a priest, Father Roy Bourgeois. "Over the past few years it's been thoroughly infiltrated—and influenced—by our global justice friends. Now it's a really interesting merging of the two movements."

"Where do I sign up?"

I've read about the horrors perpetrated by graduates of the School of the Americas, a combat training school for Latin American soldiers based at Fort Benning, Georgia. Over the course of six decades, the SOA has trained more than sixty thousand soldiers in counterinsurgency techniques, commando and psychological warfare, interrogation tactics, sniper fire, and military intelligence. These techniques have been used by its graduates against their own people, to enforce U.S. economic policies that have an uncanny tendency to benefit wealthy elites and arouse the ire of the impoverished majorities. Powerful corporate investors view Latin America as a convenient backyard to the U.S., rich with resources and cheap labor.

In this yard, the SOA graduates are the cruelest of bullies. They have been responsible for the massacre, assassination, torture, rape, and "disappearance" of hundreds of thousands of Latin Americans. Union organizers, educators, religious workers, student leaders, indigenous populations, and antipoverty activists are chief targets. More than six hundred SOA graduates are documented human rights violators. At least twelve graduates have attained the status of dictator within their home countries. In 1993 a United Nations Truth Commission reported that forty-seven of the sixty officers guilty of the worst atrocities during El Salvador's civil war — including those responsible for killing Archbishop Oscar Romero, for murdering four American Maryknoll churchwomen, and for massacring nine hundred villagers at El Mozote in 1981 — were trained at the SOA. Among its many critics, it is often called the School of Assassins.

In 1996 the Pentagon released seven manuals used for intelligence training in Latin America and the SOA. These manuals explicitly advocated torture and promoted human rights violations. On December 15, 2000, in response to public outcry, the SOA was closed by a vote of the House of Representatives. The same vote, however, approved a proposal for a new school. One month and two days later, face-lift complete, the Western Hemisphere Institute for Security Cooperation opened its doors.

On November 16, 1989, six Jesuit priests, their housekeeper, and her teenage daughter were massacred in El Salvador. A U.S. Congressional Task Force report identified nineteen of the twenty-six soldiers responsible as SOA graduates. The annual demonstration at Fort Benning takes place in late November each year, in commemoration of these murders.

Eighteen years ago, one sunny afternoon in a schoolyard on the edge of an all-white city at the very tip of Africa, I summoned up the nerve to say no. *No*, I said, I don't believe whites are any better than blacks. Six years later I did it again. *No*, sexism won't cut it. And then *no* to the violence perpetrated by my people on the Palestinians. *No* to the walls we build between us, to a globalized economy that fortifies and whitewashes those walls, to the violence that such vast imbalance incites and institutionalizes. The School of the Americas embodies all that I have spent my life fighting against. And the movement looking to shut it down exemplifies all I have been trying to do. *Yes*, says this movement, every life is inconceivably precious. Only love can end hate, so we will uproot violence with principled nonviolence. And in the face of death and destruction, we will bear witness, we will speak boldly and clearly, and we will build.

"That must be it, over there."

"There? Ma'am, I think those buildings may be abandoned."

"Probably."

Across the street: K.W. MILITARY SUPPLY. And FREEDOM HOUSE. The cab driver deposits me in the parking lot closest to building 21. I lug out my backpack and head toward the single lighted window. Apparently someone got the power hooked up.

Two kids are playing cards in the doorway. They look up as I approach.

"Excuse me, is this where the Puppetistas are staying?"

"Yeah," says one, examining me through narrowed eyes. Gauging for any red flags of the law-enforcement variety. He's about fourteen, with a disorderly array of teeth and eyes a startling blond. "I'm Quentin. Go on 'head."

I press on, through a tiny kitchen chaotic with pots and dishes, and into what was once, in its heyday, a living room. The carpet is an indeterminate shade of filthy. The walls are scored and scuffed and shedding, the windows broken. A single set of warped miniblinds dangles at a haphazard angle. I barely have time to absorb this before I'm accosted.

"Hello! And who might you be?" A puppy-eager pair of eyes peers at me from under a massy halo of brown. I take in the wide skirts, the stiletto-heeled leather boots. I'm a friend of David's, I tell her.

"Oh, yes! Are you the singer?"

Her enthusiasm renders me instantly dour. "Uh-huh. Is he here?"

"Yeah, but he's in a meeting right now. So are you in a skit yet?"

I fix her with a blank stare, but she is undaunted. "You know, a skit for our sideshows on Saturday. I know he's going to try to steal you for his, but we really need another woman in ours. I mean, we're commemorating the four churchwomen murdered in El Salvador, and so far it's only me and three men. Ridiculous. Say you'll do it. Please!"

"Uh. Okay."

"Fantastic," she says. "I'm Bonnie." She informs me that there will be a planning meeting for our skit in five minutes, and that Jamie, another member of the group, is on his way. In case you're hungry, she says, there's tons left over from dinner—brown rice, collard greens, black beans, and miso soup. She points to the meal preparation and dishwashing schedule on one wall, suggesting I sign up, and to the schedule of the week's activities on the other wall. "Meet you on the couch in five."

I lay my backpack down on the cushion-free couch.

"Hey you guys!" Enter mammoth dreadlocks attached to a human being. "Check out what we dumpster-dived! Two boxes of cookies!"

"Oh my God!" Bonnie literally jumps up and down. "Yippee! Dessert!"

"Dumpster-dived?"

"Yeah, from behind the market down the block." Both of them slowly turn to me. "Dude, are you trying to say you've never gone dumpster-diving?" His voice is low with awe.

"I suppose that's what I'm trying to say."

"Well my friend, you are missing out." Spreading his arms wide. "Every piece of furniture in this room, fresh from the dumpster." I examine the couch dubiously. And my backpack on top of it. "Great."

"I'll say. I'm Shawn." His blue eyes glint out from the narrow white patches of his face uncolonized by facial hair. "Welcome to the Puppetista Lair."

I thank him, and ask where I should set up my sleeping bag.

"Wherever." Bonnie is dismissive. "I'm in building 19, which is way worse. Officially condemned. No power or plumbing. But there may still be space in the bedroom here if you want to check."

At a rapid clip, I head toward the door she indicates.

"There aren't beds or anything, but you can just lay your sleeping bag on the floor. And hey—"

I turn. "Yeah?"

"Just to warn you, you may want to keep an eye out for the roaches. There's like a million of them."

I wake groggy, but with a clear recollection of something crawling over my belly during the night. Thankfully, the pill I took knocked me out sufficiently that I gave a few drop-kicks and went on sleeping. And the judicious employment of earplugs enabled me to sleep blissfully through the 7:30 a.m. meeting. I spoon myself some gluey oatmeal, slug down a few shots of cold coffee, and head, armed with notebook, into the Georgia morning.

While I came here to demonstrate and to make art, I also came to write. I am not sure where or what I will be publishing this time, but I want to record what happens here, so that I can tell this story to others. I'm not on assignment, and I may not get paid for it, but I have reached the point where I am doing it for myself. I feel blessed to have been witness, a number of times in my life, to what I see as history in the making. And I want to get it down on paper.

It is a dazzling day already, sunlight swiping hard over the wide expanse of green between buildings 21 and 19. The apartment right next door to ours is frenetic with activity: police march in and out, murmuring or barking at each other, radios blaring static. I inquire of a floating Puppetista what's going on.

"The cops are moving in. They're making it a base for the weekend."

Now, I wonder how that's going to affect property values. "Maybe we should send over a pound cake."

Plywood has been set atop sawhorses on the lawn to make worktables, and Puppetistas are busily stenciling and cutting out props. I peer into the bottom floor of building 19, which has been converted into a workspace. David and some others are drilling and sawing away to a curiously harmonious medley of death metal and jazz.

"What are you making?" I yell at one of them, a middle-aged man with a thick red beard, a balding pate, and a total of two red dreadlocks jutting, like a Hare Krishna gone feral, from the back of his head. He gives me a ragged, toothy grin, and holds up a narrow wooden post. "What do you think?"

"No clue. Rapiers? Vampire stakes?"

"Close but no cigar. Stilts. For the giant stilt-walking bugs."

He introduces himself as Jake and curtsies with genuine grace, plucking at the edges of his baggy pants. I introduce myself, bow deeply, and ask whether he by any chance is privy to the whereabouts of a lad named Shawn. "That fair gentle," he tells me, "was last sighted taking some sun in the meadow."

I spot the dreads skulking about on a workbench. Shawn is doing a video project, and last night we discussed teaming up on interviews. Together we head over to the building housing the SOA Watch media and communications office for the week. SOA Watch is the D.C.-based group that organizes the annual protest, along with smaller demonstrations and ongoing lobbying efforts. This office was set up days ago in one of the Southgate apartments. It contains six laptops, six harried young activists—one with a baby placidly surveying the agitation from her lap—and what sounds like seventeen phone lines beeping and ringing ceaselessly. "Christine at KPFK? 4 p.m. Pacific? Great." "*The Atlanta Journal-Constitution*. Have you spoken with—yes, of course. Of course they got the release." Punk crashes at low volume from a small stereo. Wires are taped to the walls and ceiling, congregated in bunches in the corners. Today is Wednesday. The countdown to the weekend's demonstration is just hitting its stride.

Father Roy Bourgeois doesn't look much like what I expected. Not that I realized I had expectations until he fails to fulfill them, resembling neither a priest nor a radical. He is younger than I'd imagined, dressed in a black T-shirt and a pair of jeans, and when Shawn and I knock on the door of his office asking to interview him, to my delight, he waves us in. "Sure, sure, we can chat, but just for five minutes.

This is such a busy time." He ends up talking with us for over three-quarters of an hour.

Bourgeois' home is directly outside the gates to the base. Step out the door, down the stairs, and there it is: WELCOME TO FORT BENNING, U.S. ARMY. "The movement started right here," he tells us. He gestures around him to the walls of his small office. They are adorned with photos of the assassinated: the four Maryknoll churchwomen, the indefatigable human rights defender Archbishop Oscar Romero. "Blessed are the Peacemakers," a sign reads, "for they shall never be unemployed." On another wall: Rosa Parks. Two Muslim girls, smiling from their *hijab*. "I've experienced firsthand the brutality of the military to the poor in Latin America," he explains, speaking rapidly, urgently. After five years of human rights work in Bolivia, he was interrogated, tortured, and banished from the country. During his following stint in El Salvador, he traced a string of killings—including the murders of the four churchwomen and of Archbishop Romero—to the SOA. In 1980, back in the U.S., he spent seventy days in jail after splashing a vial of his own blood on the Pentagon to protest Romero's assassination. After the report emerged that those responsible for the 1989 massacre were trained at the SOA, Bourgeois felt called to come to Fort Benning and investigate. He rented this apartment for $175 a month, and thus was born SOA Watch.

"I called up friends from the Bay Area. Our first action was a thirty-five-day water-only fast, to expose the school. Our next action took place on the first anniversary of the 1989 massacre. Three of us poured our own blood on photos of SOA graduates and instructors." Bourgeois served fourteen months for this action. In total, he has spent four years in jail for nonviolent civil disobedience in protest of the SOA. I scribble desperately as he recounts his story, trying to catch it all, overcome with admiration for this man and his commitment.

"We started to gather at the main gate in November. The first year, there were ten of us." He smiles. Bourgeois smiles a lot, like a kindly history teacher, or an affable oncologist. "The second, a hundred. Then five hundred, a thousand. Last November there were over fifteen thousand. The school became a PR nightmare for the Pentagon, so they changed its name. Now they say they're teaching democracy." He gives a hoot of a laugh, his blue eyes scorching. "You don't teach democracy behind a chain-link fence. You don't teach democracy in an undemocratic institution, from behind the barrel of a gun. It's so offensive, the Pentagon saying, 'we're putting the past behind us.' The victims — like Carlos Mauricio, who will be here — they say: you do not decide when it's time to move on." An index finger slashes through the air, pinning any argument to the desk. "There can never be healing and reconciliation without truth and justice."

The sun is setting outside his window, now, and it is not going down easy. Behind a mangle of black branches, the sky is glowing, sparking, mounting to a formidable blaze. We sit silent for a minute. I am rigid, a gritty determination rising in my chest, edged with outrage.

"So," Father Roy Bourgeois resumes eventually, his face ember-bright in the dim office, "the struggle goes on." We nod, somber. "And this weekend" — smiling again, hugely, so magnetic that I feel my face stretching involuntarily — "it's gonna be a big celebration of hope." He wags his head. "Something happens here. People start feeling more empowered to speak out. Now is the time, you know." His conviction so ironclad it can't help but carry a few thousand with it. "I've learned in this movement: we can all do something for peace, and do it well."

I walk out of that office feeling like I've been healed of a malaise I didn't know I had. Shawn and I stand together wordless, staring at the livid sky, and at WELCOME TO FORT BENNING, etched in scarlet before the yawning gates.

"Point of order."

"Yes."

"We are the Puppetistas." Jake gesticulates extravagantly at the circle. "We are therefore obliged to play games."

"Right." Bonnie is facilitating. "We'll break every fifteen minutes for a quick game to keep us on our toes. Okay, folks, it's Thursday night already, so let's get moving." She runs through the agenda for the meeting: group check-ins, review of the weekend's plans, housekeeping and workspace-related issues.

"Point of clarification." Bruce raises his hand. "In which game shall we indulge?" His caterpillar brows are lifted high. Bonnie asks him if he has a suggestion, and he deliberates briefly with the orange hand puppet on his left arm. "We humbly propose butt charades."

"Any objections?"

None. I dump a spoonful of steaming black beans over the rice on my plate and head toward an open spot on the carpet, settle down cross-legged. Some primeval relic of a survival instinct inspires me to turn my head. Jutting above the window ledge directly behind me: a writhing pair of antennae. *Fight or flight?* I screech, leap up, and swiftly relocate to a spot next to David. Safe. For now.

"All right people. Let's get started with group check-ins." Bonnie is no-nonsense. "Giant stilt-walking bugs?"

"Right here." In the corner, Abi perks up. She's fresh-faced and lovely, her cutoffs spattered with paint. "The stilts are made, but we could definitely use help with the bug-faces and bodies. Oh, and whoever's going on a supply run, we need more duct tape."

"The Madres?" Bonnie turns to me. I turn to Jamie. He looks from me to Bonnie and meekly obliges.

"Comin' along nicely." Jamie's hair curls down his neck, and his Southern accent is thick as peat. "We's about done with the four churchwomen, could use some help with the giant birds from any new folks." He glances about the circle at the people who arrived today.

"The Carlos Mauricio group?"

"We're painting up the *contestoria,* the pictures to tell his story." David taps items off on his fingers as he speaks. "Got the Carlos puppet and the church workers and the torturing generals done. Still working on the jail-turned–commemorative museum. I spoke with Carlos today and he's going to be arriving Sunday morning. He's looking forward to joining all of us."

"GI Joes?"

José rouses himself. "We've been making the guns." With crooked glasses and a paunch, José is Jerry Garcia's brown-skinned doppelganger. "Anyone feel a hankering for constructing AK-47s, come to us."

"Great." Bonnie glances at the agenda and reviews the plans for the weekend. Saturday we will be doing our sideshows, moving between three marked-out performance spaces in the crowd. Sunday we will be parading up through the crowd to the stage, where we will perform our grand pageant. On Saturday, Bonnie announces, each group will do their skit three times, except for the bugs, who will be in the crowd. And each group, she concludes, will need a clown liaison to move people out of the way and synchronize our timing.

David raises his hand and asks how the clowns will be coordinated.

"Each group," explains José, who sidelines as a clown when not full-timing as a Puppetista, "is autonomous in how they want to handle their clown liaisons." I am pondering the rich hermeneutics extractable from this seemingly simple statement when Eric, the event coordinator of SOA Watch, walks in the door. In a Pavlovian instant, the room is in uproar.

"Olé, olé olé olé," chorus the Puppetistas of yore, "shut down the SOA. Olé, olé olé olé..." Eric gamely performs a jig in the middle of the room. "Butt charades!" Bruce hollers. "It's been fifteen minutes. Eric, you're up."

"Okay, okay." He turns around, diligently proffering his rear end. "The subject is: things you find in a dumpster."

It's Friday, the last full day of art-making before the weekend's extravaganza. Sheets billow gently from a line strung across the lawn. LA VIDA reads the drying paint on one, and LA LIBERTAD on another. A black-shrouded cardboard coffin leans up against one of the trees. Beside it rests a line of cardboard rifles. A host of local kids have joined our efforts. They dip brushes contemplatively into reds and yellows, spread the paint over cardboard flowers with all the absorption and care of young neurosurgeons. Over near the worktables, Neil is getting fitted with a giant gauzy pair of green wings. At the lawn's edge, David tries out the Carlos Mauricio puppet, moving gracefully beneath its weight, slowly extending one arm to raise a giant hand.

And like a quiet benediction over all: the sun, filtering down through the massive old oaks in leisurely kaleidoscope. I discover myself awash in a coppery upswell of happiness.

"Hey you!" It's Quentin, loping toward me coltlike. Quentin lives in the Southgate apartments with his grandmother, and over the years he's become an ardent Puppetista. At one point during the week he makes off with my notebook, and when I recover it later *I love U* has been scrawled on one of its pages. Now he slings an arm over my shoulder, brings his face close to mine, narrows his eyes and cocks his head. "What you up to, girl?"

"I was going to check out the silk-screening. Looks like I got a partner now."

We climb the stairs in building 19 to another ad hoc workspace. Five women and two men are hard at work pressing, lifting, and hanging swatches of fabric with assembly-line efficiency. The ramshackle unit has been strung about with clothesline, and red RESIST flags are pegged up neatly against a backdrop of shattered windows and crumbling walls. On an ancient couch lies a pile of clothes ready to be silk-screened, my red T-shirt among them.

Back outside, Abi is about to mount her stilts.

"Don't move, Matt," she yells. "I'm in a very precarious position." She is standing atop a dumpster, Matt squatting behind her, fiddling with the segmented exoskeleton on her back. The giant bug-head and cellophane dragonfly wings are already in place. Jake supports her from below, stabilizing the stilts as she steps into them.

"Is that comfortable?" He adjusts the stilt-shoe around her foot.

"Yeah, fine." Her face is rigid, her eyes looking anywhere but down. Jake unrolls the elongated black stilt-pants until all that shows beneath her mile-long legs is a miniature pair of shoes. He peers up at her, asks her if she's ready to try it.

"I guess so." She pushes the bug-head up higher, then leans forward tentatively on her hand-poles, swallowing. "I think so."

Later, when she's back on her land-legs, I ask Abi why she comes. *I'm here because I believe in the power of creative resistance,* she says. *A lot of the activism I was involved with before was angry. But this feels joyful to me. It comes from a place of love instead of fear or anger. Rather than focusing on the negative, we are creating something different. And we're doing it collaboratively. We're living it.* "All right." She inhales sharply. "Here goes."

And she's off! The organic farmer/Puppetista/dragonfly stilt-walking natural as a calf unfolding placenta-wet onto its feet. Look up, high up, and you will witness a mystical specimen of a type common as mud—an audaciously dreamed, painstakingly realized portent of a better world, wings catching and refracting the late-afternoon light.

It's no small feat pulling together an event of this magnitude. Yesterday, Friday, Bonnie and I were the Puppetista representatives at the final coordinating meeting for the weekend. The SOA Watch facilitators began with a song and a review of consensus process, and then ran through every conceivable detail of the demonstration, from media to Spanish interpreters to the legal team supporting those who choose to scale the fence.

Today, the details that were twenty-four hours ago no more than ink on paper have assumed dimensions both material and human. The bland stretch of road in front of the gates is transformed: a high stage has been set up, strung with a banner reading CLOSE U.S. ARMY'S SCHOOL OF ASSASSINS. Thousands are already milling about expectantly before it. The army has erected three high fences just in front of the gates. Nonviolent civil disobedience is apparently as terrifying as ever to the armed-and-uniformed guardians of liberty and democracy. I spend some time browsing the booths lining the sides of the road: Veterans for Peace, Code Pink, SOA Watch, the Institute for Justice and Democracy in Haiti. Then I make my way back to the Southgate apartments. It's time to rehearse for this afternoon's sideshows.

I am standing, one flower in a row of flowers, and I am watching their faces.

"Sister Ita Ford," calls Jamie, and the giant puppet moves slowly forward. I lower my flower, read a few words from this courageous woman who was kidnapped, raped, and murdered for her work with the poor. Then I put the words away, raise my flower. *Hope*, it reads.

"Sister Maura Clarke," calls Jamie, and Bonnie reads out a quote. Then Sister Dorothy Kazel, and lay missioner Jean Donovan. When all four of the puppets are in front, a line of soldiers marches from each side, and the effigies of the women slowly descend to the ground. "We are here today to honor these four women," says Jamie. We holding the flowers settle about the fallen women as the giant doves in the back rise, wings fluttering, and glide slowly forward.

I am squatting behind my flower and I am watching the faces in the crowd before us. Watching as their expressions shape-shift from delight to horror and eventually, mirroring what I am feeling, to grief. Noting in the silent motions the ungainly choreography of the same dance I know so well, the one we are all performing these days, but generally in the craters of our unconscious, or the solace of seclusion. I am astonished at the power of our performance, at what it elicits in our audience.

One, two, three, four.

I open my mouth to sing, and feel a rush of consolation as a chorus of voices rises in harmony. *Some bright morning when this life is o'er, I'll fly away. To a home on God's celestial shore, I'll fly away...*

We rise, and walk slowly to our next site.

That night we Puppetistas head to a nearby Mexican restaurant to celebrate the success of our sideshows. We order beers and margaritas and toast to each other, the Puppetista revolution, a better world. "I have something I'd like to say," Jamie announces, rising with awkward formality, glass aloft. "I'd like to thank every one of your for your creativity and inspiration." He looks into each of our faces. "For me, coming here is like Christmas."

Olé, begins someone, and the rest of the restaurant gapes in consternation as all twenty of us plus one goggle-eyed hand puppet take up the chorus. Jamie lowers himself into his seat, eyes wet. I sat down with Jamie to interview him a couple of days ago and was profoundly moved by his story. *Most of my life I've been economically displaced,* he told me. *I was a wayward youth. I committed burglary at nineteen and served two years out of a three-year prison sentence. Generally I had manual labor jobs, which were seasonal, with no benefits. I was destitute during the worst times of the year. For a while I had a good job as supervisor at a recycling plant. Then the city privatized and I was made redundant. To achieve the*

American dream, you have to have ten pegs that fit perfectly into ten holes. You miss one, your chances are over. After dealing with it personally I began to think about how people are being treated in the rest of the world. For the past four years Jamie has been a Catholic worker at a shelter in Columbia, Missouri. *I have great faith in God,* he said to me. *For me, God is the same thing as conscience. The splinter of your soul that is a piece of God can choose to follow his ways. My mission in life is to ease suffering, and the best way is to suck a little evil out of the system and swallow it.* Tomorrow, Jamie will scale the fence onto Fort Benning property.

We exit the restaurant in small clusters. On the porch outside, two local boys are hanging out, smoking. One of them raises an eyebrow, gives us the once-over. "Hey, you all with the peace folks?"

"Yes, we're the Puppetistas," Bonnie says, executing a quick jig. She invites them to tomorrow's demonstration, telling them our pageant will begin at twelve forty-five sharp.

His head sways slightly as he mulls this over. "Well," he says, "I'm Kevin, and I'm going to Iraq in January." His words are slurred, careening into each other like boxcars in a train wreck.

Bonnie and I stare. A heretic, before our very eyes!

He twirls an index finger through the air like a lasso. "We fight so y'all can do what you wanna do, you know."

Kevin can't be more than twenty-two, with the faintest dusting of blond facial hair. He's good-looking, with the genial, skulking confidence of a high school baseball star. If he didn't win "Most Popular," surely he nabbed "Dreamiest Eyes" or "Best Smile." He's the kind of guy who would have copied my homework and minutes later forgotten I existed.

"But tell me," Bonnie says, "do you honestly want to go?" She is brimming with compassion, scouring his face for signs of possible salvation.

"Yes, I do, because two of my best friends are there. I'm going so I can make sure no more of my friends get killed. I want to come back —I got a fiancée and two kids." He looks to his friend, who nods firmly, eyes fixed staunchly on the floor. *Right on, bro.* "But I'd give it all up to protect my friends."

Bonnie asks him if he really believes that Iraq is about spreading democracy.

"Well, let me tell you," he says philosophically. "I've wanted to be in the military and fight for my country since I was three years old." This is a military town, after all. And a God-fearing one at that: the annual "God Bless Fort Benning" celebration is taking place this same weekend—not a counter-demonstration, the organizers assert, but rather a show of support for the soldiers. Held at the Columbus Civic Center, their free show with a big-name country-western star will attract a crowd of 25,000. For in addition to being a military town and a God-fearing town, this is a poor town. Driving around with Bonnie yesterday on a supply run, I eventually gave up counting the pawnshops and check-cashing outlets. Kevin takes a long drag on his cigarette, a swig from the brown-bagged forty lingering at his thigh. "Yeah, I always dreamed of being a soldier. And it's either them or you. That's what they teach us. I'd rather them than me."

I feel a stab in my chest. Tears prick, and I focus on my notebook, on my pen that keeps moving.

"Innocent people are dying, you know." Bonnie is deflated now. He's already signed over his soul.

"Nobody should die for anything. But it happens."

We nod glumly. What can we say to that? *No, Kevin. We are capable of better. Of dreaming greater and imagining greater and then creating greater. You are capable of more, and your friends—well, maybe eventually they'd understand.*

Kevin holds out his pack of cigarettes, nods for us to help ourselves, rocks forward with a lighter. "You know, you all are standing up for your beliefs. And I have to say that I appreciate that. Because it's your right. So thank you for standing up for yourselves."

Only Bonnie and I are still left on the porch, and David is waving at me to get in the car. Kevin glances at his friend, examines the glowing tip of his cigarette. "So hey, why don't you gals give me your numbers."

I thank him for talking with us, and tell him we have to go. I take his hand and shake it, forty and all. "Good luck to you." *Please don't get killed or wounded. Please look into the eyes of the mothers and the children. Please be a good father.* And I start walking away.

"Thank you. And just remember"—he's coughing suddenly, choking on his cigarette or his beer or his words—"just remember"— hacking violently now, but determined to get it out—"remember we're over there, and we're fighting for you."

Un niño de diez meses, hijo de María Argueta.

From the stage, they are calling out the names of those who have been murdered. I lay the staplegun slowly down on the table, watch as the black fabric spools off the edge. I walk to an open swath of lawn and lower myself carefully down onto the grass.

Ana María Sosa, forty years old.

I ease my bag off my shoulder, my notebook out of my bag. I start writing.

Jorge Valencia, treinta y tres años de edad.

I put the notebook down. Gaze at the final preparations going on around me: touch-ups, last-minute meetings, rehearsals. I am on the outside of a porthole, looking in, and the audio is oddly out of sync with the video.

Carmen Gómez, twenty-three years old.

Now both reels stick. The noise around me cools to static. I bring my hands over my eyes, lower my face onto my knees, and imagine her. Carmen. Thick-lipped and dimpled, black eyes startling awake as sunlight slipped slim fingers through chinks in the wall. Carmen, who loved to play pranks on her friends and sit gossiping in the fields. Who told her right hand from her left by the tiny scar whittled from a childhood of thumb-sucking. Who was one month pregnant with her second child, a boy, although she'd never know it.

Un niño de seis anos, hijo de Cristina Martínez.

A nameless child, six years old. Let's call him Tomás. A quiet and watchful boy, Tomás. He decided on the first day of school that he wanted to grow up to be a schoolteacher. He watched his mother wrestling with the washing and the maize, his father wrestling with alcohol, and he practiced his letters diligently in the dirt. When no one was watching, he stole down to the river, to the secret alcove where he stored his treasures: one speckled near-perfect blue egg, a fistful of feathers, mottled and striped, a gold button rubbed to a high shine, the impossible elegance of a hummingbird skull.

Child, age unknown, daughter of Francisca Chavarria.

A nameless ageless child. A girl. Francisca was in labor for twenty-two hours with her; this was her first and last child, and the midwife heaved a sigh of relief when the tiny dark head finally crowned. This girl, whom I will call Teresa, had the *café* skin and broad bones of her people. She sang loudly as she followed her mother through the day, and she talked to the grasshoppers, the fireflies, even the wildflowers when no one was near. When her father disappeared, she stopped talking. When the soldiers came through her village, she watched silent as they set fire to the huts, dragged her mother out ten feet past the doorstep and raped her as she screamed *ay, dios, no, por favor, no.* She watched quiet, nailed to the doorframe, when one of them turned her way, pants open and bloodied, mouth gaping like a fish drowning in air, and pointed at her, and came for her.

Un niño de cinco años, hijo de—

I stand up, wiping at my face with my sleeve. I feel like I am suffocating, like my chest has a boa constrictor around it squeezing tighter, tighter. I can hardly bear it. I can hardly bear the knowledge of what we do to each other. I gather my notepad and pen, walk rapidly across the lawn to the fence. Cling to the chain-links to steady myself. Press my face up against the cold resilience of wire. There they are: twenty thousand strong, marching in slow procession.

Lucía Márquez, fourteen years old.

Intoned from the stage in a supple, quivering female voice. There is a crack of drums, a sea of white crosses rising. And from the marchers: *Presente.* The chorus spilling out of twenty thousand throats like a lament from the earth itself. An eloping of proteins, a millennial rush of blood, a flicker of pulse.

Presente.

And they are present: their bones slackening to the tug of roots, the damp press of soil, the ministrations of blind and hungry creatures. Their souls sliding light as the wind against my cheek. They are here. They are clinging to the fence and they are watching the living march by. They are looking on as grief assumes its rightful place among the ranks of experience. They are walking slowly and holding their heads high, they are running and not looking back, they are darting among us in frantic search. *Presente.*

They are here.

I walk down the length of the fence, through the gate, into the procession. Needing to be among the bodies. Slipping into them like a robe.

Arlen Salas David, San José de Apartado.

This is a name I recognize. Arlen was a leader of San José de Apartado, the oldest and largest of Colombia's peace communities. In 1997 its two thousand war-weary residents asked the army, right-wing paramilitaries, and leftist guerrillas to stay out of their village. Fifty other communities have since followed its example, refusing to give information or sell food to armed groups. Arlen was killed three days ago.

Presente.

The mobile cemetery rising, falling, and rolling on to the next location.

Unnamed child of Bojaya, Choco, Colombia.

Presente.

Beside me walk two ancient men. One of them holds the other firmly by the arm. His friend's murky eyes leak rivers onto the front of his shirt. Before me are students, caps propped backward reading CLOSE THE SOA. They raise their crosses, which have been carefully printed with a name and an age, as have they all.

Unnamed child of Bojaya, Choco, Colombia.

Presente.

I step slowly in time, letting the familiar tide of grief rise and swamp me. Letting it seep through the seams, roll across the sand to the advancing edge of ocean, which is roiling, devouring, colonizing. For we are not separate, and neither is our suffering. And we who walk in witness are fused together in our mourning, recalled by grief.

Unnamed child of Bojaya, Choco, Colombia.

Presente.

Unnamed child of Bojaya, Choco, Colombia.

Presente.

The outermost fence blocking the gates to Fort Benning has become a thing of great beauty. A garden, blooming flowers of a most exotic nature: paper chains of orange and blue and purple, a rainbow of origami cranes, flags and ribbons and cards and photos and even the odd rose, wilting and dwarfed by its cardboard neighbors. And like wild grass, the kind that sprouts in hardy clumps and clings stubborn to the earth no matter how you pull at it: white crosses, strewn at every possible angle. A weave of crosses so dense that it obliterates the fence, leaving not even a single square inch of window to the fort within. Here is where the procession ends. Here is a garden where every flower not only has a name but also bears that name upon its petals in proud capitals. Even if it is an UNNAMED. Because we are humans, and so we name what we love, what we recognize and wish to remember. DANIEL ROMERO. INEZ MARTÍNEZ. I whisper the names, marveling over the sight before me. A holy wall, this one, like the Kotel. A wall overflowing with words. WHAT YOU HAVE DONE CANNOT BE BURIED. NO MÁS SILENCIO.

A wall of prayer. Made sacred through remembering, as is every sacred thing.

It is in darkness that we begin. In darkness the first pulse flickers, the eye blinks open. In darkness the seed splits. In darkness the stars hang, the planets wheel, the blood sings. Darkness is immense and terrifying, and no doubt darkness is chock-full of demons, but there is magic in darkness, and then there is the word. For the *no* and the *yes*, the *how* and the *why* and the *thank you*, these too issue crumpled and damp from darkness. Darkness yields myth, darkness yields all stories old and new. Only darkness knows light, and it is into our own darkness we must now venture.

"Marisa! We gotta go!" Bonnie runs up to me, grabs my arm. "It's nearly time for the pageant."

"Okay." I turn to Jamie. "Good luck, my friend. May we meet again."

"Next year in Fort Benning," he says, grinning huge. "Break a leg."

We hug, and I spin around to look at the Puppetistas, standing ready for the pre-pageant parade. The giant bugs are high up on their stilts, and the puppets of the Madres and Carlos Mauricio sway faintly in the breeze. There are the GI Joes, and the doves, and the flowers. *Hope. Imagination. Peace.* A wrench of sadness, a premature nostalgia, for the week is swiftly drawing to a close, and I will soon part from this ragtag band of dreamers and creators, they who have restored my faith in our ability to build the world we want.

"Come on, honey." Bonnie takes my hand and pulls me like a wayward child. "Let's go. The musicians are all up there already."

She steers us adeptly through the crowd, around the stage, and up to the backstage area. She tells the man at the gate that we're the singers for the Puppetista pageant, and he smiles and lets us through. We climb the stairs up to the stage and hover at the back. Now I have a bird's-eye view, and I am overwhelmed with awe at all these people, twenty thousand of them from across the nation, saturating this bleak street with color and song and humor and prayer. Then I feel a pang of terror. That's a whole lot of people to sing in front of.

One of the musicians points me at a microphone, and I take small tentative steps toward it, hum a note into it. Yes, it's definitely on.

"*Hola Marisa. ¿Cómo estás?*" I turn to my left, to the person standing at the next mike.

"*Hola Carlos, estoy bien. ¿Y tú?*"

"*Bien.*" Carlos Mauricio smiles at me, pats me on the shoulder. He points ahead, beyond the crowd. "*Mira*, here they come."

What a sight. Dragonflies tall as trees spindling delicate down the road. Faces large as my body, faces of grieving and fear and serenity and joy rocking gently forward, silent and eloquent as mystics. Doves skating through the air, flowers bobbing, coffins bumping, soldiers marching. An entire jail jogging rawboned toward us. And finally the drummers, pounding away, holding the entire cavalcade to swaggering lockstep. The crowd parts before them like the Red Sea, in gleeful cahoots with the forces of liberation. Down toward us they proceed, and when they reach the stage they spread out. Flourish on the drums, and then silence.

It is time for Carlos to speak.

"I was in the classroom teaching when the men came," he begins, and the giant puppet sways forward. "I was blindfolded, handcuffed, and taken to a place where I was tortured." He speaks rapidly, holding in front of him the text that is the barest summary of his life, pausing between sentences as the pageant is acted out below us. "I was a science professor, but everyone knew I was against the government's killings. I spent nine days in the chamber of torture."

For me it is difficult to talk about torture, Carlos told me this morning, when I interviewed him. *But I have to do it. I speak for those who can't because they were killed and tortured.* Carlos was blindfolded, deprived of sleep and food, and left hanging by his arms. If he leaned against a

247

wall he was beaten. His torturers broke two of his ribs and permanently damaged his vision in one eye. But unlike the estimated seventy thousand people killed during El Salvador's twelve-year civil war,
Carlos miraculously survived. He fled to the U.S. Together with two
other torture survivors, Carlos sued two of the generals in charge of
Salvadoran security forces during his imprisonment, men who had
since settled in Florida. In July 2002, a U.S. federal court found the
generals guilty, and the three plaintiffs were awarded $54.6 million.
Carlos used his share to expand the Stop Impunity Project, a group
he founded in order to organize the survivors of torture and fight the
amnesty granted to Salvadoran combatants. *We are seeking to bring the
perpetrators to justice, and also to preserve the historic memory of what
happened in El Salvador. We want to establish a museum so none of this is forgotten. If it's forgotten, it will be repeated.*

Last week the former Salvadoran vice minister of defense was
found guilty of crimes against humanity.

"Thousands have been killed by death squads, by soldiers trained
right here at the School of the Americas," Carlos cries, and the GI
Joes raise their flags, and the soldiers move in, and the Madres slowly
go down. I look at Bonnie to my left, and Bonnie looks back at me,
and I count us in. *Some bright morning when this life is o'er, I'll fly away.*
The guitar swings in, and the banjo twangs, and the drums kick
steady. *To a home on God's celestial shore, I'll fly away. I'll fly away, oh
Lordy, I'll fly away.* We sing through the chorus once, and then halt
abruptly. Silence.

"But while we grieve for the victims, we also hold the perpetrators
accountable," Carlos declares, looking up from the paper, out into
the crowd. "The people are rising in the name of justice. In the name
of peace we are making our voices heard."

The flowers shoot up. The birds take wing. The walls of the jail
open out; when they close again, it is a Museum of Human Rights.
The Puppetistas are whooping and ululating, the crowd is cheering
and clapping, and on every face hope beams fierce as the sun and joy
glitters like a river. This is it. These too come from darkness, the hope
and the joy. From walking into it, with courage and with friends. Listening to the names, moving through the anger, moving through the
grief, we emerge dazed and squinting and emptied and ready. For

anger and grief have their place, but so do joy and celebration, and if they are not present, nothing will grow. Nothing will dance, or sing, or stretch its arms to the sky. Tragedy birthed this event, tragedy heaped upon tragedy, and most of us run mute from such horrors. But there are those who pointed the way into tragedy, who walked boldly into the night, and discovered that in the night the moon rises ivory, and the water mirrors or transforms it, and the curling night-flowers blossom fragrant. I am quiet, taking in the jubilation. I am thinking of the country of my birth, of the Truth and Reconciliation Commission, of how the people took a good long look at the atrocities and the pain, and then were freed to move on. Out of the tragedies we are mourning this weekend has emerged an event of great beauty, and when this brand of tragedy ends, as it will, so shall the event. But we will carry its legacy forward with us, unfold it like a rainbow tent at the next carnival of salvation. We will lay out our pens and our paint-brushes, our pots and our shovels, and we will only dream bigger. For what are creation and faith without each other?

I look down, and I realize David is staring up at me urgently, and that the musicians are waiting, and that it is time. Fear hits me clean in the groin and I buckle, for an instant, but then I remember that fear is just fear and it's not real, that this is what is real, these faces be-fore me, these words. I step toward the microphone and sing.

> *Many lives on the line*
> *Reckoning in pennies, buying time*
> *Too many lost, too many mourned*
> *Families broken, communities torn*

I look to Bonnie, and to the circle of musicians, and then down to the Puppetistas. I can't stop smiling.

> *Hey hey hey*

and Bonnie lilts in with the harmony

> *Justice is on her way*

the Puppetistas belting it out raucously

Close the gates on the SOA, close the gates on the SOA

I wonder when I'm going to get a chance to breathe, but I manage to holler "sing with us" out at the audience anyway, and a few hundred new voices join in, then a couple of thousand more, and by the fourth chorus everyone is singing and bouncing to and fro, and as for me I'm not just dancing I'm soaring, bounding miles off the stage and back again.

Hey hey hey

and the Puppetistas are starting to move

Justice is on her way

dancing around the stage and past the fence and out

Close the gates on the SOA, close the gates on the SOA

I look down and wave. There goes Abi, there go Shawn and Jake and Bruce and José and David. I lift my face to look at the tossing, rollicking sea before me, but my vision is blurring, and a peculiar thing is happening because the faces out there are growing familiar, like I am remembering I used to know them. There among the crowd stands Mario, and next to him Maureen is doing the *toyi-toyi*. Kiran has his arm slung around Abdul Bakr, and Rufo is laughing with Miguel.

Hey hey hey

And the largest of the coffins is passing the fence now

Justice is on her way

where it pops open, and a human being clambers out

Fort Benning, Georgia

Close the gates on the SOA, close the gates on the SOA

and is propelled above the crosses to the top, where he lays cardboard over the barbed wire and perches, for a minute, hand raised in a peace sign as the crowd cheers, and then hops over, to join the 181 others who have been arrested over the years, who have served an average sentence of six months for that splinter of their soul known as conscience or God.

Hey hey hey
Justice is on her way
Close the gates on the SOA, close the gates on the SOA

I shut my eyes, retreat back to the place where I end and voice begins. Softening, listening as the melody is carried. Then I open them wide—I want to miss no part of this—and keep on singing.

Imagine no weapons
no fences too
billions are dreaming that dream
that dream is

you

Epilogue:

Home

As a child, I asked the people I trusted what God was. I wanted to understand God because I wanted to understand the universe. I wanted to know why I was here, what my purpose was. I wanted to figure out why people do what they do to each other, which was so often so cruel. I wanted clear answers.

I asked the *rebbitzen*, the rabbi's wife, who taught me in Hebrew school. I asked my mother. I asked God. None of what came back to me—when I got answers, that is—made much sense. At first I got answers that were so clear that upon even cursory examination they were proven false. Then I got answers that were a little more abstract, and I struggled to grasp them. Later, as my observations of the world matured, even these bottomed out. So I decided I didn't know. Probably there was no God, because God had to be some kind of sadistic freak to let the world suffer as it does.

In my early twenties I discovered solitude and nature, and those twin blessings led me to—and through—a third: experiences that could only be called spiritual. I started meditating and reading "spiritual" books. At the age of twenty-four, I went to India, spent ten days meditating, and found my version of God. I found that God is all of us—all of it—and that separation is illusory. But this God had few answers. Mostly this God inspired a series of questions followed by silence.

Eventually I learned my role: to listen. I'm still listening.

This book explores my life and work as an activist. But as much as it is about my journey outside—my journey to raise hell where I believed it was most needed—it is about my journey inside. It's about my struggle to come to terms with the world, and also my struggle to come to terms with myself. The two are not separate. They are different paths to the same place, be it heaven, hell, or Timbuktu. (All of the above, if you ask me.) At each point in this journey I eventually let go of fear just enough to test out my new truths by speaking them. But it didn't come easily.

I have come to believe that every one of us is an activist, and that every action taken in the name of our interconnection—every action that brings us closer to ourselves, to each other, to the planet—births a better world.

It is my hope that you found something here that moved you, that aroused some sense of kinship with the people you sit next to on the bus or those you read about in the newspaper. And I submit that whatever may have moved you in this book simply echoed a voice that is already speaking inside you.

Listen to that voice.

Discussion Guide

1. In *Loyal to the Sky*, Handler writes about saying no to social and economic injustice. What have you said no to in your life? Did that choice affect decisions you made later? If so, how? Did it eventually get easier, as Handler maintains, to say no? What have you said yes to? How has that shaped your life today?

2. In Chapter Five, Abdul Bakr speaks of the "old hatred" between Hindus and Muslims in India. What "old hatreds" exist in your family, community, or culture? Are they openly acknowledged? Have they been addressed or examined? What old hatreds may you or your community be the object of? Have these been acknowledged, addressed, and examined? What "new hatreds" might you have witnessed or been subjected to?

3. Alienation is a theme that arises repeatedly in *Loyal to the Sky*. Do you experience our society as fragmented? How may that manifest in your daily life? Do you feel capable of bridging the gaps? How? When do you feel most connected with those around you? When do you feel most grounded and in touch with yourself?

4. Do you believe it's possible, as Handler asks in Chapter 11, to build a movement without a common enemy? Is such a thing already in existence? Which issue would you pick to structure this movement around — the environment, human rights, economic justice, or something else entirely? What people, or kinds of people, do you envision as allies in your effort? Can you think of an example of an action that raises consciousness while adhering to the guiding principle of "no enemy"? What do you think we would be risking, as Handler wonders, "if we tried something different"?

5. In the community in which you live, is there a general awareness of issues related to corporate globalization? How does that awareness or lack of awareness affect cultural and community activities? Do the activities and events that take place in your community generally express a range of political convictions or a narrow stripe? A range of cultures or a single culture?

6. Do you have a spiritual practice? How does that inform or affect your work in the world? Your actions and choices on a daily basis? Does your work in the world enter into or inform your spiritual practice? If so, how? If not, do you see ways to build that connection?

7. In the final chapter Handler writes: "It is into our own darkness we must now venture." Do you see value in examining and exploring what is painful? In unearthing what is hidden or pushed away? How would or do you do that, as an individual? How can or do we do that, as a society? What of guilt—how do you think it affects this process?

8. Think of a powerful experience you have had at a demonstration. Was this a positive or negative experience? What emotions arose in you? How did your experience guide or affect your thinking about the issue the demonstration was addressing? Since then, has your involvement in this issue increased or decreased?

9. What is the issue or cause closest to your heart? How did you become aware of this issue or cause? Why does it move you? Have you taken action to help others become aware of it? If not, what kind of action could you envision doing? If so, what do you see as the next step in raising awareness or bringing about positive change?

10. We talk about a better world, but we seldom take the time to imagine it. What would a better world look like to you? What would you do on a typical day? Where would you be living? What kind of work would you be doing? How would you spend your

leisure time? What would your community look like? Who would be running your community, and how would they run it? What about schools, hospitals, and clinics—what would they look like? What would you eat for dinner, and where would your food come from? What would you read, watch, and listen to? Are there steps you can take now to align your life with your vision of a better world?

Index

Index

About the Author

Marisa Handler is a writer, activist, and singer-songwriter living in San Francisco. She has worked as an organizer in the global justice and peace movements and has traveled the world writing about sociopolitics and globalization. Her work has appeared in *Orion Magazine, Tikkun* magazine, Salon.com, the *Earth Island Journal,* Alternet.org, *Bitch,* the *San Francisco Chronicle,* and anthologies. Marisa plays regularly around the Bay Area, and her music, as well as more on the book, can be accessed at marisahandler.com.

About Berrett-Koehler Publishers

Berrett-Koehler is an independent publisher dedicated to an ambitious mission: Creating a World that Works for All.

We believe that to truly create a better world, action is needed at all levels—individual, organizational, and societal. At the individual level, our publications help people align their lives with their values and with their aspirations for a better world. At the organizational level, our publications promote progressive leadership and management practices, socially responsible approaches to business, and humane and effective organizations. At the societal level, our publications advance social and economic justice, shared prosperity, sustainability, and new solutions to national and global issues.

A major theme of our publications is "Opening Up New Space." They challenge conventional thinking, introduce new ideas, and foster positive change. Their common quest is changing the underlying beliefs, mindsets, and structures that keep generating the same cycles of problems, no matter who our leaders are or what improvement programs we adopt.

We strive to practice what we preach—to operate our publishing company in line with the ideas in our books. At the core of our approach is stewardship, which we define as a deep sense of responsibility to administer the company for the benefit of all of our "stakeholder" groups: authors, customers, employees, investors, service providers, and the communities and environment around us.

We are grateful to the thousands of readers, authors, and other friends of the company who consider themselves to be part of the "BK Community." We hope that you, too, will join us in our mission.

A BK Currents Book

This book is part of our BK Currents series. BK Currents books advance social and economic justice by exploring the critical intersections between business and society. Offering a unique combination of thoughtful analysis and progressive alternatives, BK Currents books promote positive change at the national and global levels. To find out more, visit www.bkcurrents.com.

Be Connected

Visit Our Website

Go to www.bkconnection.com to read exclusive previews and excerpts of new books, find detailed information on all Berrett-Koehler titles and authors, browse subject-area libraries of books, and get special discounts.

Subscribe to Our Free E-Newsletter

Be the first to hear about new publications, special discount offers, exclusive articles, news about bestsellers, and more! Get on the list for our free e-newsletter by going to www.bkconnection.com.

Participate in the Discussion

To see what others are saying about our books and post your own thoughts, check out our blogs at www.bkblogs.com.

Get Quantity Discounts

Berrett-Koehler books are available at quantity discounts for orders of ten or more copies. Please call us toll-free at (800) 929-2929 or email us at bkp.orders@aidcvt.com.

Host a Reading Group

For tips on how to form and carry on a book reading group in your workplace or community, see our website at www.bkconnection.com.

Join the BK Community

Thousands of readers of our books have become part of the "BK Community" by participating in events featuring our authors, reviewing draft manuscripts of forthcoming books, spreading the word about their favorite books, and supporting our publishing program in other ways. If you would like to join the BK Community, please contact us at bkcommunity@bkpub.com.